FRIULI

CHE

ABRUZZI
MOLISE

AZIO

CAMPAGNIA

BASILICATA

PUGLIA

CALABRIA

SICILY

LUIGI CARNACINA PRESENTS
ITALIAN HOME COOKING

Luigi Carnacina Presents Italian Home Cooking

BY LUIGI CARNACINA

Introduced, edited and translated by
PHILIP DALLAS

1972

Doubleday & Company, Inc., Garden City, New York

ISBN: 0-385-06458-6
Library of Congress Catalog Card Number 72–76143
Copyright © 1972 by Luigi Carnacina
All Rights Reserved
Printed in the United States of America
First Edition

FOR MY WIFE, GERMAINE

Contents

N.B. For information on oven temperatures, see note on Ovens under Notes on Special Preparations and Ingredients.

For recipes indicated by an asterisk (*), see Index.

Introduction

It is often the case that a man, after a lifetime of struggles and hard work, gains recognition when he is embittered and no longer cares either for the fame or the money which accompanies it.

Luigi Carnacina, however, has worked hard all his life from the age of seven—and today at eighty-three is still working hard—but has become neither cynical nor embittered. Rather, he is happily enjoying his fame, which has flowered after a long and stern discipline of making others happy during fifty-five years in the hotel profession. He has dedicated the last fifteen years to writing and he now is no longer making only the rich happy, but is passing on all his experience to a world audience through his books.

The great reputation which Carnacina has earned, first making the rich happy and then making millions of people happy, is his pride: for him, the money which has accompanied his fame is not important. It is, of course, the current coinage of success and prestige, but for him it is something he uses to bring happiness to his family, his children and his grandchildren. He personally has not changed his simple way of life (he still does his own marketing and his own cooking), though fame has caused this simple way of life to be interspersed with invitations to all parts of Italy and Europe from people who wish to give banquets in his honor.

As a good Roman, he tries to keep to the rule of moderation in all things. He does not let anything turn his head and he maintains a level-eyed yet warm equilibrium in his daily life: he does his best to conserve his energies for his work and his family, but in fact is often prodigal with them due to his innate spontaneity of character.

At eighty-three, he still initiates new ventures and, at table, can do justice to great banquets which can stop others in their tracks. One can say, therefore, of Luigi Carnacina that he has lost neither his appetite nor his zest for life.

Despite his international life, Carnacina is essentially a Roman. He was born there in 1888 in a Rome very different from today's. For only eighteen years, Rome had had a king instead of a pope ruling it. The city was developing fast and, though the Via Veneto was still green and virgin fields, there was a new railroad station and a new residential area around it to accommodate the rush of Italians arriving in search of fortune in the newly founded kingdom's capital. Carnacina's father, from Rovigo, was among these and Luigi was born near what is now the Air Terminal. His father first had good fortune as the owner of a *café-chantant* (bar-cabaret) and then met with failure, but not before a very small Luigi—or Giggetto as he was called—had seen the glitter and learned that there was a good life to be led even if you were the person to polish the silver and serve the champagne.

At the age of seven, little Giggetto was put to work for a bookbinder: at nine, he earned his pennies singing in the choir at the German church near Piazza Navona and in St. Peter's Sistine Chapel Choir—he even sang in opera, in *Carmen* in the children's ballet scenes in the second and fourth acts.

His father died when he was twelve. As eldest son and head of a family of five, he went to work seriously as a ganymede in a hostelry. By taking French lessons every morning at 6 o'clock, he quickly improved his position, moving first to a café, then a pension and then to a hotel. By the time he was fourteen, he was a professional and he set out to conquer the world. He left Rome with a cardboard box and no money. He returned three years later to Rome speaking four languages to become a captain at the Excelsior Hotel.

Once promoted and established, he set out again on his travels. This time to the Claridge in Paris, the Savoy in London and the Bayerischer Hof in Munich to return again to Rome where he became maître d'hôtel at the Palace Ambasciatori Hotel on the Via Veneto. After yet more globe-trotting, Carnacina, from 1933, started his career of directing luxury hotels which he did for the next twenty-six years.

To put Luigi Carnacina into proper perspective, perhaps the best way is to say that he is a few days older than the late Maurice Chevalier and that when he was working at the famous Ciro's Restaurant in Monte Carlo in 1921, he was chosen by Auguste Escoffier and invited by him to return with him to Ostend and to manage Escoffier's restaurant there. During his years in Ostend, he not only married a very beautiful Belgian girl, Germaine, who is still at his side, but he learned Escoffier's gastronomic philosophy and his practical arts of cooking. This meeting will perhaps find its place in history, since Carnacina brought back to Italy some of that genius which the French have expended in the culinary arts and which the Italians first gave to the French when Catherine de' Medici took her Florentine cooks to France many centuries ago.

Luigi Carnacina, himself, has never been a professional cook, but discovering the culinary arts and experimenting with the raw materials has been his overriding lifetime passion. As proof of this he points out that his wife has never cooked a meal in her life.

Carnacina crossed the Atlantic twenty times on the *Conte di Savoia* and the *Rex* as director of the Luxury Class restaurant during the 1930's and made the high reputation of Italian shipboard cuisine which has lasted till today. He went on to organize the food for the Paris Exhibition in 1937, for the New York World's Fair in 1939, and, in 1957, for the Brussels World's Fair. From 1956 onward, he has sat at his desk eight hours a day most days of the week and has written some thirty-five books and booklets.

He has recently completed an encyclopedia of world cuisine which contains over 8000 recipes. His publications have been varied: there are modest paperbacks which aim to help the teenager onto the same ladder that he himself has climbed and others which head chefs and gourmets keep by their side.

The recipes, therefore, which follow are the result of a long experience. They are all fairly simple, as the Italian cuisine should be: but they are also full-flavored. There is wide use of garlic throughout Italy but, as you will find trying out the recipes, the quantities suggested by Luigi Carnacina are such that the garlic only carries out its essential task which is to bring out the flavor of the other ingredients, rather than stand out alone and offer an aggressive flavor. Do not, therefore, omit the garlic on principle or prejudice.

Although cooking times and the like have been mentioned throughout the book, these can never be definitive. They vary for many reasons: they vary according to the calorific value of the fuel, the thickness of the pots and pans, the sort of metal they are made of and even the height above sea-level of your home. There is a note on temperatures under Ovens in the front of the book.

The art of cooking, therefore, also lies in keeping a wary eye on what is cooking: turning down the heat if the liquids are drying out prematurely or adding more liquids. Here, too, the art of tasting should be practiced. This is essential for adjusting for salt, since the saltiness of salt varies, as do individual tastes: and tasting is especially important with pasta during the last few minutes of cooking. One should nip out strands of pasta with pincers and bite them so that cooking can be stopped at the proper al dente stage. Good cooks keep a few spoons in a cup of warm water on the stove, close to hand, so that they can check on the food while it is cooking and make the necessary adjustments for a successful final result.

In northern Italy, there is a general use of butter in all preparations. As one moves south, olive oil becomes more important: and then as one reaches Rome and southern Italy, lard increases its domain. Salt pork, in suitable recipes, however, is used throughout Italy due to its noted flavoring qualities. If, in the past, there was an excessive use of fats in Italy, this no longer obtains. The Italian diet, on the whole—particularly in central and northern Italy—is almost daily becoming lighter. Seed oils are increasingly being used, particularly for frying, but good olive oil for salads is still an imperative. As Luigi Carnacina says, it is up to the cook to decide whether to use butter, margarine, olive oil, seed oil, lard or a mixture of any of these in the preparation. Although these fats have their effect on the final gastronomic result of a recipe, the cook, whether in Italy or in the United States, retains the right to balance out these fats as he or she thinks fit.

Food markets are as good as the use we make of them. Luigi Carnacina is one who keeps them on their toes. At 8 o'clock every morning, he takes a little walk to the open-air market near his home where he does his shopping. He looks over the offerings at all the stalls without buying anything. Then he returns and buys the best he sees for sale with a complete indifference to proprietors' blandishments or long acquaintance. In a market, the seasons have a real meaning: there the fresh vegetables, the herbs and the fruit arrive, and they themselves suggest what to have for lunch.

Though the supermarkets are a magnificent convenience, good food does require that the cook not only keep tabs on the season (at the supermarket, the seasons scarcely seem to change) but search out specialty stores for cheeses, sausages, olives, hams, mushrooms and other imported Italian products.

The marrying of Italian regional dishes with Italian regional wines is a very happy arrangement and one which is nowadays being practiced a great deal in Italy outside of the respective regions. This may not be so easy in parts of the United States, but it is well worth the effort. But, in all event, wine is the natural partner of Italian food and, no matter where it comes from, provided it is genuine, it is more than welcome.

Luigi Carnacina is a traditionalist regarding drinking the correct wine with each specific dish, and though this is ideal it is often—almost usually—not possible. Though a strong red wine goes best with a roast and a sweet white one goes best with dessert, this writer feels that an exaggerated involvement in the mystique of wine is a mistake. The important thing is to find, by trial and error, wines that one likes and to drink them: honest wine enhances any dish by awakening the taste buds and refreshing the palate: it also tends to mitigate the acerbities of modern life and to make the dining table the peaceful place of enjoyment that it should be. As can be seen from the recipes which follow, small quantities of wine are an essential ingredient for a great number of the more characteristic Italian dishes: and it is the wine which, more than anything, gives that *je ne sais quoi* of adult satisfaction to the palate.

Plenty of people drink dry white wine always, even with a rare steak: plenty of people drink dry red wine with fish. They are not right, but they are not wrong—at least they are drinking wine, which is right. The most important thing is not to freeze the taste and bouquet out of the wine. White wines are best served cool but not chilled, if their qualities are to be enhanced. Reds should be drunk at about 65° Fahrenheit and should be opened half an hour before mealtime to allow them to breathe.

The refrigerator, like the supermarket, is a magnificent convenience, but it should be used with equal caution. It is designed to preserve food: but once that food is to be eaten, it should be removed and allowed to find its natural temperature. This is particularly important with cheeses, which, if eaten straight from the refrigerator, have no flavor at all, even if they are the finest imported Gorgonzola.

The reader, looking at the contents page, may shy at the large number of freshly made pasta dishes and rightly say that nobody has time to make ravioli, for example, any more. This is true, and even in Italy homemade pasta has become a luxury. In fact, fresh-pasta shops have been set up, with great success, in the last few years in the major cities, which specialize in fettuccine, tortellini and the rest. The standard dried pasta is recognized as one of the very best vehicles for a sauce in the sense that it brings out the qualities of a sauce (and the cook). But homemade pasta is even better: it is a luxury in the sense that it takes time and trouble to make, but it is one of the great simple joys of the Italian cuisine and one which should, at least, be remembered on Sundays and holidays, as in fact it is, nowadays, in Italy.

The famous Carnacina recipes which follow are just a sampling of the huge swath of recipes he has invented, or saved from extinction or perhaps made definitive where there have been a variety of regional recipes of a similar nature. But this book is not definitive, its aim is to offer a fair number of recipes, but much more importantly to bring Carnacina's philosophy of culinary method and principle to the reader. Once learned, these can be used over a much wider field in the art of giving gastronomic pleasure and human contentment which has been Carnacina's life work.

In sum, what is Luigi Carnacina's gastronomic philosophy? What has he learned from the days of being a ganymede in a trattoria, to dealing daily with Escoffier and living for decades involved with the haute cuisine of the whole world?

First, perhaps, that French cooking is the best in the world: then that Chinese comes second (he says, however, that perhaps Chinese cooking is best, but that he has never had the opportunity to visit China and to meet their chefs) and that Italian food is a close runner-up to both. However, he has some reservations to make about the first two which are of an entirely practical nature. One is, obviously, that Chinese cooking is not everybody's cup of tea and, in any case, is relatively little known in the homes of the Western world.

As for French cooking, he feels that unless it is superbly done, it can be a disappointment: and to do it superbly not only requires great skill but kitchen logistics which are laborious and, nowadays, usually skimped except in the most expensive of restaurants. Fine French food demands time, money and talent such as is not readily available now and, in fact, have been becoming less available since the *belle époque* when French cooking reached its peak.

Carnacina's gastronomic philosophy has been that the Italian cuisine is more in line with modern times and he has spent decades weaning his clients to Italian food, particularly when top French food was not available. His point is that Italian cooking is within the scope and conditions of present-day cooks and—and this is important—offers the palate an equally mature gustatory satisfaction.

Italian cooking is not haute cuisine which requires that the cook shall have slaved in a steaming kitchen from the age of twelve until he is thirty-five and then graciously allowed by an avuncular yet stern chef to make his first mayonnaise and thus start his career. It is something within the reach of all of us. Italian cooking is not a cuisine invented on a banqueting level by chefs of genius and which, in a simplified form, can be prepared by lesser mortals: it is something which has grown out of the life and history of the Italian people and been conditioned by the local products of the soil and the fruits of the rivers, seas, and lakes.

Over the centuries, or one could say millennia, since the ancient Romans loved their food, Italian cooking has evolved, been influenced by most of the nations of Europe and North Africa and, in turn, has influenced them: and yet it has always remained a home-cooking style, an outdoor style, something which you can usually do relatively easily and quickly, at least not in the style of some French dishes which require two or three days' preparation.

The recipes in this book are, for the greater part, not those that you will even find in Italian restaurants in Italy; they are essentially home cooking—off-the-hob home cooking, with no pretentiousness, that can be prepared successfully by anybody with a love and understanding of good food. Italian home cooking is not a new sacred cow to kow-tow to; rather it is a good friend ready to help out in the kitchen.

Italian cooking is in an active period of expansion in the world, as a result to a great extent of the renaissance of interest in cooking in Italy itself. The greater wealth of present-day Italy, too, has had its effect in a richer diet and the use of finer wines. This new and imaginative approach to Italian cooking, now so widely spread, has been promoted by Luigi Carnacina over the last forty years and its flowering in the last decade is, therefore, his greatest triumph.

PHILIP DALLAS

Notes on special preparations and ingredients

BY LUIGI CARNACINA

ANCHOVIES

How to desalt them

Salted anchovies are desalted by plunging them in a basin full of running water and rubbing off the external salt. Remove head and tail and discard. Fillet the anchovy and discard the bone. Do not wash the inside of the anchovy; dry with a cloth. If it is to be preserved, place anchovies in a glass jar and cover with oil.

BACCALÀ AND STOCCAFISSO

Baccalà is a particular type of cod which is fished in the North Atlantic, especially off Newfoundland, Nova Scotia, and New England. It is eviscerated, salted, and dried. It has a bigger head, belly, and eyes than normal cod as well as having more and larger teeth. One should take care in selecting baccalà: the flesh should be very white: this means it will be tender, not overly salty, and should flake easily.

Baccalà must be soaked for a minimum of twelve hours, changing the water frequently: it is better to put the baccalà in an enamel or plastic basin under a continuous trickle of water for twelve hours or more until the salt is removed. Needless to say, checking for saltiness is essential and can only be done by tasting.

Stoccafisso (stockfish) also is cod, but from Irish and Norwegian waters. Unlike baccalà, which is salted, stockfish is only dried. After pummeling to soften it up (this process should not be overdone), immerse in cold water for three to four days, changing the water frequently. The best stockfish is called *weste:* it is large, white and quite without smell.

BEANS

How to cook dried beans

Wash the beans and put them in cold water to soak overnight. Drain, and place them in a fireproof pot, covering them with lightly salted water: boil slowly for about two and a half hours and they are ready for any requirement that a recipe may call for.

How to cook fresh beans

First shell the beans. Then, to give them flavor, brown a carrot and a chopped onion with a little butter in a casserole. Add water and a bouquet garni of rosemary and bay leaves and some chopped salt pork: bring to the boil, remove scum, and continue boiling for a further 30 minutes.

Add the beans to the boiling liquid and cook for about 30 minutes or more (according to the type of bean).

If you toss in some small pasta and cook till al dente, you have an excellent pasta-and-fagioli (pasta and bean) soup. Serve with grated Parmesan.

BÉCHAMEL

(Besciamella)

4 tablespoons butter
½ tablespoon chopped onion
3½ tablespoons sifted flour
1 pint warm milk
Salt and white pepper

Grating of nutmeg
Bouquet garni:
3 bay leaves
2 sprigs thyme

Heat all the butter in a casserole, add the onion, and cook very slowly till translucent; mix in the flour and allow to cook for a few seconds before adding the warm milk. Season with a pinch of salt, a pinch of pepper, a grating of nutmeg and the bouquet garni. Bring to the boil, turn down heat, and simmer for 15 minutes, stirring often. Remove the bouquet garni and discard. The béchamel should be a rather thick sauce.

BEEF

The fat of prime beef should be white; if yellow, the animal is old. The best beef comes from steers slaughtered at between four and five years of age. The meat should be coarse-textured but very soft both when cutting and when pounding to break up its fibers.

Choosing the correct cut for a particular recipe is very important: knowing your meat can also save money if you know how to choose suitable economical cuts.

The fillet is always tender and an excellent cut as a roast or casseroled, or cut into 8-ounce fillet steaks and grilled. The middle portion of the fillet is the famous châteaubriand; then come the tournedos, followed by the top-and-tail slices which make good little steaks, though they tend to be rather fibrous. They make the best ground meat for making a real Bolognese sauce, which is one of the basics of the Italian cuisine.

The flank and rump braise well and also make good boiled beef. The sirloin is most suited for roasting. The rump steaks, from the lower part of the haunch, also make a good roast beef. An excellent roast can also be obtained from the boned rib—the part after the sirloin.

For mixed boiled-meats *all'italiana,* the most suitable and economical cuts are sirloin tips, lean short ribs, the round and the rump and the hocks.

The tail, chopped into thick slices, braises well with celery hearts as the Roman oxtail vaccinara*; it can also be boiled to good effect. The leg muscle and the shinbones make a good basis for stock, sauces, and gelatin.

BEETS

Thoroughly scrub and wash some young and tender beets. Place them in a fireproof dish for about 30 minutes in a moderate oven. They are cooked when they "give" a little when pressed. Cool, peel, slice, and store in a cool place in a marinade of herb vinegar.

EGGS

Eggs—since the beginning of time—have been a source of strength for man and viewed with confidence. There are, of course, bad eggs, but they are rare nowadays and, on the whole, eggs are not subject to the trickery to which other foodstuffs lend themselves so easily.

The really new-laid egg is without price, but hard to come by if one does not live in the country. Freshness—which means that the egg is only a few days old—is an essential for all culinary uses except one: that is for whipping an egg white. If you only have fresh eggs in store, there is an easy and quick remedy for this: add a drop of lemon juice and a pinch of table salt.

Eggs, over and above their great role in pastry making, are the cook's best friend in emergencies: not only are they highly nutritious and satisfying, but they are also valuable for diets and in time of sickness, except in some special cases.

How to fry eggs

An egg, fried all'italiana, must be puffed up and the white brought to a golden brown. Only by cooking the eggs one at a time can this condition be obtained.

Break the egg into a plate and season it with a little salt. Pour plenty of oil into a frying pan (sufficient to cover the egg): heat till smoking. Slide the egg into the pan, spooning the oil around the yolk to prevent its spreading. When the egg has set and colored suitably, remove with a slotted spoon and drain: keep warm and continue operation with the other eggs.

EGGPLANT

The eggplant is a tropical plant, originally imported from India in the seventeenth century. Before being sautéed, stuffed, or cooked au gratin, it must be thoroughly drained, because of its very high water content.

Cut it in half lengthwise, and place on a paper towel for about 30 minutes, remembering to add plenty of salt to help this drying process. Then wipe off the salt with a cloth and dice and sauté (if used as a garnishing) or cut into thick slices if to be browned in butter, or leave in halves if to be done au gratin or served with Parmesan alla napolitana.

FISH

Fish is one of the joys of the Mediterranean cuisine. Though the species differ from those of the Pacific and Atlantic Oceans, many recipes can be transferred satisfactorily to similar types of fish. Though fish is an excellent food, both from a gastronomic and health point of view, and although there exist dozens of delicious recipes, it has always taken second place to meat when it comes to the honors.

However, with the widespread use of frozen fish in the cities, a new interest in fish recipes has emerged which is more than welcome. Though frozen fish is not comparable to fish straight out of the water, it is far better than "fresh" fish which has been on display for many days. The freshness of fish can be judged not only by the smell, but by the brightness of the eye, the pinkness of the gills and the firmness of the flesh. It is usually best to cook fish as soon as possible on purchasing, but, in the case of big soles and turbots, for example, a couple of days' "hanging" is advisable. This maturing process is done by putting the fish on ice, with no covering, in the refrigerator. Fresh soles and turbots are found in only a few East Coast markets and then at high prices. You can substitute these with flounder and halibut. If you use frozen fish, allow to thaw out very slowly and completely before

cooking. Fresh-water fish tend to keep their freshness in the refrigerator longer than do salt-water fish.

How to prepare fish for cooking

First the fish must be scaled and eviscerated. Scale by holding the
tail (wrapped in a cloth to prevent slipping) with the left hand
and, with the right, scrape away the scales downward toward the
head either with a knife or a proper fish scaler. Care should be
taken not to damage the skin. Then clip off the gills and the fins,
if of a prickly variety; and, finally, cut into the abdomen and
remove the entrails. Wash out well with running water.

With fish of the eel family, it is best to skin them. This entails
making an incision around the head; then, holding the head
wrapped in a cloth to prevent slipping, peel off the skin around the
head, and when sufficient has been lifted so that you can grip it
firmly, pull the whole skin toward the tail in one long, determined
motion; the skin should come off whole. Cut off the head. If the
eel is not to be cooked immediately, sprinkle lightly with salt,
wrap in a cloth, and keep in a cool place; but do not put it in
water.

How to roast fish

Most fish can be roasted, but it is better if they are large and
meaty ones such as carp and pike.

Having been cleaned, salted, and generously buttered, they
should be put in a hot oven and basted as often as possible with
their own juices and the hot butter in the pan.

How to braise fish

Butter a fireproof dish, line it with a layer of sliced carrots
and onions, and add a bouquet garni of parsley, a sprig of thyme,
and bay leaves. Lay the fish, already cleaned and prepared for
cooking, on this bed and sprinkle with salt and pepper. Cook
slowly for 15 minutes and remove from the oven. At this point
either a prepared fish fumet* or dry white wine is added: enough
of either should be added to half-cover the fish. Replace in the
oven and continue cooking on a very low heat, basting every now

and then. When the fish is cooked, the pan liquids can be reduced to form the base of a sauce.

How to fry fish

The best fat for frying is either olive oil or a vegetable oil. Butter has a lower burning point, and since high temperatures are required for frying, butter is less suitable. Oil which has been used for frying fish can be used twice (of course only for frying fish), but should be filtered through a cheesecloth before being used a second time, to remove any remnants of flour, bread crumbs, etc., which can compromise the success of the second operation.

The oil must be plentiful and very hot—smoking slightly. Only in this way is the surface of the fish quickly sealed so that the fish does not absorb too much oil. Absorbing oil not only makes the fish indigestible but spoils the flavor.

With larger fish, to facilitate frying, incisions should be made along the flanks: then dip them in lightly salted milk (or beer), dust in flour, and shake off any excess. When cooked, serve with parsley, lemon, sauce tartare, or mayonnaise.

How to broil fish

Having cleaned the fish, sprinkled it with salt and dipped it in or brushed it with oil, place on a grill or broiler which has been well preheated. If put on cold metal, the fish will stick to the metal and break when being turned. During the cooking, baste frequently with oil, or melted butter, if you prefer it. The flame and the heat of the broiler should be in inverse proportion to the size of the fish: that is to say, use a high flame for a small fish (since it cooks through quickly) and a small flame and moderate heat for a big fish (so that it cooks through slowly without burning the skin). In the case of very large fish which are too big to broil, they should be cut into inch-thick "steaks" and treated with a high flame as with little fish.

How to poach a fish

The proper poaching of fish (that is to say "boiling" fish at just below boiling temperature) depends chiefly on the use of the correct liquid: this varies according to type. Bass, mullet, and cod, for example, are best poached in simple water with only 2 teaspoons of salt for every quart of water. Salmon and trout, however, require a court bouillon made from:

4 quarts water	*Pinch of thyme*
¼ pint vinegar	*1 teaspoon freshly ground*
1 sliced onion	*pepper*
3 sprigs parsley	*4 teaspoons salt*
1 bay leaf	

which is brought to the boil, and simmered for 45 minutes.

To poach lobsters, crayfish, or other shellfish (and eels), first sauté a sliced carrot and 2 sliced onions in butter: add 2 pints of water, a bouquet garni of parsley, thyme and bay leaves and a few bruised peppercorns. Bring to the boil, add the shellfish and poach for about 30 minutes.

With shrimps, salt water with thyme, bay leaves, peppercorns, and parsley is recommended. Two or three minutes cooking in boiling water is all that is needed.

While they are poaching, fish must always be well covered with liquid. For a 3-pound salmon, for example, 6 quarts of liquid are required. Cooking times can be calculated on a basis of 10 minutes for the first 1½ pounds, 15 minutes for a 4-pound fish, 20 minutes for 7 pounds and 30 minutes for a 9- to 11-pound fish.

For soles and other fish of that type, 7 to 10 minutes are sufficient for the first 2 pounds: with larger fish of 8 to 12 pounds, the cooking time drops to less than 3 minutes per pound from the moment the water reaches boiling point.

Remember always to poach on a low heat so that the fish does not burst and thus spoil its appearance when presented at table. When poaching slices of a big fish (the slices should never be thin), drop them into fast boiling salted water (or a prepared court bouillon*) and then reduce the heat sharply to a simmer. This system has the effect of sealing within the fish the juices which would, if the fish were cooked from the beginning in cold water, be dispersed into the water.

How to cook au gratin

For a light gratin, a few minutes before a fish is fully poached, remove it from its liquid and sprinkle it with bread crumbs which have been lightly browned in butter. Then dab with softened butter, dotting it here and there; put in a hot oven till there is a crisp, golden crust.

A fuller way of doing a gratin is to cover the fish, when poached, completely in béchamel sauce* and sprinkle with grated Parmesan. Spray lightly with melted butter and put in a hot oven. This will produce not only a light golden crust, but the Parmesan will also melt to perfection. A few browned bread crumbs, grated very fine, can be added to the Parmesan to good effect.

The former method can also be used with leftover pieces of fish which are put in shells and heated in the oven: or used as an all-purpose garnishing. The second method is best for a whole poached fish, where the cooking liquid is being reduced to serve as a sauce.

FISH FUMET

2 pounds raw fish, heads,
   bones, trimmings
1 carrot, sliced
1 onion, sliced
1 stalk celery, chopped
Salt and pepper
5 pints water

Cook the above ingredients together over a moderate heat for about 20 minutes. Filter through a warm, damp cheesecloth. This fumet may be further reduced, if required.

COLD BASS ITALIANA

(Dentice freddo all'italiana)

3-pound bass
3 hard-cooked eggs
6 lettuce hearts
2 lemons

Dressing:
   ½ cup oil
   Juice of 1 lemon
   Salt and pepper

Scale, eviscerate, and wash the fish well. Place in a pan of cold water with no herbs or flavorings. Poach slowly and allow to cook in its own liquid.

Drain the bass and transfer to a serving dish. Decorate it with hard-cooked eggs, cut in half, quartered lettuce hearts, and lemon wedges. Prepare the dressing of oil, lemon, and salt and pepper and pour over. Serves 6.

FRIED SOLE ITALIANA

(Sogliola fritta all'italiana)

6 soles (½-pound each)	Salt
Flour	3 lemons quartered
1 cup oil	

Raise a corner of the black skin of the sole and strip it off with one movement, using a kitchen cloth to hold the tail; scrape the white skin lightly with a knife. Eviscerate, wash, snip off fins and tail tips of the soles. With a sharp knife, lift the fillets very slightly from the backbone to facilitate cooking.

Dust the soles lightly in flour; heat plenty of oil in a frying pan till smoking and fry on both sides till crisp and golden. Drain, transfer to a serving dish, sprinkle with salt, and serve with lemon quarters. Serves 6.

FRITTATAS

How to make frittatas

The history of the frittata goes back to Roman times, as is confirmed by the ancient writer Petronius; in later centuries, the frittata has served as the vehicle for the genius of uncounted chefs and housewives the world over.

The frittata differs from the omelet in that the filling is combined with the eggs, whereas, with the omelet the filling is folded into egg mixture while it is cooking.

The secret of making a real Italian frittata is having a good, thick iron frying pan which is absolutely flat and with low sides; and in not using it for anything except making frittatas. Further, it must never be washed: clean it with a cloth while it is still warm. If, however, the eggs stick to it, you should oil it, heat it, and with a little table salt rub it vigorously with a heavy absorbent paper and then with a rough cloth.

The frittata must be crisp and golden outside and soft inside. This point is reached by heating the butter as much as possible without blackening it. If you use oil, make it smoke. In either case very hot fats ensure an immediate hardening of the frittata surface. When the fat is at the right high temperature, pour in the eggs, beaten with a little salt. When the eggs begin to set, shake the pan lightly so as to prevent the eggs' sticking to the bottom. Toss the frittata—or turn it over with the aid of a plate or saucepan lid—and cook the other side. All this should be done over a very high flame. Then slide the frittata onto a plate and serve immediately.

GRANDMOTHER'S FRITTATA

(Frittata delle nonne)

½ cup butter
9 eggs, fresh
1 tablespoon salt

Heat the butter in a frying pan; beat the eggs with the salt and pour into the pan when the butter is foaming. Turn when cooked underneath. Serve hot. Serves 3.

MUSHROOM FRITTATA ITALIANA

(Frittata coi funghi all'italiana)

2 tablespoons chopped
    mushrooms
1½ tablespoons butter
Salt and pepper

3 tablespoons oil
6 fresh eggs
12 slices mushroom
2 tablespoons butter

Sauté the 2 tablespoons mushrooms lightly in a little butter, salt, and pepper. Pour the oil into the same pan and add the beaten eggs, shaping up the frittata according to the Note. When cooked on one side, turn it.

At the same time, sauté the mushroom slices in the butter and reserve till the frittata is ready. When the frittata is golden brown on both sides, serve and top with the sautéed slices. Serves 3.

FRYING BATTER

FRYING BATTER FOR VEGETABLES

½ pound sifted flour
4 tablespoons melted butter
2 eggs, beaten with a pinch of salt

Combine the flour, the butter and the 2 eggs in a mixing bowl. Add a little water, mixing constantly, until a soft paste is obtained. Allow it to stand for about one hour before use.

FRYING BATTER FOR SWEET FRITTERS

3 eggs   *Salt and pepper*
2 tablespoons sifted flour   *¼ pint milk or, better, cream*

Beat the 3 eggs in a bowl, combining in the 2 tablespoons of flour and a pinch of salt and pepper. Pour in, then, a little at a time, the milk or cream, mixing constantly.

GELATIN

There are several ways of making gelatin or aspic; one can use stock on hand or canned beef bouillon and commercial gelatin or go through the whole and correct process. The essence of this recipe is in the use of 2 tablespoons of white wine with a fine bouquet for every quart of gelatin so that the gelatin gains in character.

GELATIN STOCK

½ pound leg of veal
½ pound veal bones, chopped
1 calf's foot, blanched in
    boiling water 10 minutes
1 carrot, chopped
1 onion, chopped

1 stalk celery, chopped
Bouquet garni:
    1 sprig thyme
    1 bay leaf
    2 sprigs parsley
2 quarts water

First brown the meat and bones in a very hot oven for 15 minutes. Put all the ingredients in a large fireproof pot, bring to a rapid boil, turn down heat, and simmer for six hours. Remove the scum from the surface; add extra water if needed, and when the stock has become almost syrupy, pass through a cheesecloth to remove every trace of fat. Makes 1 quart.

WINE GELATIN

1 quart gelatin stock*
2 tablespoons white wine
2 tablespoons chopped
    tarragon

2 tablespoons chopped chervil
1 egg white, beaten
1 eggshell, crushed

Bring all the ingredients to the boil, stirring constantly, turn down heat and simmer for 5 minutes. Remove from heat, allow to stand for a few minutes then pass one or more times through a fine cheesecloth to remove all alien substances and produce an absolutely clear gelatin.

ICE CREAMS

Ice cream is a generic term which includes many completely different delights: there are cream ices, water ices, cassate, coupes, semi-freddi, granite, spumoni, et al, all of which demand a different system of preparation.

With the aid of electric refrigerators, making ice creams at home is no longer the heavy task that it was not many decades ago. In the past, homemade ice creams were produced in an ice cream box, but nowadays they are easily made in the freezer compartment of the refrigerator, in a simple system requiring only that the refrigerator be calibrated to maximum chill, that the ice cream mix be whirled in a blender for about thirty seconds and poured into a metal container and put in the freezer for an hour or so until it has solidified. It should, then, be again put in the blender and whirled for a minute and then poured into suitable metal molds in the freezer until it has reached the correct consistency, usually about an hour.

Here are a few rules to follow: The containers and equipment used must be absolutely clean; wash them in boiling water and detergent. The milk must be boiling before being added to the egg yolks. The mixture should not be oversugared since oversugaring makes freezing difficult and produces an ice cream that melts easily and is, in any case, less palatable.

When making ice creams without vanilla—i.e., with liqueurs such as maraschino, kirsch, rum, Strega, etc., or with tea, coffee, or wine—the flavorings should be added after the first freezing.

Although fresh fruit is always best for flavoring ice cream, canned fruit may be used, especially when one wishes to make an ice cream with an out-of-season fruit. It is often economical to prepare fruit flavoring in quantity and keep it in store, particularly if you have a lot of ripe fruit to use up. First pass the fruit pulp through cheesecloth, avoiding physical handling. Sweeten the fruit purée with 1½ pounds sugar for every 1 pound of fruit, then mix well until the sugar blends with the fruit. Pour into jars, close hermetically and store in a cool place. The ices you make with this preserve will have the same aroma and taste as those made with fresh fruit.

LAMB

A lamb becomes a sheep when it is one year old and, consequently, in culinary terms, mutton. Between three and five months of age, it is usually called spring lamb or baby lamb.

When buying lamb, one should look at the loins: these should be broad and well covered with firm meat. The freshness of the meat can be judged by pressing the leg and by the pale rose color of the kidneys.

A good roast can be obtained from the leg, either with or without the saddle. Chops and cutlets come from the saddle. Stews and spezzatini come from the shoulder, neck, and breast. The liver is particularly tasty.

MAYONNAISE

(Maionese)

1 pint oil
3 egg yolks
Salt and pepper

1 tablespoon vinegar (or lemon juice)

If the weather is cold and the kitchen implements equally so, the latter must be warmed with boiling water, otherwise mayonnaise cannot be made. Also, the oil must be warmed slightly; however, with the ordinary summer room temperature or central heating, these precautions are not necessary.

Put the egg yolks into a mixing bowl, adding a pinch of salt and pepper and a few drops of vinegar. Begin beating this mixture with an appropriate whisk, adding the oil, a little at a time, in a thin trickle. As soon as the egg yolks have absorbed 4 or 5 tablespoons of oil, the mayonnaise will begin to take body.

At this stage, do not pour in more oil, but combine in a few drops of vinegar or lemon juice; this prevents the mayonnaise from thickening too much and too quickly. After this operation, the oil can be added with little fear of the sauce "separating" (when it looks as though it is curdling) though if, on the other hand, the sauce thickens too much, a further few drops of vinegar or lemon juice should be added.

If the sauce does "separate," due to an exaggerated use of oil, start the process again by beating a raw egg yolk in a bowl and pouring in the "spoiled" mayonnaise as though it were the oil.

MUSHROOMS

These can be field or cultivated, dried or fresh. In practice, one uses the Italian dried mushrooms mainly (these slivers come from the big porcini mushrooms) and fresh cultivated mushrooms which are available almost everywhere.

If you have fresh porcini, they are prepared for cooking by first removing any earthy parts and then skinning the caps and stems. Without washing them, they should be dried with a cloth, chopped or left whole according to the recipe; this should be done as soon after they are bought or gathered as possible.

With fresh cultivated mushrooms, it is a good rule to do a preliminary cooking as soon as they are bought. Having removed earthy roots, wash and drain them carefully: snip off stems as close to the cap as possible. Skin both caps and stems and place in a pot of cold water with a squeeze of lemon.

Taking, say, 2 pounds of mushrooms, put them in a casserole and cover with water. Add 2 ounces of butter, a pinch of salt and bring to the boil. From that moment, continue boiling for 5 minutes in the case of small mushrooms and for 7 minutes for medium-sized ones. Drain and reserve covered with a buttered greaseproof sheet. They are ready for final cooking.

If the mushrooms must be prepared quickly to garnish a fish, meat, or other dish, just wash them in running water, dry them well, and, without peeling them, chop and sauté them in butter over a high flame for a few minutes.

Dried porcini mushrooms should be placed in tepid—or even hot—water for 30 minutes to bring back their flavor and substance. Drain, wash, and dry them, and they are ready for use.

For some sauces which are made with fresh mushrooms, if some dried porcini mushrooms are added, the flavor is improved considerably.

FRESH MUSHROOMS ITALIANA

(Funghi freschi all'italiana)

1 pound mushrooms	3 cloves garlic, finely chopped
(preferably wild)	6 tablespoons chopped parsley
½ cup oil	Juice of ½ lemon
2 teaspoons salt	Cubes of day-old bread,
Pinch of pepper	sautéed in oil

Prepare the mushrooms according to the Mushrooms Note*. Slice them. Heat the oil to smoking in a frying pan, add the mushrooms, salt, and pepper, and as the mushrooms begin to brown, turn down the heat and add the garlic. When the garlic is golden, add the parsley and lemon juice and combine. Pour into a serving dish, decorate with the bread cubes. As a main dish serves 2 to 3.

MUSSELS

Edible mussels come in all shapes and sizes. One should, however, avoid only those with a fragile shell and which tend to bluish and yellowish tints, since these may be infected. Since infection (particularly in the case of harbor-bred mussels) can easily occur, it is wise to add a little vinegar to the cooking water to kill off any bacteria.

Be sure the mussel is alive before cooking: tap the shell, and if the mussel is alive, the shell will clamp down tightly. Then soak them in a basin of water before cooking: discard any which float to the surface. Then clean and beard the shells well and place in a covered pan with a little water over a high flame. Do not throw away the liquid which comes from the shells; it is rich in flavor and can be the base of an accompanying sauce.

FRIED MUSSELS ITALIANA

(Cozze fritte all'italiana)

2 *pounds large mussels*	*½ cup oil*
2 *eggs, beaten*	3 *sprigs parsley, chopped*
2 *tablespoons bread crumbs*	3 *lemons, quartered*
Flour	

Scrub and beard the mussels; shuck them raw, remove from their shells and dry them with a cloth. Beat the eggs and dip the mussels, one by one, in the beaten eggs and then dust in bread crumbs; pass them again through the beaten egg and dust them in flour.

Sauté the breaded mussels in plenty of smoking oil in a pan until golden brown: remove with slotted spoon and drain: keep warm. When all are cooked, pass to a serving dish, decorate with parsley and lemon wedges. Serves 4 to 6.

OVENS AND OVEN TEMPERATURES

In some old ovens, there were two systems for controlling the heat source: a flame at the bottom and one at the top. The lower flame was used for pastries—to raise them—and the higher flame for roasting and broiling. In most ovens, today, there is only one heat source—the lower one: one must, therefore, put the food to be "raised" on the lower grid and what is to be broiled, braised, or roasted on higher ones.

For example, a cake or pastry is put on a low grid near the flame to make it rise: on a higher grid it would not rise, but only a crust would be formed. However, when it has risen satisfactorily, it can be put on a higher grid to brown.

Roast meats in general—and fish too—are best put on the central grid in a moderate oven, so that they cook through evenly. The temperature of the oven must be carefully regulated. For the purposes of this book, moderate heat means 300° to

325° Fahrenheit; a hot oven means from 350° to 400° Fahrenheit, while a very hot oven means 450° and above.

Pizzas, for example, should be cooked in a very hot oven and require usually from 15 to 20 minutes. This goes for most buns, croissants, pastry, etc., in which yeast or baking powder is used.

A cake, however, should bake in a hot oven, so that it cooks through to the center without burning. Meringues and all other cakes and cookies in that category should receive only moderate heat, since they do not need to color, but must only harden.

PASTA

Over and above the classic homemade pastas, made with fresh eggs, there are innumerable dry pastas made on an industrial scale; these include spaghetti, macaroni, maccheroncelli, bucatini, perciatelli, zite, mezze zite, linguine, trenette or lingue di passero, maltagliati or penne, rigatoni, vermicelli, cannolicchi, cannolic-chietti o avemarie, etc.

How to cook pasta

Cooking pasta is very easy, but it requires some care. First, there must be plenty of water: the rule says, use from a pint to a quart for every ¼ pound of pasta. My preference is for a quart or more as this ensures that the pasta will not become tacky and stick together. For the same reason, it is as well to use a disproportionately large pot: that is to say, so big that the pasta can move freely in the water without fear of strands sticking together. The water should be salted in the proportion of about 1½ tablespoons for every quart of water.

The pasta is added to the water when the water is boiling fast, but not all at once. Add the pasta a little at a time, sprinkling it in carefully and stirring continuously so that the strands do not stick together. Adding the pasta will cause the temperature of the water to drop: bring the water, therefore, back to a fast boil, turn down the heat and continue cooking. Stir every now and then.

It is not possible to lay down a specific time for how long pasta should be cooked. This depends not only on the type of flour used, the shape and thickness of the pasta, whether it is fresh or dried, and whether there are eggs in the mix, but also on the personal preference of those who will be eating the pasta.

Our advice is to cook it al dente. This means halting the cooking when the pasta is still consistent and not cooked right through. Al dente (literally "to the tooth") means that the pasta is not soft, but presents still some resistance when being bitten or masticated. Sample the pasta, therefore, while it is still cooking and when it reaches that point, remove from the stove (add a little cold water to prevent further cooking from its own heat—this is very important with very thin pasta like vermicelli) and drain as quickly as possible in a colander, pass to a mixing dish, and serve.

In the case of pasta being served simply with butter and Parmesan, one should retain a little of the cooking water so that a spoonful or two can be added in case the pasta has been drained too well and the strands are dry and sticking together; this occurs, particularly, after the butter and parmesan have been added.

It is a habit (and a bad one) even in Italy of adding the sauce first to the pasta in the mixing dish and following with the Parmesan. This is a plain technical error. First the cheese should make contact with the hot pasta, liquefy and, in this way, regain its full flavor; then add the sauce and mix well.

How to prepare homemade egg pasta

Heap 1 pound of sifted flour onto a pastry board or marble-topped kitchen table. Whip 5 eggs with a few drops of oil and a teaspoon of salt. Pour the mixture into a well, scooped out of the mound of sifted flour. Kneading manually, bring the flour to the center and continue until the dough reaches a fairly consistent texture. Dampen a white kitchen cloth with warm water, wrap the dough in it and allow to rest for a half hour.

Then, with a rolling pin, roll out the dough into sheets of the thickness required by the recipe. Where possible, it is often better to make the sheets of dough on the thick side and to make the dough mixture "porous" with the addition of a little extra flour.

This egg pasta dough offers itself for a very wide swath of possible recipes: which, in their turn, offer further variety according to the way in which the dough is shaped and stuffed. Here, for example, one can mention tortellini, agnolotti, cappelletti, ravioli, cannelloni, tortelli, tortelloni, etc. All these have different fillings, but the dough is generally the one described above, though it can vary in the number of eggs used and the sheets of pastry can be thicker or thinner according to taste.

Cappelletti, for example, are tortelloni, but bigger. The dough used for these should be smooth and well-kneaded: after a brief rest, it should be rolled out into sheets and cut into 1½-inch diameter circles with a metal cooky cutter or glass. The filling is put in the middle of the circles, which are folded over lightly and pinched and twisted into the traditional shape of a little hat, which is the meaning of *cappelletti*.

The dough for tortelli and tortelloni should be very thin and allowed to rest for almost an hour. Then cut it into rounds of 2 to 3 inches in diameter: lay the stuffing on one half of each roundel and fold over the other side so that a half-moon shape is obtained.

The people of Genoa make their dough for ravioli in this way—i.e., as above—but they use only 3 eggs for every 1 pound of flour, plus a little water and a pinch of salt. The dough is then made very thin and the stuffing (rolled into little Lima-bean-sized balls) is put regularly on a sheet of dough and a second sheet of dough is laid on top of this first one and, with a fluted pastry cutter, squares or rounds are cut from the sheets. Squares, for example, should not be bigger than 1½ inches.

Agnolotti are made and filled in much the same way as ravioli, but are bigger and always round.

The dough used for cannelloni, also, is usually the same as for ravioli. It is rolled out into sheets and cut into rectangles 3 inches wide and 4 inches long. These are then cooked in plenty of boiling lightly salted water, drained and laid out on a damp (but well wrung-out cloth). Allow to cool before filling and rolling.

Tagliatelle, which are called fettuccine in some parts of Italy, and lasagna are simple strips of dough used without a filling. They differ only in their dimensions. Fettuccine or tagliatelle are less than ½ inch broad and spaghetti-length, while lasagna vary from 1 to 3 inches in width, and are often shorter: the broader types are preferred for the various methods of making baked lasagna (lasagne pasticciate).

POLENTA

Traditionally, a big copper pot is used to make polenta; this round-bottomed caldron is called a *paiolo* and is hung over a wood fire. But, of course, one may substitute a casserole.

One starts by putting the pot (or casserole) with 4 pints of water and 2 teaspoons of salt to boil; at the same time, put another kettle or pot of water to boil, as this extra boiling water will be needed during the cooking.

Then take 1½ pounds of polenta flour and sprinkle it "like rain" (as they say in Italian) into the pot so that there is no sharp drop in temperature of the water: if the water stops boiling, even for a moment, the polenta forms into lumps and is spoiled.

Which polenta flour is best? Polenta, in fact, is a maize flour comparable to American corn meal. The traditional countryman's food is coarse-grained polenta, which is almost gritty to the palate; the Verona and Bergamo varieties are the best in this category. The lighter, smoother polenta, however, is the classic one for fine cooking. In either case, having "showered" the polenta into the boiling water, a little at a time, start stirring and do not stop. A wooden spoon is needed to stir and one must, without letup, keep stirring—traditionally always in a clockwise direction—till the polenta is cooked.

The polenta will begin to thicken slowly at first; and then more rapidly. You must help it not become too thick. This is done by adding a ladle of the extra boiling water which was prepared. The art of polenta making lies entirely at this point: that is to say, one should let the polenta thicken and then soften it by adding boiling water—and, of course, stirring constantly in a clockwise direction.

After 15 minutes of this process, sprinkle another pound of polenta into the pot in the same way as before. You may, at this point, take a few moments off from the continuous stirring: but then the hardening and softening process of the polenta starts again.

In about another 15 minutes, you will sense that the polenta is reaching the right consistency, because it comes away from the side of the casserole easily as you stir. It is, in fact, cooked, and nobody can say that it isn't.

But, for connoisseurs, this is not enough. They insist on a further 30 minutes with the wooden spoon and boiling water process. The reason for this is that the extra cooking makes the polenta much more digestible, as well as improving its flavor. This extra work also removes the slightly bitter taste which can be noted when the cook has taken the shorter route.

However, after a full hour in the pot, the polenta is finally ready. If coarse-grain polenta has been used, this should be poured out and cut with a white thread and not with a knife: it is then eaten with butter and fresh or grated cheese. Or better, it can be used as the foundation (cut into squares and fried or crisped in the oven) for ragouts, stews, and other intingoli of fish or meat. Remember, however, that polenta must always be served very hot or it loses its flavor. It can also be eaten with broth or well-soaked in milk. There are, in fact, no limits to the uses of polenta, since it replaces bread, potatoes, and other basic starch foods.

PORK

Pork should be white with a light pink tint, firm and finely textured. It should always be well-cooked for hygienic reasons, but that is no reason to overcook it till it is dry and tasteless.

Fresh leg of pork, the chops, the fillets can be prepared in many ways but are best roasted or grilled. Pork sausages, the feet, the ears, the belly, and the rind should not be ignored by a good cook, nor should the liver which, when enhanced with bay leaves and wrapped in its own net and grilled is very appetizing, though somewhat heavy.

The shoulder butt, the spareribs, and the neck offer excellent stewing meats for intingoli and spezzatini. In all cases when pork knuckles and feet are used, they must be blanched, cleaned, stripped of skin and superfluous fat before use: then boil with herbs and aromatic vegetables.

Suckling Pig

The definition of suckling pig is a piglet of between six and eight weeks old which has not yet been weaned. It is slaughtered in the normal manner and then bled till the meat is white. It is then plunged into boiling water; the exterior is cleaned, the hoofs removed and the animal eviscerated (reserve only the liver).

Suckling pig is best cooked on the spit or in the oven with garlic, rosemary, oil (or lard), and with plenty of salt and even more pepper. It is also excellent stuffed: in this case, one should let the pig hang for twenty-four hours and then stuff it with a well-peppered filling including its own liver. After a generous larding (or use oil) the pig should be roasted whole.

POULTRY

This category includes not only squab chicken, pullets, broilers, fryers, roasters, capons and boilers but wild and farm-raised duck, turkey, guinea hen, geese, pigeon and game birds generally.

How to choose a bird

A fowl is young and fresh if, when it has been plucked, its skin is smooth to the touch, the flesh tender and elastic but not soft. The spur should be short and smooth: if it is hard, pointed and scaly, this is a sure sign that the bird is old. The rump should be white and slightly pink and have some fat on the upper part. A poor bird is easily recognized, not only from its skinny neck, but by its having well-formed spurs and calloused feet.

How to prepare poultry for cooking

Pluck the feathers and pass the bird over a flame to remove any remaining hairs; dry well with a kitchen cloth and complete the external cleaning. Remove the head. With an incision under the neck, remove the gorge: then, with another incision from the tail to the abdomen big enough for your hand to reach in easily, remove all the entrails and vital organs, being particularly careful not to break the bile sac (gall bladder), which is attached to the liver. Then wash out well with running water. Bend back (or break) the leg above the knee joint and truss up well and tie with string, or cut the bird into pieces according to the recipe. Reserve the liver and heart.

How to bone a fowl

The choice of bird for this operation is most important: it must be a good plump specimen of its type. Pluck it and pass it over a flame to sear off remaining feathers and hair, but taking care that the actual skin is not charred. Dry well with cloth. Cut through the neck in the middle, break the wings, and either break or bend back the legs at the joint. Then with a sharp knife, open the bird along the back of the neck to the tail and, from the inside, very gently remove the bones from the wings, stripping away the meat with great care. Working still from the inside, lift the meat from the legs, the back and the breast and continue this operation till the whole carcass, with all its innards, is removed.

How to obtain poultry breasts

Prepare the bird in the normal manner for cooking and then make a circular incision around the neck. Make another incision from the first cut to the base of the neck and along the top ridge of the breastbone and continue down each side to separate the flesh from the bone in one piece. Carefully remove the skin from around the neck and then cut the neck off where it joins the body. Raise the skin from the neck toward the breast and pass the point of a longish and very sharp knife along the breastbone, lifting the meat. Then, very gently, so as not to damage the fillets, lift them off the bone leaving the skin attached to the meat.

Then, from the inside, with a firm movement of a knife or poultry scissors, cut the breastbones away from their anchorage and remove: proceed carefully removing all the smaller bones which remain. This done, close the opening with the skin from the neck which was raised at the beginning of the operation. The bird will then appear to be whole and presentable. It is also ready to be stuffed, trussed, and cooked.

RICE

Rice is not only healthful and nutritious, but is the most easily digestible of all the starchy foods. It has an important place in the Italian cuisine because there is a very large production of rice in the Valley of the River Po: this high-quality, large-grain Italian rice is widely obtainable in the United States.

In Italy, rice is used in a variety of ways, but chiefly it is served in soups and in the form of risottos; but also as a filling for vegetables, in salads and as a side dish. It is also used a great deal in dessert making.

Broadly, it can be said that rice has four main culinary uses:

1. Boiled in stock, for soups—usually called minestra.

2. Boiled or steamed, for making dry rice for use in salads, timballi, pilafs, etc.

3. Sautéed and browned in the casserole to make the famous, traditional Italian risotto.

4. Sautéed and browned in the casserole, then baked in the oven for certain regional dishes.

SALADS

Salads, in the raw state, are not only refreshing, full of minerals, vitamins, etc., but tend to balance out an overly rich diet. Salads, with raw or mixed with cooked vegetables, are most versatile: they can be eaten alone or as a side dish to almost any fish or meat course. The standard dressing for salads is a simple sauce made of 2 parts olive oil and 1 part wine vinegar or lemon juice, a pinch of salt and a pinch of pepper, but the range of possible salad dressings is infinite and limited only by one's own ingenuity.

There are entrée-type salads which are usually composed of slices of shellfish, fish, seafood, chicken slivers, various cooked and raw vegetables and bound with a mayonnaise sauce. These require careful preparation and often almost constitute a meal in themselves.

MIXED SALAD WITH POTATOES, EGGS, ONION, CELERY

(Insalata mista all'italiana con patate, uova, cipolla e sedano)

½ *pound onion rings, raw*	*6 eggs, hard-cooked*
½ *pound salad tomatoes,*	½ *cup oil*
sliced	*2 tablespoons vinegar*
½ *pound boiled potatoes,*	*Salt and pepper*
sliced	*1 teaspoon Dijon mustard*
½ *pound celery, chopped*	

With the exception of the onions, clean and prepare the vegetables, reserving them in a cool place. At mealtime, shell the eggs and divide the whites from the yolks; chop the yolks and cut the whites into strips. Put both into a salad bowl into which the prepared vegetables have already been placed. Mix a dressing of oil, vinegar, salt and pepper, and Dijon mustard; peel the onions, slice them and lay them on top of the other ingredients in the salad bowl. Pour in the dressing, toss the salad and serve. Serves 6 to 8.

MIXED SALAD WITH LETTUCE AND CHEESE

(Insalata all'italiana con lattuga e formaggio)

1 pound lettuce hearts	*A mixture of:*
4 tablespoons grated	*1 sprig chervil, chopped*
Parmesan	*1 sprig tarragon, chopped*
½ *cup cream*	*Salt and pepper*
½ *cup oil*	*Juice of* ½ *lemon*

Clean and dry the lettuce hearts, quarter them lengthwise, and lay them in a salad bowl; reserve in a cool place.

Put 4 tablespoons of Parmesan in a mixing bowl: pour in the cream, mixing well with the cheese. Then pour in the oil, as though making a mayonnaise, whipping with a wire whisk or fork. Finish by combining into the bowl the mixture of chervil, tarragon, salt, pepper, and lemon juice. Pour this thick, creamy dressing over the lettuce hearts, mix well, and serve. Serves 4 to 6.

MIXED SALAD WITH ASPARAGUS, STRING BEANS, AND LETTUCE

(Insalata all'italiana con asparagi, fagiolini e lattuga)

½ *pound asparagus tips*	*Dressing:*
½ *pound string beans*	½ *cup mayonnaise**
½ *pound cauliflower*	*1 tablespoon chopped basil*
flowerets	*2 tablespoons oil*
4 lettuce leaves, chopped	*1 teaspoon vinegar*
fine	*Salt and pepper*
¼ *pound radishes, sliced*	

Wash and cook the asparagus, the string beans and the cauliflower. Chop off the tips of the asparagus, chop the beans into 1-inch lengths and break the cauliflower into flowerets. Put all these, in layers, in a salad bowl, and sprinkle over the finely chopped lettuce leaves and the little slices of radish.

Prepare in a mixing bowl a dressing of mayonnaise, with some basil and combine this with the oil, vinegar, and a pinch of salt and pepper. Pour this dressing over the salad and toss well. Serves 6.

MIXED SALAD WITH LETTUCE, BEETS, AND HAM

(Insalata mista all'italiana con lattuga,
    barbabietola e prosciutto)

½ *pound crisp lettuce leaves,*	¼ *pound pickled veal*
coarsely chopped	*tongue*
½ *pound beets, sliced and cut*	½ *cup mayonnaise**
in strips	½ *cup cream*
½ *pound celery, chopped*	*2 tablespoons tomato ketchup*
A mixture of:	*Salt*
¼ *pound Italian ham*	

Clean and prepare the vegetables and chop the ham and tongue. Reserve all these in a salad bowl in a cool place. Prepare a generous mayonnaise sauce with cream and a little ketchup to color it a delicate pink. Pour over the salad, toss and serve. Serves 8.

MIXED SALAD WITH LETTUCE, BEETS, AND HORSE-RADISH

(Insalata mista all'italiana con lattuga, barbabietola e rafano)

½ pound beets,* sliced
6 lettuce leaves, crisp
3 eggs
Dressing:
  6 tablespoons oil

2 tablespoons lemon
Salt and pepper
1 teaspoon chopped parsley
2 tablespoons grated horse-
  radish

Bake the beets in the oven till done. Wash the lettuce leaves. Hard-cook the eggs, dice them, and crush them with a fork.

Prepare a dressing of oil, lemon, salt, pepper, and chopped parsley. Combine the crushed hard-cooked eggs with the 2 tablespoons of grated horse-radish.

On each of 6 plates, put 1 lettuce leaf; onto each, spoon some slices of baked beets. Spoon a little of the egg and horse-radish mixture onto beet slices and pour over each dish the dressing. Serves 6.

MIXED SALAD WITH LETTUCE, ARTICHOKES, AND SWEET PEPPERS

(Insalata mista all'italiana con lattuga, carciofi e peperoni)

½ pound lettuce hearts,
  chopped
½ pound salad tomatoes,
  sliced
½ pound artichoke hearts,
  sliced
½ pound sweet peppers,
  sliced

6 eggs
Dressing:
  ½ cup oil
  2 tablespoons vinegar
  Salt and pepper
  Dijon mustard

Clean and prepare the vegetables: put them in a large salad bowl and reserve in a cool place. Hard-cook the eggs and reserve.

At mealtime, shell the eggs; chop the yolks and cut the whites into strips. Add both to the salad bowl. Prepare the dressing of oil, vinegar, salt, pepper and Dijon mustard. Pour this over the salad, toss, and serve. Serves 8.

CELERY SALAD

(Insalata all'italiana con sedano)

1 pound celery stalks, white and tender	*½ cup oil*
Dressing:	*1½ tablespoons salt*
1 teaspoon Dijon mustard	*Pinch of pepper*
3 tablespoons vinegar	*1½ tablespoons chopped parsley*

Wash the celery well; chop it into 2-inch lengths and then lengthwise into little "matchsticks." Bring a pot of water to the boil and blanch these celery sticks, drain and allow them to cool. Reserve in a salad bowl in a cool place.

Two hours before serving prepare the dressing of Dijon mustard, vinegar, oil, salt, pepper, and chopped parsley and pour over the salad and toss. Serves 4 to 6.

SALAMES, HAMS, AND SAUSAGES

The following are some of the better-known dried sausages, salames, and hams which play important roles in Italian regional dishes.

1. Bologna *coppa,* made from boiled and spiced pig's head.

2. Lombardy *cotechino,* made chiefly from pork rind: the best known is that of Cremona in which vanilla is also added.

3. Parma *culatello,* made from pork hindquarters: although originally from Busseto, the best is now matured at Zibelle.

4. Tuscan *finocchiona,* a special dried pork sausage, flavored with wild fennel.

5. Roman or Veneto *lingua salmistrata,* sweet-and-sour pickled tongue.

6. Abruzzo *lonza,* spiced and matured pork back.

7. Monza and Veneto *luganega* are the best-known Italian dried sausages.

8. Bologna *mortadella* is famous throughout the world. There is, however, also mortadella from Rome and Amatrice. Roman mortadella can be recognized by its oval, flattened shape, Amatrice mortadella by the square strips of matured pork fat which are inserted lengthwise into this delicately spiced sausage.

9. Campania or Calabria *capocello* or *capicello* is made from well-matured lean pork back which, to be perfect, on being sliced, should emit drops of liquid which are romantically described as "tears."

10. Marches' *clauscolo* should be so soft that it can be spread on bread; it is in its prime condition in the two months before Easter.

11. The Piacenza and Parma *biondole* and *coppe* are round and made of lean meat only; these are strongly recommended.

12. The types of ham are unending: the best known are those of *Parma,* closely followed by *Langhirane, San Daniele, Friuli, Acri, Grimaldi, San Fili, Sant'Agata, Esare* and a variety of "mountain hams"; these last come from many parts and are all prepared and matured in such a way that they are only lightly salted and, in fact, come into the category of "sweet hams."

13. Milan *salame* is a very finely ground and well-spiced (with red peppers) pork sausage.

14. Fabriano salame is a sausage of spiced lean meat, ground with a little fat: in the Marche and in Rome, this salame goes under the name of *corallino.*

15. *Sorpressate* are produced in Calabria, Puglia, Sicily, Sardinia, and in the Veneto.

16. Modena *zampone* is the glory of the Modena sausage makers: it is prepared with a mixture of ground and spiced meats and stuffed into a pig's foot which has been boned and dried.

SAUCES

Sauces enhance and round out almost all Italian dishes. Tomato sauce,* especially when made with fresh tomatoes, is the basis of many dishes. Béchamel* is needed for many recipes, while mayonnaise* is a war-horse which plays its role in an infinite number of dishes, particularly with fish and salads.

Among the more important sauces are the famous green sauce,* which is served with boiled meats; bagnacauda,* pride of the Piedmontese; pesto,* the glory of Liguria; Roman sugo finto* (mock sauce), the joy of the Romans; and the peverada,* much loved by the cooks of the Veneto, who serve it with all types of game, whether bird or beast. There are also a series of meat sauces, lamb sauce, pork sauce, mushroom sauce, and many others to add to the joys of the table, which will be found throughout the text of this book.

To be a successful sauce maker, one needs passion and some creative talent: and this is rarely lacking in those who love good food. It is not easy to amalgamate the various ingredients, but this ability grows with practice.

Sauces should be simmered on a moderate heat: real boiling should always be avoided. When ready, sauces should be kept warm, preferably in a double boiler: if they are to be preserved, a film of butter should be poured over the surface to prevent a skin forming.

As well as the sauces mentioned above, there are to be found also in the text of this book the following:

Amatrice sauce
Bagnet sauce
Bolognese sauce
Braised beef sauce
Braised pork sauce
Calabrian red wine sauce
Carbonara sauce

Cherry sauce como style
Clam sauce
Court bouillon
Duck sauce
Emilian béchamel
Emilian meat sauce
Family meat sauce (Romagna)
Fish fumet
Fresh anchovy sauce
Gremolada sauce
Horse-radish sauce
Hot red pepper sauce (all'arrabbiata)
Italian meat sauce
Jugged hare sauce
Lamb sauce
Marches' tomato sauce with basil
Mushroom sauce
Rabbit sauce

ITALIAN MEAT SAUCE

(Sugo di carne all'italiana)

3 tablespoons chopped ham
  fat
3 tablespoons chopped pork
  or bacon rind, blanched
1 pound lean beef
1 carrot, sliced
Salt and pepper
½ pound veal leg muscle
¼ pound salt pork, cut in
  strips
1 tablespoon chopped dried
  mushrooms, soaked
A mixture of:
  8 tablespoons finely
    chopped onion

4 tablespoons finely chopped
  carrot
1 stalk celery, finely chopped
1 clove garlic, finely chopped
1 clove
Salt and pepper
Bouquet garni:
  2 springs thyme
  3 bay leaves
  2 sprigs marjoram
½ cup dry red wine
1½ tablespoons flour
¼ pound peeled tomatoes,
  drained
Salt

Put the ham fat in a casserole, add the pork or bacon rind, followed by the pound of lean beef into which have been inserted slivers of carrot. Sprinkle with salt and pepper.

Lard the veal leg muscle with salt pork strips and add to the casserole. Add also the mushrooms and the finely chopped mixture, seasoning with the clove and some salt and pepper.

Put this prepared casserole, covered, onto a moderate flame and stir every now and then. As soon as the meat begins to color, add the bouquet garni (tied with a white thread) and pour in ½ cup of dry red wine: reduce the wine almost completely and then, off the heat, mix in the flour. Put the casserole back on the heat, mixing well for a few minutes; then add the peeled tomatoes. Pour in sufficient boiling water so that the meat is just covered: adjust for salt and stir well so that all the ingredients are well mixed. Bring to the boil, turn down heat and simmer for about four hours in the oven.

Remove the casserole from the oven, reserve the meat (this can serve for minced meat), pass the sauce through a sieve into another casserole or saucepan and bring to the boil on the stove. Skim off fats which come to the surface: if the sauce is too thin, continue boiling until it reaches the right consistency. Pour into a suitable jar and reserve in a cool place. This will remain good for several days: and, in fact, will be more savory on the second day than on the first.

SOUPS, BROTHS, AND STOCK

How to prepare stock

2 pounds beef
Giblets and neck of 1 chicken
2 carcasses of roast chicken
1 marrowbone
8 pints cold water
4 small carrots
2 leeks
1 stalk celery

Bouquet garni:
  3 sprigs parsley
  3 sprigs thyme
  2 bay leaves
1 clove garlic, bruised
3 peppercorns, bruised
2 tablespoons coarse salt

The choice of meat is very important. The following cuts are recommended: the rump and the round; the short ribs next to the pot-roast area; and the sirloin. Any of these make a fine stock, especially if strengthened with a veal shank. The shank (the whole part above the shin, which is also called the short plate), the meat on the shinbone and the lower part of the breast, around the brisket, all make a very rich stock.

Truss up the meats well with string and put in an fireproof kettle and cover with water. Bring the water *slowly* to the boil over a moderate heat. As soon as the scum rises to the surface, skim it off carefully and add the vegetables, the herbs, garlic, and peppercorns and 2 tablespoons of coarse salt. Simmer over a low flame for about three and a half hours.

Remove kettle from stove, remove meat, and reserve; pass the stock through a damp cheesecloth to filter, then adjust for salt.

The most important point in preparing a good stock is to bring it to the boiling point very slowly. In fact, this slow heating of the water encourages the dissolving of the albuminous substances in the meat and allows them to incorporate themselves in the stock, while the scum rises to the top as a foam and is easy to remove.

The nearer to boiling point the water gets, the more the foam comes to the surface, especially if, from time to time, a tablespoon of cold water is added to help this process.

Cooking should never be started in hot water, nor should the boiling be done over a high flame as this would make the albuminous substances solidify and block the fibers of the meat, preventing the meat juices from incorporating themselves in the stock. A low heat dilates the fibers of the meat and gives flavor to the stock. A high heat means a mediocre and cloudy stock—and stringy meat.

SOUPS

Zuppe, with some exceptions, are characterized by garnishings of bread, rice, pasta, and vegetables in their final preparation. Vegetables play an important part and must first be slowly sautéed in butter (or whatever fat you prefer). This is done for two reasons: first to eliminate the water from the vegetables and then to impregnate the fat (preferably butter) with the aroma of the vegetables.

VEGETABLE BROTH

1 pound potatoes, peeled,
    sliced
2 onions, chopped
1 stalk celery, chopped
3 carrots, chopped
3 tomatoes, drained and
    chopped
1 clove

Bouquet garni:
    3 sprigs parsley
    2 sprigs thyme
    1 bay leaf
Oil
1 teaspoon salt
¼ teaspoon freshly ground
    pepper

Having cleaned and chopped the vegetables, sauté them and the other ingredients in a kettle. Add salt, pepper and plenty of water.

Bring to the boil and allow to simmer for one and a half hours. Filter through a fine sieve.

VEAL

Milk veal comes from calves which have been slaughtered at around three months of age—that is, before weaning. The meat is white, close-grained and very digestible because of lack of fat. It is hard to find in the United States and very expensive. Even in Italy, it is becoming rarer: the finest comes from Piedmont, where it goes under the name of *sanato*.

As for normal veal, the best cuts come from the loin. This is then sliced lengthwise into two. Then veal chops are obtained in two ways—either by removing the chops with a perpendicular stroke so that each cutlet retains a part of the fillet and the kidney (these are called *nodini* or *arrostini*), or by removing the cutlets without the fillet and the kidney, in which case they are called *lombatine*. The loin, with or without the bone, makes an excellent roast veal: and the veal chops, with the bone, are excellent grilled, fried or egg-and-bread-crumbed alla milanese.

The leg, the rump, and the noisettes furnish excellent roasts: the last makes good scaloppine, particularly from the inner noisette and the fesa (the point of the inner noisette) which is also much used for involtini and piccata and other small-slice dishes.

The breast, including the arm-steak area, can be stuffed in various ways, when it becomes a rollé. The shoulder, with the skill of the Genovese cooks, is used to make rolled veal cima Genoa style.* All the leftover parts can be used for stews, spezzatini and intingoli.

The shanks supply the raw material for the Milan ossobuco, the marrowbone "steak," while the shinbone meat is suitable for fricassées and other intingoli with tomatoes, vegetables, etc.

The veal fillet, being small, is normally used for saltimbocca, messicani, vitello all'uccelletto and other recipes of this nature.

All the variety meats can make first-class dishes: brain, sweetbreads, kidneys, and especially the liver. The tongue, too, when well prepared and cut into slices makes an excellent dish.

Piedmont and the Aosta Valley

Piedmont is somehow a strange region—little known to foreigners and Italians alike; yet it made Italy. Over one hundred years ago, it was ruled by the Dukes of Savoy, who were also Kings of Sardinia; it was a little state, advanced in its thinking and with an army as disciplined as that of the Prussians.

With a hand from Garibaldi, they made Italy one country instead of six; and put their own ruler on the throne in Rome. From then on, everybody seemed to forget that Piedmont even existed. Were it not for its gastronomy, Piedmont's only claim to fame would be that Fiat motorcars are made there.

Piedmont is, in fact, a land many times blessed gastronomically. It has the finest wines of Italy. Their names—Barolo, Ghemme, Gattinara, Grignolino, Barbaresco, Barbera, Dolcetto, Carema, Cortese, and many more—are dulcet sounds in the ear of any gourmet. Piedmont has also Italy's best veal and magnificent game —from pheasants to wild boar—and they have that jewel of gastronomy, the white Alba truffle, the price of which often sails beyond its base price of thirty dollars a pound to close to sixty dollars over Christmas and the New Year in Rome.

It should also be remembered that, in Turin, vermouth and grissini (breadsticks) were invented about a century ago: and that the Piedmontese have the most delicious cheese fondue in the world which, if married to some slices of Alba truffle, is exquisite beyond words.

Turin's having been a capital city for so long, of course, has played an important part in enhancing what might otherwise have been a provincial cuisine. Being so close to France, one might expect to find some French influence, but strangely Piedmontese cooking stands much on its own and, unlike most of Italian food, is particularly robust. Piedmont's wines are equally masculine.

Bagnacauda,* for example, is the most singular dish: it is a savory dip which, once tasted, is unlikely to be forgotten, based as it is on salted anchovies and garlic marinated in milk. It is eaten with raw vegetables and never fails to delight and satisfy.

Piedmont is more a risotto-eating land than a spaghetti land, but it has one great pasta specialty—agnolotti.* These are the big brothers of Genoa's ravioli and they are usually filled with a stuffing of chicken, sausage, onions, and cheese: their reputation is well established throughout Italy.

Piedmont has one dish which is fit for heroes. This is the bollito,* the classic dish of boiled meats—beef, veal, capon, turkey, zampone, cotechino, calf's head and calf's tongue—served with a piquant green sauce* or the bittersweet mostarda di Cremona, which is spiced mixed fruit. As served in Piedmont, one should allow for a two-hour sleep after enjoying a real bollito.

But even a delicacy like salmon is given a very masculine treatment: it is poached and served with a strong red wine sauce and sautéed mushrooms. This Barolo red wine sauce is widely used also with meat and game dishes.

It was all this good eating that Napoleon was thinking about when he urged his ragged, hungry, and despondent army into Italy and told them to resolve their immediate troubles in "the most fertile plains in the world." They followed his advice, swallowing up Piedmont and Lombardy, and went on to conquer the whole of Italy. When one thinks of the tender veal of Piedmont, such as one finds nowhere else, one cannot but see how right Napoleon was. The veal is so tender that the Piedmontese "cook" paper-thin slices of it in lemon juice and eat it raw.

There is something essentially male in the specialties of Piedmont; and one has a nagging suspicion that this is due to Piedmont's post-Napoleonic military tradition and that gourmet officers with huge mustaches a century ago laid down the gastronomic law—and good laws they were too. They also saw to it that good, manly wines were produced—Barolo for the officers, Barbera for the troops—both of which are stern and unsuited to frivolous palates.

This unexpected characteristic is a novelty to both Italians and foreigners who have a priori ideas and prejudices about the Italian cuisine: but it is not the only surprise we shall come across as we move south down the peninsula to Sicily.

Sauces
> GREEN SAUCE   46
> (Salsa verde)
>
> BAGNACAUDA DIP   46
> (Bagnacauda piemontese)

Antipasti
> STUFFED TOMATOES HORS D'OEUVRES   47
> (Pomodori ripieni per antipasto)
>
> RAW STEAK SALAD   48
> (Insalata di carne cruda alla piemontese)

Soups
> CABBAGE AND CHEESE SOUP VAL D'AOSTA STYLE   48
> (Zuppa alla maniera della Val d'Aosta)

Pastas and other farinaceous dishes
> AGNOLOTTI   49
> (Agnulet alla piemontese)
>
> AGNOLOTTI WITH MELTED BUTTER   50
> (Agnolotti con burro fuso)
>
> CANNELLONI LIMONE STYLE   50
> (Cannelloni alla maniera di Limone)

GREEN SAUCE

(Salsa verde)

8 sprigs parsley
3 fillets desalted anchovy*
3 pickled gherkins
1 small boiled potato, cold
1 clove garlic

1 tablespoon onion, chopped
Pinch of salt
Oil
Vinegar

Pound the parsley, the anchovy fillets, the gherkins, the potato, the garlic, onion, and a pinch of salt in a mortar until a paste is obtained. Put this paste in a mixing bowl and dilute slowly, stirring continuously, with oil until a creamy sauce is obtained. Finish off the operation by combining a little vinegar into the sauce. Yields 1½ cups. Serve with boiled meats.

BAGNACAUDA DIP

(Bagnacauda piemontese)

8 fillets desalted anchovy*
5 cloves garlic
2 cups milk
Raw vegetables:
    choice optional—cardoons,
    celery, green, yellow, or red
    sweet peppers, green salad,

tomatoes, endives, artichokes,
    etc., suitable for eating raw
Juice of ½ lemon
3 tablespoons butter
1½ cups olive oil
Thick slices of Italian or
    French bread

Pound the anchovy fillets in a mortar. Chop the garlic fine and marinate it in milk for at least two hours (this reduces the garlic taste and makes it more digestible). Trim, clean, remove fibers, seeds, etc., from the raw vegetables. In the case of the traditional cardoons, these should be cut into 3-inch lengths and put in a basin of cold water with the lemon juice.

At the table: melt the butter in olive oil in a warm chafing dish: add the anchovy paste and the garlic marinated in milk. Cook the mixture over a low flame for about 20 minutes, stirring often.

At this point, either the whole company dips vegetables into the communal dish or the bagnacauda is poured into individual earthenware chafing pots which are kept warm by a lighted candle under the sauce.

This is always a cheerful ceremony and is helped along with a prickly young red wine, which still has the taste of the grape in it. The Piedmontese peasants, reluctant to waste such of the sauce as is left over when there are no more vegetables, scramble an egg or two in it. The result is sublime. Serves 8.

STUFFED TOMATOES HORS D'OEUVRES

(Pomodori ripieni per antipasto)

8 medium-sized salad tomatoes,
 firm-fleshed and ripe
Bagnet sauce:
 2 tablespoons parsley, finely
  chopped
 1 clove garlic, finely chopped

2 fillets desalted anchovy,*
 finely chopped
2 tablespoons bread crumbs
Vinegar
5 tablespoons oil
Pinch of table salt

Wash and dry the tomatoes well: cut them in half horizontally. Scoop out the seed and residual liquids and reserve upside down, to drain, in a cool place.

Sauce: This is a filling made from the mixture of parsley, garlic, anchovy, bread crumbs and vinegar, oil and a pinch of salt; the quantity of vinegar should be only that amount which can be absorbed by the bread crumbs. Fill the scooped-out tomatoes with the mixture. Serves 8.

RAW STEAK SALAD

(Insalata di carne cruda alla piemontese)

Sauce:
- ¼ *cup oil*
- 2 *tablespoons lemon juice*
- 3 *cloves garlic, finely chopped*
- 1 *small Alba truffle, finely sliced* or
- 6 *small mushrooms, finely sliced*

- 1 *pound beef fillet, well hung and tender*
- *Salt and pepper*

Make a sauce of the oil, lemon juice, garlic, and truffle (or mushrooms). Chop the meat coarsely and pour the sauce over it, seasoning with salt and pepper. Allow to marinate for at least one hour before serving. Serves 4.

CABBAGE AND CHEESE SOUP VAL D'AOSTA STYLE

(Zuppa alla maniera della Val d'Aosta)

- 1 *medium-sized cabbage*
- 3 *quarts strong meat stock*
- 24 *thin slices bread, crusts removed*

- 6 *ounces Fontina, or other soft cheese*
- 1 *cup grated Parmesan*
- 2 *tablespoons melted butter*

Separate the cabbage into leaves. Wash them all well; blanch them and drain them and cut into thin strips. Bring a pint of stock to the boil in a casserole, add the cabbage and cook until tender, but not mushy.

Line a fireproof dish with a layer of bread slices, cover with a layer of cabbage, then a layer of slices of Fontina cheese and a sprinkling of Parmesan. Repeat until all ingredients are used, finishing with a top layer of cabbage. Pour the rest of the stock over all, sprinkle with the remaining Parmesan and top with melted butter. Bake for about an hour in a moderate oven. Serve hot. Serves 8.

AGNOLOTTI

(Agnulet alla piemontese)

Dough*:
  1¼ pounds flour, sifted
  5 eggs
  1 teaspoon oil
  Pinch of salt
  1 egg, beaten with few drops
    warm water
Filling:
  1½ tablespoons chopped
    onion
  1 tablespoon chopped celery
  1½ tablespoons chopped
    carrot
  1 tablespoon chopped parsley
  3 tablespoons butter
  ½ pound lean beef, chopped
  6 ounces sausage meat,
    crumbled

  3 ounces prosciutto, chopped
  ½ cup dry white wine
  ¼ pound peeled tomatoes,
    drained
  2 tablespoons rice, browned
    in butter
  ¾ pound cabbage, boiled
    and chopped
  Salt and pepper
  Grating of nutmeg
  2 tablespoons grated
    Parmesan
  2 eggs
Salt
5 tablespoons butter
1½ cups Italian meat sauce*
1 cup grated Parmesan

Dough: Mix the dough and allow to rest for 15 minutes: roll out into sheets. Brush the surface of the sheets with beaten egg.

Filling: Sauté the mixture of onion, celery, carrot, and parsley in the butter; when golden, add the beef, the sausage meat and the ham and cook for a few minutes. Then add the wine and let it evaporate almost completely; add the tomato, the rice, the cabbage, all seasoned with a little salt, pepper, and a grating of nutmeg. Simmer till the mixture thickens; transfer to a mixing bowl, add the 2 tablespoons Parmesan and bind with the 2 eggs; allow to cool and reserve.

To combine: Put the filling, when cold, into a pastry bag and squeeze out little mounds (the size of a Lima bean) on the pastry sheets about 3 inches apart. Cover this sheet with another and, pressing down with the fingers around the filling, make the sheets stick together. With a 3-inch-diameter glass or a cooky cutter, cut out circles or squares or ovals, laying these on a floured cloth. Reserve.

At mealtime, cook the agnolotti in plenty of lightly salted boiling water. When al dente, transfer them to a large warmed serving dish and pour over them the remaining butter and the Italian meat sauce. Serve the grated Parmesan at table. Serves 6.

AGNOLOTTI WITH MELTED BUTTER

(Agnolotti con burro fuso)

Prepare the agnolotti as in agnolotti* and transfer them to a warmed serving dish: then add 1 cup grated Parmesan and 10 tablespoons of melted butter.

This butter, if desired, may be browned lightly and mixed with a dozen little fresh sage leaves. Mix well at table and serve in deep soup bowls. Serves 6.

CANNELLONI LIMONE STYLE

(Cannelloni alla maniera di Limone)

Dough:
  ¾ pound sifted flour
  4 eggs
  Pinch of salt
Filling:
  10 ounces cold roast beef, chopped
  ¼ pound cooked ham, chopped

1 pound spinach, boiled and chopped
½ cup grated Parmesan
*½ cup Italian meat sauce**
Salt and pepper
2 eggs
2 tablespoons butter
*2 cups béchamel**

Dough: Mix the dough as for pasta* and allow to rest for 30 minutes. Roll out thin sheets and cut into 4-inch by 5-inch rectangles. Cook these in plenty of lightly salted boiling water. Drain when al dente, lay out on a damp cloth, and reserve.

Filling: Combine in a mixing bowl the meat, the ham, the spinach, 3 tablespoons Parmesan, the Italian meat sauce, a sprinkle of salt and pepper and the eggs. Mix this all into a smooth paste.

To combine: Place 3 tablespoons of this mixture on each pasta rectangle and, lifting the edges, turn them into little tubes. Lay these tubes out in a pan smeared with 2 tablespoons of butter, pour béchamel over all and sprinkle with remaining grated Parmesan. Put in hot oven until golden brown (about 15 minutes) and serve hot. Serves 8.

GNOCCHI WITH FONTINA CHEESE

(Gnocchi alla bava)

4½ pounds mealy potatoes	*¾ cup butter*
1 pound sifted flour	*½ pound Fontina cheese, or*
Salt	*mozzarella, sliced*

Boil the potatoes without peeling them. Peel them, pass them through strainer and onto the tabletop. Mix together with the flour until a delicate and smooth paste is obtained. With floured hands, roll out ½-inch-diameter rolls: cut them into 1-inch lengths and press each piece with the prongs of a fork on one side only with sufficient force to mark but not to squash the gnocchi.

Cook the gnocchi in plenty of lightly salted boiling water; drain them al dente as they come to the surface (after about 5 minutes) and transfer them to a buttered fireproof pan, interspersing the gnocchi with slices of cheese and, finally, top off with softened lumps of the remaining butter. Cover the dish with a lid and put in warm oven for 8 to 10 minutes. Serves 6.

PIEDMONTESE RISOTTO

(Risotto alla piemontese)

2 ounces salt pork, minced
1 tablespoon chopped onion
¼ pound butter
A mixture of:
  1 small carrot, grated
  1 stalk celery, chopped
  2 sprigs parsley, chopped
4 slices Italian salame,
  chopped

¼ pound chicken livers and
  hearts, sliced
1 pound large-grain rice
4 cups chicken stock
Salt and pepper
1 cup grated Parmesan

In a deep saucepan, large enough to hold the rice, fry the salt pork
and onion in half the butter. When the onion is golden (not
brown) add the carrot, celery, and parsley mixture. Cook for a
few minutes and add the salame, chicken livers and hearts. Continue cooking the mixture for about 10 minutes on a moderate
heat, then add the rice. Stir for a minute or two and pour in 1 cup
of stock, stirring constantly. When the rice has absorbed the stock,
add another cup and so on until all the stock has been used. Cover
the pot and cook over a slow heat for about 20 minutes, checking
occasionally to see if more liquid is required (water may be used
instead of stock at this point). Add salt and pepper to taste.
At the end of the cooking, add the rest of the butter and 2 tablespoons of cheese; mix well, cover again, remove from heat and
leave the risotto to rest for a few minutes. Put into a heated serving
bowl and sprinkle a tablespoon of grated cheese on top. The remaining cheese is served at the table. Serves 6.

SALMON BRAISED IN BAROLO WINE

(Salmone brasato al barolo)

3½-pound salmon
3 pints fish fumet*
Sauce:
   1 small onion, chopped
   1 small carrot, chopped
   1 stalk celery, chopped
   5 tablespoons butter
   2 tablespoons oil
   3 cups Barolo wine (or
     other strong red wine)

24 stalks fresh mushrooms
Salt and pepper
2 tablespoons butter mixed
  with 1½ tablespoons flour
24 caps fresh mushrooms,
  cleaned and simmered in
  butter, salt, and a little
  water until cooked and
  firm

Clean and prepare the salmon and place in a deep pan; cover with fish fumet and simmer for about 20 minutes. Pour half of the fumet into another pan and reduce it by half; strain through a damp cheesecloth and reserve.

SAUCE:

Fry the onion, carrot, and celery in 1½ tablespoons of butter and 2 tablespoons of oil; drain off the fat and add the wine and mushroom stalks. Season with a little salt and pepper and simmer for 20 minutes. Pass through a fine sieve. Then heat the butter and flour paste and pour in to thicken the sauce. Add the remaining 3½ tablespoons of butter and the fish fumet, mixing well with an egg whisk. Drain the salmon and remove its skin from head to tail. Place on a serving dish, cover with sauce, surround with cooked mushroom caps, and serve hot. Serves 6 to 8.

SOLE IN WHITE WINE TURIN STYLE

(Sogliola al vino bianco alla torinese)

6 soles (¾ pound each)*	½ cup burtter
3 tablespoons butter	Fish fumet*
2½ cups dry white wine	Juice of ½ lemon
Salt	
Sauce:	
1½ tablespoons flour mixed	
with 1½ tablespoons butter	

Prepare the 6 soles for cooking. Smear a fireproof dish with 1½ tablespoons butter; lay in it the soles and distribute 1½ tablespoons soft butter in little lumps on the soles. Pour over all 2½ cups dry white wine and season with a sprinkling of salt. Put in a moderate oven for 12 minutes: remove the soles, drain them, and put them on a serving dish and keep warm.

SAUCE:

Reduce the pan juices to about 1 cup and combine with them, using a wire whisk, a mixture of butter and flour (1½ tablespoons each): bring to the boil for a moment and remove from the heat. Finish the sauce by adding ½ cup of soft butter (added in lumps), a few tablespoons fish fumet and the juice of ½ lemon. Pour this sauce over the fish and serve immediately. Serves 6.

DEVILED LOBSTER

(Aragosta alla diavola alla piemontese)

3 lobsters (about 1½ pounds	1 shot brandy
each	2 tablespoons oil
Salt and pepper	½ cup bread crumbs
4 tablespoons butter	3 lemons, halved
1 tablespoon Dijon mustard	

Divide the lobsters lengthwise, remove sand sac and entrails; season with salt and pepper. Mash the liver and coral with the butter and Dijon mustard in a saucepan over a low heat; add the brandy and, after 30 seconds, ignite it. Stir the mixture well until it becomes smooth and creamy; remove from heat.

Oil a pan well and lay lobsters in it, shell side down; spread them generously with the creamy sauce and put the pan in a moderate oven for nearly 20 minutes. During the cooking, mix the remaining creamy sauce with the bread crumbs and spread on each lobster to obtain an au gratin effect. When golden brown, remove from oven and serve each with half a lemon. Serves 6.

CHEESE FRITTATA

(Frittata al formaggio alla piemontese)

6 fresh eggs	*½ tablespoon salt*
2 tablespoons julienne-sliced	*Pinch of pepper*
Gruyère	*5 tablespoons butter*
2 tablespoons grated Parmesan	

This frittata must be soft internally and golden crisp externally. First mix all the ingredients, except the butter, in a bowl and beat well together; then sauté the mixture in butter following the frittata* instructions. Serves 3.

HAM FRITTATA ON FRIED BREAD VAL D'AOSTA STYLE

(Frittata con prosciutto sul crostone)

3 ounces ham, chopped	*3 slices day-old bread,*
(prosciutto crudo or cooked	*browned in butter*
ham)	*6 fresh eggs*
6 tablespoons butter	*½ tablespoon salt*

Sauté the ham for one minute with a tablespoon of butter. Brown the slices of bread in the same pan, adding 3 tablespoons of butter, and put them in a buttered fireproof dish. Combine and beat together the eggs, the ham, and salt. Preheat a very hot oven, pour the mixture over the fried bread, and place in oven. This should not overcook, but be served while the egg mixture is still soft. Serves 3.

FRESH MUSHROOM SALAD

(Funghi di serra freddi alla piemontese)

1 pound fresh mushroom caps*	*2 egg yolks*
Salt	*¾ cup olive oil*
½ pound raw shrimps, shelled	*¼ tablespoon Dijon mustard*
and deveined	*1 tablespoon lemon juice*
½ pound asparagus tips	*1 teaspoon brandy*
1 celery heart	*½ teaspoon Worcestershire*
2 artichoke hearts, if desired	*sauce*
Dressing:	*1 teaspoon tomato ketchup*

Having prepared the mushrooms according to Note, boil them in salted water for 15 minutes. Drain and let them cool. Boil the shrimps for 3 minutes; drain and cool. Cook the asparagus until tender, being careful not to overcook them; drain and cool. Slice the celery heart finely; also the 2 artichoke hearts, if you wish.

At serving time, bring the ingredients to the table in a salad bowl; pour the salad dressing made of egg yolks, olive oil, mustard, lemon juice, brandy, Worcestershire, and tomato ketchup over all, and mix well. The addition of a little sliced Alba truffle is welcome. Serves 6 to 8.

FONTINA CHEESE CROQUETTES VAL D'AOSTA STYLE

(Crocchette di Fontina della Valle d'Aosta)

2 eggs and 4 egg yolks, beaten	Pinch of salt
½ cup flour	Pinch white pepper
½ cup rice flour	Grating of nutmeg
1 pound Fontina, or other soft melting cheese, diced	2 beaten eggs
	½ cup bread crumbs
1½ cups milk	Vegetable oil for deep-frying
¾ cup butter	

Beat the 2 eggs and 4 egg yolks in a heavy fireproof casserole, adding the flour, the rice flour, the cheese, milk, butter, salt, pepper, and nutmeg. Bring the mixture to the boil, stirring constantly; cook at a high heat for 5 minutes.

Remove from heat, pour into another recipient and allow to cool. Make croquettes about the size of a large walnut. Dip them in beaten egg, roll them in bread crumbs twice and deep-fry in oil until they are golden. Serve hot. Makes about 16.

CHEESE FONDUE WITH TRUFFLES

(Fonduta con tartufi alla piemontese)

10 ounces Fontina, or other soft melting cheese	3 egg yolks (very fresh)
	2 tablespoons softened butter
½ cup milk	2 tablespoons hot milk
Pinch of salt	1 small white Alba truffle

Cut the cheese into thin strips and mix it with the milk and the salt in the top of a double boiler. Keep the water in the bottom of the boiler hot but not boiling. Stir the mixture constantly, and always in the same direction, until the cheese melts and the mixture becomes creamy.

Gently beat the egg yolks, butter, and hot milk together, add 2 or 3 tablespoons of the cheese mixture, stirring constantly until creamed. Add this mixture to the cheese mixture in the double boiler and stir in until absorbed. Pour into individual ramekins, slice a few slivers of white Alba truffle on each, and serve hot. Serves 4.

TAPULON HASH BORGAMANERA STYLE

(Tapulon alla borgamanerese)

A mixture of:
1 tablespoon chopped garlic
½ tablespoon chopped rosemary
1 bay leaf, chopped
2 cloves
¼ cup oil
½ cup butter

2 pounds lean beef (or veal), chopped
2 pounds cabbage leaves, blanched, drained, chopped
1½ tablespoons salt
Pinch of pepper
1½ pints dry red wine

Sauté the garlic mixture in the oil and butter; when golden, add the meat and combine for 2 minutes. Add the cabbage, seasoned with 1½ tablespoons salt and a pinch of pepper, and pour in the red wine. Bring to the boil, turn down heat, simmer until liquids are almost evaporated and the meat is cooked. Serves 6 to 8.

STUFFED LAMB LIMONE STYLE

(Agnello ripieno alla limonese)

15-pound hindquarters of lamb (without kidneys)
1½ pounds spinach
¼-pound calf brain
2 cups grated Parmesan

6 eggs and 3 egg yolks
Salt and pepper
3 bay leaves
¾ cup butter

Clean and dry the lamb. Wash, chop, and blanch the spinach in boiling water for 5 minutes. Blanch the calf brain in boiling water for 3 minutes, remove outer skin, chop, and allow to cool.

Combine in a mixing bowl the chopped spinach, the chopped calf brain, the Parmesan, the eggs, the egg yolks, seasoned with a little salt and pepper, and the bay leaves; knead this mixture until a smooth paste is obtained. Stuff the lamb with this filling and sew up the opening with white thread.

Butter a large pan, preheat a very hot oven, rub the lamb with salt and pepper, dot with lumps of softened butter and roast for about 1 hour in a moderate oven. When the lamb is crisp and well-browned, remove from oven. Cut it into pieces, slice the stuffing, and transfer both to serving dish. Strain the pan juices and pour them over both meat and stuffing. Serve with a mixed salad. Serves 10.

MIXED BOILED MEATS

(Bollito misto piemontese)

2 pounds beef sirloin tips	1 pound pork rind, blanched
1 calf's foot	Coarse salt
1 young turkey, readied for cooking	2 stalks celery
	1 large onion, stuck with 2
1 calf's head	cloves
2 pig's feet, blanched	1 large carrot

Put all the meats in a large earthenware pot, with some coarse salt and cover with 10 or more pints of cold water. Bring to the boil and add the celery, onion, and carrot; turn down heat and simmer.

As each of the meats reaches its respective point of doneness, remove from the pot, keep warm, moistened with some of the cooking liquid. When all the meats are cooked, transfer all to a large serving dish or dishes: serve with green sauce,* Cremona mustard,[1] or tomato sauce.* Serves 10.

[1] Cremona mustard is an Italian specialty, obtainable readymade in jars; it consists of fruit, treated with spices to make a sweet-and-sour sauce.

BRAISED BEEF RIB TIPS

(Punta di culaccio di manzo brasato alla piemontese)

2½ pounds beef rib tips
3 ounces salt pork, cut in
 strips
Marinade:
 2 cups dry red wine
 2 shots brandy
 ½ tablespoon salt
 Pinch of pepper

1½ tablespoons chopped
 parsley
4 tablespoons butter
1½ tablespoons oil
1 tablespoon flour
2 cups stock
Salt

Put the beef and salt pork in the marinade for 30 minutes, turning often. Remove salt pork, dry, and roll it in chopped parsley. Using a larding needle, insert salt pork strips in the beef. Dry the beef and brown it on all sides in a large casserole with the butter and oil; remove and reserve.

Add the flour to the pan juices, a little at a time, over a low heat; as soon as it colors, pour in the marinade and the stock; bring to the boil slowly, replace the meat, seasoned with 1 tablespoon of salt. Cover the casserole with a sheet of buttered greaseproof paper and a lid, and simmer for three hours.

Drain the meat, pass the pan juices through a fine sieve, and replace both meat and sauce in the casserole; continue simmering for another hour or till the sauce is reduced by half. Serves 8.

TURKEY BREASTS WITH TRUFFLES

(Filetti di tacchino con tartufi)

6 turkey breasts, trimmed and
 flattened
1½ tablespoons flour
Salt and pepper
¾ cup butter

½ cup sweet marsala wine
2 tablespoons stock
1 Alba truffle, walnut size
½ cup grated Parmesan

Flour the turkey breasts, season them with salt and pepper, and sauté them in 6 tablespoons of butter until golden brown on both sides; drain, reserve, and keep warm.

Pour the marsala into the pan juices and reduce; add the stock and 2 tablespoons butter, stirring continuously. Reserve and keep warm.

Place the turkey breasts in a fireproof dish, distribute on each little lumps of softened butter, thin slices of truffle and a sprinkling of grated Parmesan; pour the pan juices over all and put dish in a hot oven until the cheese melts. Serve immediately. Serves 6.

NOTE: Lacking truffles, a thin slice of Italian prosciutto can be substituted.

COLD WAR GOOSE

(Oca di guerra fredda)

1 young goose, 3 pounds after	*6 cloves garlic, crushed*
evisceration	*3 sprigs rosemary tied with*
1½ tablespoons coarse salt	*white thread*

Pluck, eviscerate, and pass the goose over a flame to remove residual feathers. Remove head, neck, feet, and wing tips. Wash and dry the bird and cut it into pieces; place the pieces in a large earthenware pot.

Pour water into the pot until the goose pieces are just covered; season with 1½ tablespoons salt, the garlic cloves and the rosemary. Cover the pot with a lid and put it in a moderate oven: after three hours, the goose will be cooked and all the fats settled on the bottom. Transfer the meat to a deep bowl, discard the rosemary and pour all the cooking juices and fat over it. Allow to cool and reserve. This dish is traditionally eaten cold, but may be heated and served with boiled green vegetables, which have been sautéed in some of the goose fat. Serves 6.

PARTRIDGE ZABAIONE

(Pernice allo zabaione)

3 partridges (about ¾ pound each)	*Dry white wine*
	3 egg yolks
1 ounce salt pork (3 thin slices)	*4 tablespoons dry white wine*
	6 slices day-old bread,
½ cup butter	*sautéed in butter*

Pluck, eviscerate, clean the 3 partridges and cut off their feet. Wash and dry well. Truss up legs around the body and affix a thin slice of salt pork around each of the partridge breasts with the aid of string.

Heat 5 tablespoons of butter in a casserole, cook the partridges in it for 25 minutes in a moderate oven, occasionally pouring over a little white wine. Remove from oven, discard string and salt-pork slices. Cut the partridges in halves, reserve, and keep warm.

Pass the pan juices through a fine sieve into a warm double boiler; add the remaining butter and the 3 beaten egg yolks. Continue beating as though making a zabaione, adding the wine a little at a time. As soon as the sauce thickens, remove from heat. Put the fried bread on a serving dish, half a partridge on each slice, and cover with the sauce. Serves 3.

RABBIT WITH SWEET PEPPERS

(Coniglio coi peperoni)

6 sweet peppers, yellow or green	*½ cup butter*
	Bouquet garni:
4 tablespoons oil	*1 sprig rosemary*
Salt	*2 bay leaves*
3 cloves garlic, sliced	*2 sprigs parsley*
¼ cup vinegar	*1 plump young rabbit, chopped into chunks*
6 fillets desalted anchovy, mashed	*Pepper*
3 tablespoons lard	*Stock*

Char the sweet peppers over a flame, plunge them in cold water, and peel them; remove seeds, dry peppers, and cut into squares. Sauté them lightly in 2½ tablespoons oil, and season with salt; reserve. Heat 1½ tablespoons oil in a pan and brown the sliced garlic; pour in the vinegar and simmer for a few minutes until the vinegar is reduced by ⅔ meanwhile mixing in the anchovy fillets; reserve.

In a larger pan, heat the lard with 3 tablespoons of butter and add the bouquet garni: after a moment or two, add the rabbit pieces and season with 1 tablespoon of salt and a pinch of pepper. Brown rabbit well over a lively heat. Remove from heat and pour off all the fats; replace these fats with sufficient stock to cover the pieces of rabbit completely and add the remaining butter. Cover the pan with a lid and simmer for one and a half hours, adding tablespoons of stock, if and when needed.

Fifteen minutes before removing the rabbit from the stove, mix in the anchovy and vinegar, and, after another 5 minutes, add the sweet pepper squares.

Remove from heat, transfer the rabbit pieces to a warmed serving dish, surround with the sweet peppers, pour over all the pan juices and serve. Serves 4 to 6.

FRESH MUSHROOMS AL FUNGHETTO

(Funghi freschi al funghetto)

1 pound fresh mushrooms	*Pinch of pepper*
(fresh porcini preferably)*	*Grating of nutmeg*
½ cup olive oil	*½ teaspoon chopped orégano*
1 tablespoon salt	*2 cloves garlic, finely chopped*

Chop the mushrooms coarsely. Heat the oil in a frying pan, add the mushrooms, season with salt, pepper, and nutmeg, and toss them vigorously over a lively flame until all the moisture has evaporated. As they brown, reduce the heat, add the chopped orégano and garlic and cook for 4 to 5 minutes more. Serve immediately. As a main dish, serve with fried bread sautéed with the minimum of oil. Serves 3.

STUFFED PEACHES

(Pesche ripiene piemontese)

6 ripe peaches	*Whipped cream*
½ pint dry white wine	*3 small macaroons*
¾ cup sugar	(amaretti), *chopped*
Pinch of vanilla bean	*1 egg yolk*

Peel the peaches, cut in halves, and remove the stones; scoop out a part of the peach flesh and reserve.

Prepare, in a large saucepan, a hot syrup with the wine, the sugar, and the vanilla, and reserve. Prepare a paste with the removed peach flesh, the whipped cream, and the chopped macaroons combined with the egg yolk.

Reheat the wine syrup in a large pan and remove from the stove; lay in the peach halves and marinate for 5 minutes. Remove them, drain them and place on a serving dish. Fill each of the peach centers with the paste of peach flesh, whipped cream and chopped macaroons. Pour the syrup over each peach. Serve hot or cold. Serves 6.

Lombardy

Lombardy is, on the whole, not the most attractive part of Italy; mostly it consists of dull plains, chilly and damp in winter and broiling in summer, and the inelegancies of pulsating industry. The beauty of Lombardy is to be found among the lakes and mountain valleys to the North—the Valtellina, Lake Como, and Lake Maggiore. But these dull plains, to their credit, not only produce the money which makes most of Italy tick, but also the cheeses, from Gorgonzola to Bel Paese, and great quantities of butter and even of rice. It is difficult to think of heavy industry cheek-by-jowl with rice paddies, but this strange juxtaposition exists through much of the Po River valley. The rice fields are, of course, now as mechanized and automated as the industries and nobody stands knee-deep in water any more.

The people of Lombardy, and particularly of Milan, are considered by the rest of Italy to be much too busy working and making money to think about food and wines. There is some truth in this, but not much. Lombardy's wealth and energy has, in fact, been the driving force behind the great improvements in Italian living standards of the last two decades and in the production of more and higher-quality foods and wines. This has been especially felt in the wine sector where whole new areas, which twenty-five years ago were producing mediocre peasant wines, are now bottling fine matured ones. In the past, only the red wines of the Valtellina (Sassella, Grumello, Inferno, and Fracia), which are close cousins of Piedmont's Barolos, along with the Lake Garda clarets and the Lugana whites had a high reputation; today, the Oltrepò Pavese (beyond-the-river-Po-Pavia area) wines have more than made their mark: Frecciarossa, Pinots, Rieslings and a sparkling red dessert wine called Judas' Blood (Sangue di Giuda). Not only this, but the Milanese have invested heavily in wine production throughout Italy to the benefit of all.

The food of Lombardy, like the region itself, is tending to get automated, but changing times are not all bad. Milan, for example, prides itself on having the best fish in Italy. Now there is nothing traditional about this, since this great inland city, in the past, had no fish except dried cod and what little fresh-water fish (trout and lake sardines mostly) came out of Lake Como. Today, fast trucks and six-lane highways mean that fish reaches Milan from the Italian Riviera in a matter of hours.

The traditional dishes of Lombardy are risotto, the famous rice dish flavored and colored with saffron and cooked in stock; minestrone, which is eaten hot, cold or tepid according to the weather; ossobuco, which is veal shinbone with plenty of marrow in it and plenty of meat around it and which is gently stewed and served with a Gremolada sauce* of rosemary, garlic, lemon, sage, and parsley.

More should be said about the cheeses. There is also a Gorgonzola without the green holes called Taleggio, which, like Gorgonzola, should be allowed to mature well before serving: there is the simple Stracchino, a delicious cream cheese, and a whipped-cream delight called mascherpone, which is equally loved by the Romans; and the various robbiolas, which are extensions of the Gorgonzola family and usually stronger: and finally Lombardy's Parmesan, called Grana, which is very fine and can be substituted for "Parmigiano."

Spaghetti is not the rule of the day in Lombardy. Rice wins out and second comes corn-meal polenta, which is the bread of much of north Italy; however, lasagna baked in the oven is very much a favorite.

Lombardy, as shown by its dairy produce, is a major cattle-raising area: however its meat is not comparable to Tuscany's fine beef nor to Piedmont's young veal (called "sanato"). Most Lombardy meat dishes are based on young—but not very young—veal: the famous Milanese breaded cutlet, if made according to rule, is a succulent dish; if made badly, it can be one of the most depressing offerings of the Italian cuisine. Piccata di vitello can equally easily go down the long slide if not made with the tenderest of meat and the freshest of ingredients, whereas Milanese Mexicans (Messicani alla milanese) are a good solid standby, which can take some rough handling. Another cook's-best-friend from Lombardy is zuppa pavese*; this is made with stock, poached eggs, fried bread, and cheese, and it cheerfully resolves the problem of unexpected guests, particularly on a cold winter night.

Sauces

Soups

Pastas and other farinaceous dishes

Fish

CHERRY SAUCE COMO STYLE

(Salsa di corniole alla comasca)

1 pound cherries
Peel of ½ lemon (no pith)

Juice of ¼ lemon
Superfine sugar

Wash the cherries, but do not stone them. Put them in a casserole with ½ cup water, the lemon peel and the lemon juice and bring to a low simmer; maintain this for two hours.

Remove from heat, allow to cool, and pass through a fine sieve. Weigh this cherry purée and replace it in the casserole along with ½ the weight of the purée in superfine sugar. Cook again on a moderate heat for 5 minutes, stirring constantly; allow to cool. This sauce is served with boiled meats.

SOUP PAVIA STYLE

(Zuppa pavese)

2 slices bread
Butter
1 tablespoon grated Parmesan
1½ cups hot beef stock*

2 fresh eggs
Pinch of white pepper
1 tablespoon grated Parmesan

Place the slices of bread, spread with butter and sprinkled with Parmesan, in a moderate oven. Put them on a soup plate when golden: keep warm.

Pour the hot stock into a fireproof saucepan, slide in 2 shelled eggs and a pinch of white pepper. Put the pan in a hot oven for just long enough for the eggs to set, about 5 minutes.

Pour the stock and the eggs carefully over the bread slices in the soup plate. Sprinkle with Parmesan. Serves 1.

MINESTRONE MILANESE STYLE

(Minestrone alla milanese)

¼ *pound lean salt pork*
¼ *pound potatoes*
¼ *pound carrots*
¼ *pound zucchini*
¼ *pound asparagus*
A mixture of:
  ½ small onion, chopped
  1 leek heart, chopped
  1 small celery heart,
    chopped
Bouquet garni:
  3 sprigs parsley
  3 sprigs rosemary
¼ *pound butter*

½ *pound peeled tomatoes,*
  drained
Salt and freshly ground pepper
¼ *pound cooked dried white*
  beans (or raw fresh)
4 pints stock
½ *pound rice*
A mixture of:
  1 tablespoon chopped basil
  1 tablespoon chopped parsley
  1 clove garlic, chopped
  ½ *bay leaf, chopped*
1 cup grated Parmesan

Dice the salt pork. Dice the vegetables—potatoes, carrots, zucchini, and asparagus and reserve. Put the onion, leek, and celery mixture, with the salt pork in a casserole with the sprigs of parsley and rosemary and sauté in 1½ tablespoons of butter. Simmer for about 10 to 15 minutes. Discard the bouquet garni, add the tomatoes, season with salt and pepper.

Sauté the potatoes, carrots, zucchini, and asparagus and the beans in the remaining butter; when colored, add the pork and onion mixture and simmer together for a few minutes. Then add the stock and simmer for about one hour until all the vegetables are well cooked. Turn up the heat and add the rice. Cook for about 20 minutes but, about 4 minutes before removing from the heat, add the mixture of chopped basil, parsley, garlic, and bay leaf. Remove from stove, allow to stand for a few minutes and serve with Parmesan cheese at table. Serves 8.

COLD MINESTRONE MILANESE STYLE

(Minestrone alla milanese freddo)

For the cold version of minestrone Milanese* style, which is a great favorite in Italy in summertime, season it with grated Parmesan. Then pour it into individual soup bowls and decorate the surface with very thin slices of lean breast of salt pork. This salt pork is greatly improved if it has been cooked in the same minestrone. Cool and keep in the refrigerator until ready to serve. The Parmesan should be neither too soft and fresh nor hard and mature.

RISOTTO MILANESE STYLE

(Risotto alla milanese)

½ pound butter
2 tablespoons beef marrow
2 tablespoons onion, chopped
    fine
Pinch of pepper
1¼ pounds rice, cleaned with
    cloth, not washed

Salt
Pinch of saffron
Stock
1 cup grated Parmesan

Heat 5 tablespoons of butter, the beef marrow, the onion, and the pepper in a casserole over a very low flame. As soon as the onion is translucent, but not in any way browned, toss in the rice, and season with salt. Allow the ingredients to simmer together for a few minutes to gather flavor; then add the pinch of saffron and pour in 2 pints of stock and mix well. Turn up the heat; as the rice liquid thickens and begins to dry out, add more stock, a little at a time. Continue cooking over a lively heat, stirring frequently, without a lid, until the rice is al dente.

At this point, remove the casserole from the stove, add the remaining butter and a few tablespoons of grated Parmesan; allow the risotto to settle for a minute on the corner of the stove, then pour it into a serving dish and serve hot with the remaining Parmesan passed at table. Serves 6.

NOTE: An old recipe for risotto Milanese style recommends that before the rice is tossed into the casserole, a glass of dry white wine (or even dry red) be added to the butter-and-onion mixture and that the wine should be reduced by half; only then, it says, should the rice be added.

LOBSTER WITH VERMOUTH

(Astaco al vermut)

2 lobsters (2 pounds each, preferably alive)	2 tablespoons sweet vermouth
	1½ cups cream
Salt and pepper	4 egg yolks
3 tablespoons oil	Pinch red pepper
2 tablespoons chopped onion	¼ pound butter
1 scant cup dry vermouth	2 lemons, halved

Cook the lobsters in boiling water; wash and divide them in half lengthwise. Remove the sand sac. Season with salt and pepper. Smear all over with oil and put on a hot grill (meat toward the heat) and cook for 25 minutes. During the grilling, baste with oil now and then.

Meanwhile, mix the onion and the two vermouths in a saucepan and bring to the boil. Simmer till the liquids are almost evaporated.

Pour the cream into another saucepan and reduce to ⅓, simmering gently. Pour in the onion-and-vermouth mixture and the egg yolks, previously mixed with 2 tablespoons of the reduced cream. Season with salt and red pepper and pass through a sieve into another saucepan. Melt the butter, mix in a little at a time with a wire whisk over a low heat. Place the hot lobster halves on a serving dish, decorate with lemon halves, and serve the sauce separately. Serves 4.

VEAL OSSOBUCO WITH RISOTTO MILANESE STYLE

(Ossobuco alla milanese con risotto)

6 ossobuchi (veal-shin steaks),
  1½ to 2 inches thick
Flour
8 tablespoons butter
A mixture of:
  2 tablespoons chopped onion
  1½ tablespoons chopped
    carrots
  1 tablespoon chopped celery
  1 clove garlic, chopped
  1 level tablespoon chopped
    marjoram (or parsley)
  1 slice lemon peel (no
    pith), thin
1½ tablespoons salt

Pepper
½ cup dry white wine
¼ pound peeled tomatoes,
  drained
Stock
Gremolada sauce:
  Pinch rosemary
  Pinch sage
  1 clove garlic, chopped
  Grated peel of ½ lemon
    (or the grated peel of ¼
    orange)
  1 tablespoon chopped parsley
Dish of risotto Milanese style*

Dust the ossobuchi in flour; melt about 6 tablespoons of butter in a pan and arrange veal-shin steaks in it, but not too close together. Fry them until a light golden brown on both sides; add the first mixture and season with salt and a little pepper. When the mixture colors, pour in the wine and simmer till reduced by ⅘.

Add the tomatoes and a few tablespoons of stock (or water). Cover the pan and simmer for an hour or more; add more liquid, if the sauce becomes too thick.

A few minutes before removing from heat, add the Gremolada sauce and the remaining butter: stir in well and simmer for a few more minutes. Put the steaks on a serving dish, cover with the sauce and decorate the dish with risotto Milanese style. Serve hot. Serves 6.

VEAL PICCATA

(Piccata di vitello alla lombarda)

1½ pounds veal, fillet or noisette	Flour
	½ cup butter
2 ounces prosciutto, fat and lean	1 lemon
	1½ tablespoons chopped parsley
Salt and pepper	

Cut the veal into thin 1-ounce slices, all of equal size and shape. Cut the prosciutto into thin strips. Pound the veal lightly and season with a little salt and pepper, then dust in flour. Heat 6 tablespoons of butter in a pan and add the veal slices; turn up the heat a little and sauté the slices on both sides till golden. Transfer to a warmed serving dish.

Add the remaining butter to the pan juices, add the ham strips and when the ham begins to color, add a squeeze of lemon juice. Pour the pan juices over the piccata slices and sprinkle chopped parsley over all. Serve very hot. Serves 6.

STEWED PORK CHOPS

(Bottaggio alla lombarda)

1 pig's foot	½ scant cup prosciutto, chopped
¼ pound pork rind	
1 pound pork chops	2 tablespoons chopped onion
1 pound raw pork sausages	2 cloves garlic, chopped
3 medium Savoy cabbages	1 tablespoon chopped parsley
¼ cup oil	Salt and ¼ teaspoon pepper
A mixture of:	

Split the pig's-foot bone lengthwise, wash well: remove any bristles from both foot and pork rind by holding over a flame. Cover both with water and simmer gently for one hour. Remove the rind and leave the pig's foot for another 30 to 40 minutes. Cut the rind into small squares and reserve. Having skimmed the fat from the surface of the cooking liquid, reserve several cups of the liquid. Reserve pig's foot.

Cut the meat from the chops into medium-sized pieces; pierce the sausages; clean and wash the cabbages and divide them into quarters. Sauté the chopped mixture till golden, add the pork chunks, the rind, and pig's foot. Season with salt and pepper. Pour in the reserved liquid and bring to the boil. Simmer for one hour. Add the sausages and cabbage. Continue simmering until everything is cooked and the sauce fairly thick. Transfer the pork chunks to a serving dish, skin the sausages, chop into chunks, and transfer to the serving dish. Surround with the thick cabbage sauce. Serve hot. Serves 4 to 6.

VEAL CUTLETS MILANESE STYLE

(Costolette di vitello alla milanese)

6 veal cutlets	2 eggs, beaten
Salt and pepper	1 cup bread crumbs
Grating of nutmeg, if desired	¼ pound butter
2 tablespoons flour	3 lemons, halved

Trim the meat and remove gristle. Gently flatten and season with salt and pepper and a little nutmeg if desired. Flour and dip the cutlets in the beaten eggs and coat with bread crumbs; reserve.

About 15 to 20 minutes before serving, melt the butter in a pan and sauté the cutlets at a moderate heat till a light golden brown on both sides. Put on a hot serving dish and cover with the butter from the pan. Sprinkle each cutlet with salt and decorate with lemon halves. Serves 6.

VEAL (or PORK) ROLLS IN GELATIN
ST. AMBROSE STYLE

(Messicani in gelatina all'ambrosiana)

2½ pounds loin of veal (or
   pork)
¼ pound bread, soaked in
   stock
¾ pound lean veal
¼ pound prosciutto, fat and
   lean
2½ tablespoons grated
   Parmesan
1 clove garlic, chopped
Salt and pepper
Grating of nutmeg

3 egg yolks
1 cup butter
Flour
Stock
¼ pound carrots, scraped and
   sliced
¼ pound green olives, pitted
¼ pound mushrooms, sliced
¼ pound peas, shelled
Sprigs basil, chervil, or parsley
1 pint of warm gelatin*

Cut 12 thin slices, about 4½ inches long and 2½ inches wide, from the loin of veal or pork. Flatten them with meat cleaver.

Drain and remove crusts from bread soaked in stock. Mince the ¾ pound of lean veal, the ham and the bread together and mix in the Parmesan, the garlic, ½ tablespoon of salt, and a pinch of pepper; add a grating of nutmeg, if desired. Combine with egg yolks to obtain a compact, smooth filling.

Lay the flattened meat slices on a table and put an equal amount of filling on each. Roll them up so that they look like sausages and secure them with wooden skewers.

Melt the butter in a pan and, having lightly dusted the rolls in flour and seasoned them with salt, sauté until golden brown all over. Add a cup of stock, stirring with a wooden spoon; continue cooking slowly for about 30 minutes. When done, put the rolls on a warm serving dish and cover with the pan juices and allow to cool.

Simmer separately the carrots, the pitted olives, the mushrooms, and peas (or other suitable vegetables in season) until tender in a little stock and allow to cool. Arrange these vegetables on the serving dish alternately with the messicani. Decorate each meat roll with a sprig of herbs (basil, chervil or parsley) and pour warm gelatin over all. Reserve in refrigerator until serving time. Serves 6.

SAUTÉ OF VEAL WITH WHITE WINE

(Arrostini annegati al vino bianco)

6 veal cutlets, 1 inch thick,	*½ cup stock**
bone and fillet	*A mixture of:*
Salt and pepper	*1 clove garlic, chopped*
¼ cup flour	*1 tablespoon chopped sage*
¼ pound butter	*and rosemary*
½ pint dry white wine	*Juice of ½ lemon*

Trim and bone the cutlets to about equal size: season each with salt and pepper and dust in flour. Melt 6 tablespoons of butter in a pan and sauté the cutlets to a light golden brown. Turn the meat occasionally while cooking. Add the wine, reduce the heat and simmer until the wine is reduced by ⅘. Then add a little stock from time to time. One minute before serving, add the chopped herbs and the juice of ½ lemon. Transfer the cutlets to a warmed serving dish, strain the pan juices and pour them over the cutlets. Serves 6.

BEEF CERTOSINA

(Manzo alla certosina)

2½ ounces lean breast salt	*A mixture of:*
pork, sliced	*2 cloves garlic, chopped*
¼ cup oil	*6 fillets desalted anchovy,**
1½ pounds rump or round of	*chopped*
beef	*1 tablespoon chopped parsley*
1 tablespoon salt	*and basil*
½ teaspoon cinnamon	
1 pint stock (more if	
necessary)	

Lightly brown salt pork in the oil. Add the meat and brown it all over. Season with salt and the cinnamon; pour a few tablespoons of stock over and cook gently for about a half hour, adding a little stock and turning the meat from time to time.

After it has cooked for one hour, add the chopped mixture. When the meat is done (after about a further 30 minutes), drain well, reserving the sauce. Slice and arrange the meat on a hot serving dish. Pass the sauce through a sieve and pour sauce over the meat slices. Serve immediately. Boiled potatoes go well with this. Serves 4 to 6.

ASPARAGUS AND FRIED EGGS

(Asparagi con uova alla lombarda)

2 pounds asparagus	3/4 cup grated Parmesan
Salt	1/2 cup melted butter
6 eggs	

Trim and scrape the asparagus stalks carefully so as not to damage them; wash them and tie in 6 bundles with thread. Poach in plenty of lightly salted water. Thin asparagus requires 12 to 14 minutes from the time the water boils: thick asparagus can require as much as 18 to 20 minutes.

While the asparagus is cooking, fry the eggs* in butter, one at a time. Reserve and keep warm.

Drain the asparagus, remove the thread, and lay out on a warmed serving dish. Sprinkle the grated Parmesan. Heat the butter in a saucepan; when it turns golden, pour over the asparagus. Place a fried egg on each portion and serve. Serves 6.

SPINACH MILANESE STYLE

(Spinaci alla milanese)

2½ pounds spinach	3/4 cup grated Parmesan
Salt	6 eggs, fried*
½ cup butter	

Clean and prepare the spinach, removing the stalks and washing the leaves in running water. Cook in a small quantity of fast boiling water, lightly salted, for 10 minutes. Drain and press well to remove excess water.

Melt 4 tablespoons butter in a frying pan and sauté the spinach in this for a couple of minutes to flavor it and evaporate remaining water. Then pass the spinach to a fireproof dish, which has been greased with 1 tablespoon of butter. Sprinkle the Parmesan cheese; melt the remaining butter and pour over. Put the dish into a hot oven and remove when the cheese is thoroughly melted. Serve with fried eggs. Serves 3.

PARADISE CAKE

(Torta del paradiso alla lombarda)

1 pound butter, softened	*8 eggs*
1 pound superfine sugar	*½ pound flour*
Grated peel of ½ lemon (no pith)	*1½ generous cups potato flour*
	1 tablespoon baking powder
1½ tablespoons potato flour	*Butter*
10 egg yolks	*Vanilla-flavored sugar*

Put the softened butter in an earthenware pan which is warm and dry; beat the butter with a wire whisk until it is reduced to a cream. Add the sugar and continue beating until combined. Add the grated lemon peel and 1½ tablespoons potato flour, and mix in well until a smooth paste is obtained. Reserve.

Beat the egg yolks in a bowl; add the eggs, beating constantly and energetically for 10 minutes or more.

Sift the flour along with the 1½ cups of potato flour; mix in the baking powder and pass all 3 ingredients through a sieve. Reserve.

Returning to the butter-and-sugar mixture, start beating this, again adding, a little at a time, the beaten eggs and the sifted flour, making sure that no lumps form.

Butter a low baking pan and pour the mixture into it. Put in a moderate oven until well browned. Allow to cool. Remove from pan, sprinkle with vanilla-flavored sugar, and serve.

Veneto and
Trentino–Alto Adige

Venice holds a special place in the hearts of all Italians; it still remains the most romantic of honeymoon resorts. Nearby lies historic Padua and that delight of delights, Verona, which of course was the scene of Romeo and Juliet's tragedy and has changed little since those days.

The Veneto is a land of delights, both visual and gastronomic, while the lilting accent of the region and the language of Goldoni's comedies is an added *je ne sais quoi* to garnish them. It is a land of lovely cities, renaissance country villas, beautiful fishing villages, hills and fertile plains and, to the north, the magnificent Dolomite mountain ranges and the vine-clad Alto Adige Valley.

Yet the Veneto is among the quietest and least flag waving of all the Italian regions; surely nobody has ever seen a Venetian restaurant abroad? Nobody boasts of Venetian cooking and yet, as a result of its fine farm products and its Adriatic fish, it is among the best in Italy. The only flag waving to be found in the Veneto is, perhaps, for the wines and it must be admitted that Valpolicella, Valpantena, Bardolino, and Soave are something to boast about. And if you add the Alto Adige Valley which is contiguous, the list of fine wines is formidable though, except in Germany, they are, so far, little known.

Real Veneto food is not easily found. Often one is offered Bolognese cooking as being, perhaps, more acceptable to non-Veneto palates. And, in fact, Fegato alla veneziana (calf liver Venetian style*) is the only dish which is well known outside of the region though, as you will see from the recipe, the stewed onion and liver which so often goes under that name is a far cry from the original dish.

Venice itself has delicious seafood dishes, such as one finds almost nowhere else in Italy: Verona is the city of haute cuisine, while Vicenza prides itself on its creamed dried cod, its river trout and guinea fowl and Treviso on its game from hare to venison, grilled eels, and sausages. The whole area has a great wealth in market-garden products ranging from peas, and string beans to asparagus and mushrooms as well as huge chicken, duck, and turkey farms.

Polenta was once the staple of the mountain people and the very poor; since this has now been refined and improved, it has become a popular adjunct to the table of all classes.

As one goes more to the north, to the hill country, to Trento and Belluno, to Asiago and Cortina, the food becomes simpler: lamb roasts, cheeses, game birds, venison and sausages, while toward Lake Garda one enjoys trout, carp, and tench from the lake and a lightness of Italianate cuisine which is matched by the Soave wine of the area. Farther north, toward the Austrian border around Bolzano, the regional food becomes Alpine and Teutonic with sauerkraut, smoked pork, and würstels; but, at the same time, one finds good Italian food in the restaurants because most of the cooks come from other parts of Italy, especially to cope with the big tourist season.

This enormous sweep of styles of cooking is followed closely by an equally enormous swath of wines. The famous wines of the Veneto proper have already been mentioned, but to these must be added the names of the Alto Adige wines which grow on some 50,000 acres of hillside, many of which are now reckoned to be among the best in Italy; the most noted are Caldaro, Santa Maddalena, Casteller, Marzemino, Teraldego, Lagrein, Black Pinot, Sylvaner, Traminer, Riesling, and Cabernet. Also here, there are Germanic overtones (often the wines are in gothic-styled bottles), but despite the vineyards often being at 1500 feet above sea level and under snow in winter, the hot Italian sun quickly produces a rich grape for making strong, rounded wines. Particularly worthy of special mention is the relatively small production of white, well-aged sparkling wine which is made according to the French champenois method by the Giulio Ferrari Winery of Trento and which is considered to be comparable to anything in the champenois category.

The unusual gothic characteristics of the Alto Adige are due to its history; after the fall of the Roman Empire, the Alto Adige was ruled by the Bishops of Trent and Bressanone for the next eight centuries. After a brief dominion by the Venetian Republic in the fifteenth century, it was ruled from Vienna till the end of World War II. Its flourishing as a tourism and wine-producing area, however, is of a much more recent date; since the construction of huge hydroelectric and irrigation systems and good communications over the last two decades.

Sauces

Antipasti

Soups

Pastas and other farinaceous dishes

RABBIT SAUTÉ   97
(Coniglio fritto dorato alla veneta)

Vegetables

PORK AND BEANS ZERMEGAI   97
(Fagioli Zermegai)

FRIED ZUCCHINI   98
(Zucchine alla veneta)

Desserts

FRIED CUSTARD SQUARES   99
(Crema fritta alla veneta)

PEVERADA SAUCE

(Salsa Peverada alla veneta)

10 ounces poultry liver	*2½ cups strong stock**
(chicken, pheasant, duck or	*2 tablespoons chopped parsley*
guinea fowl)	*Juice of ½ lemon*
½ pound Veneto soppressa	*Salt*
(dry salame-type sausage)	*Freshly ground pepper*
¼ cup oil	

Having cleaned the poultry livers, chop them finely, and dice the soppressa. Heat the oil in a pan and sauté the chopped liver and soppressa mixture, adding parsley, a pinch of salt, and a very generous grinding of black pepper.

Pour the stock, a little at a time, into the pan: mix well. Turn down heat and simmer for a half hour: add a generous squeeze of lemon juice and the sauce is ready. This is also eaten with simple slices of bread browned in the oven, but it is chiefly used with all game and dark meats. Yields 2 cups.

NOTE: Peverada sauce is among the oldest sauces in Italian culinary history: it is well documented from medieval to renaissance times in Venice. It was widely used by the aristocracy and the people to season boiled beef and chicken, game birds, wild boar, and all dark-meat fowl. Peverada used to be prepared with bread crumbs, a generous sprinkling of cinnamon, raisins from Smyrna, pine nuts, salt, and plenty of freshly ground pepper. This mixture was added to meat pan juices or to a reduced stock: or in the case of boiled meats, it was cooked in strong wines from Greece. Sometimes, the livers of the game birds or chickens were pounded in a mortar and added to the pan juices. The addition of soppresse would seem to date from much later times.

CRAB HORS D'OEUVRES

(Antipasto di granzeola)

2½ pounds fresh crab meat	Worcestershire sauce
4 egg yolks, hard-cooked,	1 cup heavy cream
chopped	Juice of ½ lemon
1 tablespoon chopped basil	¾ pound lettuce hearts
Salt and pepper	Vinegar

Boil the crabs, drain, and allow to cool; remove the meat. Combine the egg yolks with the basil in a mixing bowl. Season with a little salt and pepper, a few drops of Worcestershire sauce and beat in, a little at a time, the heavy cream. When a smooth paste has been obtained, mix in the lemon juice, also.

Chop the lettuce hearts very fine and put in a large salad bowl; sprinkle with salt and vinegar. Add the crab meat and pour in the sauce. Mix at table. Serves 6 to 8.

SALTED HERRINGS WITH ONION RINGS

(Aringhe salate con cipolla e olio alla veneta)

4 salted herrings (about ½	Juice of 2 lemons
pound each)	Freshly ground pepper
½ pint milk	2 cloves garlic, sliced
Sauce:	lengthwise
2½ cups oil	1 small onion, sliced

Scale, eviscerate, and clean the salted herrings, removing heads and fins. Boil them for a minute in plenty of water; drain and fillet them. Marinate the fillets in milk for three hours.

Dry fillets with a cloth, lay them in an hors d'oeuvres dish and pour over them a sauce made of the oil, lemon juice, and a generous pinch of pepper beaten well together. Decorate the fillets with very small slivers of garlic and little onion rings. Serves 8.

BEAN AND PASTA SOUP

(Minestra di fagioli con la pasta alla veneta)

1 pound dried brown beans	*2 tablespoons chopped*
1 ham bone, with some meat	*celery*
on it	*1 tablespoon chopped parsley*
½ pound pork rind	*Oil*
1½ tablespoons salt	*¼ pound peeled tomatoes,*
Freshly ground pepper	*drained*
A mixture of:	*½ pound egg pasta (2-inch*
¼ pound ham fat, chopped	*lengths) or*
1½ tablespoons chopped	*½ pound cannolicchietti (or*
onion	*other small or broken*
1 clove chopped garlic	*pasta)*

Soak the beans overnight in plenty of cold water. Boil the ham bone and pork rind together for 10 minutes; drain, allow to cool, and then clean both well, cutting away unappetizing-looking pieces and scraping the pork rind with a knife and cutting it into strips.

Wash the beans in cold running water, place in an earthenware pot and cover with 6 pints of cold water; add salt, a pinch of pepper, the ham bone and the pork rind. Bring to the boil and simmer for two hours.

Meanwhile, sauté the ham fat, onion, garlic, celery, and parsley mixture in a little oil; add the tomatoes and allow to cook together gently for 10 minutes.

When the beans are cooked, remove the ham bone, scrape off remaining meat, chop it and put it and the tomato sauce into the bean pot; bring to the boil again, stirring, and sprinkle in the pasta. Remove from heat when the pasta is al dente. Allow to rest for a few minutes. Serve hot. Serves 6 to 8.

DUMPLINGS IN BROTH TYROLESE STYLE

(Knödl in brodo alla tirolese)

A mixture of: *1 pint milk*
  2 tablespoons chopped onion   *½ cup sifted flour*
  1 tablespoon chopped parsley *2 eggs*
½ cup butter   *Salt*
¼ pound bacon slices chopped   *4 pints beef stock*
1 pound day-old bread, diced

Simmer the onion and parsley mixture in a pan with the butter, and add the bacon. Sauté these together for a few moments before sprinkling in the bread. Sauté all lightly; allow to cool.

Using an electric blender, combine the milk, the flour, the eggs, and a pinch of salt; pour this mixture and the onion-bacon-bread mixture into a bowl and combine until a smooth, creamy consistency is obtained.

Taking small quantities of this mixture, using your hands, roll out walnut-sized balls. Drop these, a few at a time, into lightly salted boiling water for a few minutes until the flour is cooked; drain and reserve.

Bring the stock to the boil, drop in the knödl balls, and, after a few moments of simmering, serve in deep soup bowls. Serves 6 to 8.

BROTH VENETIAN STYLE

(Brodo dei veneziani in tazza)

8 egg yolks   *3 pints beef stock*
Juice of 1 lemon   *6 ounces day-old bread, diced*
Salt and pepper   *and browned in oven*

Put the egg yolks in a fireproof casserole, beat them with an egg whisk, adding the lemon juice, a pinch of salt and a little pepper.

Transfer the casserole to a low heat; beating continuously, add, a little at a time, the cold stock. Increase the heat slowly and bring the mixture to the boil, stirring constantly. As soon as the stock begins to show signs of boiling, remove casserole immediately from the stove.

Distribute the bread cubes in soup bowls and pour the broth over them. Serves 6 to 8.

SPAGHETTI WITH DUCK SAUCE

(Bigoli in salsa d'anitra)

1 young duck	*¼ pound mortadella,*
1 small onion, stuck with a	*chopped*
clove	*3 cloves garlic, crushed*
1½ tablespoons chopped carrot	*4 sage leaves*
1½ tablespoons chopped celery	*3 tablespoons butter*
½ tablespoon salt	*3 tablespoons oil*
1½ pounds spaghetti	*1 cup grated Parmesan*
Sauce:	

Pluck and eviscerate the duck; pass it over a flame to remove any residual feathers, etc. Wash and dry well. Place in a very large casserole of cold water; bring to the boil, skim off scum, add the onion, the carrot, and the celery; season with ½ tablespoon of salt, and simmer for 40 minutes.

Remove the duck, drain, and reserve for later use such as duck and horse-radish sauce* recipe. Strain the cooking liquid through a damp cheesecloth and replace in casserole. Add more water if needed and bring to the boil; toss in the spaghetti and cook till al dente. Drain and transfer to a warmed serving dish.

Sauce: While the pasta is cooking, sauté the chopped mortadella, garlic, and sage in the butter and oil. Pour this mixture over the drained pasta along with ½ the grated Parmesan; mix well and serve remaining Parmesan at table. Serves 6.

PASTA WITH RICOTTA BELLUNO STYLE

(Paste conze con ricotta alla bellunese)

1¼ pounds dry pasta
Salt
¾ pound fresh ricotta
1½ tablespoons sugar

1 teaspoon powdered cinnamon
2½ cups Italian meat sauce*
(or use the pasta's cooking
water)

Cook the pasta in plenty of lightly salted boiling water; meanwhile place the ricotta in a big serving dish with the sugar, the powdered cinnamon, and the Italian meat sauce (or an equivalent quantity of boiling water from the pasta pot), and combine well. When the pasta is al dente, drain and pour into the serving dish and mix well, allowing the ricotta time to soften, serve hot, with grated Parmesan, if desired. Serves 6.

PASTA WITH PEAS

(Paste conze coi bisi)

2 ounces peas, shelled
Salt
Pinch of sugar
1¼ pounds spaghetti (or
  other dry pasta)

1½ cups grated Parmesan
6 ounces butter, melted
Pinch of pepper

Shell the peas and boil them quickly with a pinch of salt and a pinch of sugar. Meantime cook the pasta in plenty of lightly salted boiling water; drain when al dente and pass to a warmed serving dish. Mix in the peas, followed by the grated Parmesan and the melted butter and season with pepper. Serves 6.

RICE AND PEAS

(Risi e bisi)

6 ounces lean salt pork,
   chopped
1½ tablespoons chopped onion
1½ tablespoons chopped parsley
1 pound shelled peas
3 tablespoons butter

2 pints stock
1¼ pounds rice, cleaned with
   a cloth
Salt and pepper
1 cup grated Parmesan

Lightly brown the salt pork, the onion, and the parsley in a casserole; add the peas, the butter, and the stock, and bring to the boil. Toss in the rice, season with salt and pepper and bring to the boil again and continue boiling fast for 20 minutes, adding extra boiling water if the liquids evaporate prematurely. Immediately before removing from the stove, mix in the grated Parmesan. Serve hot. Serves 6.

EEL BRAISED IN DRY MARSALA

(Bisato in tecia alla veneta)

2½ pounds eel
½ cup oil
3 tablespoons butter
Salt and freshly ground pepper
A mixture of:
   3 cloves garlic, chopped
   1 tablespoon chopped parsley

2 tablespoons chopped sage
   leaves
½ cup dry marsala wine
1 pound peeled tomatoes,
   drained
3¼ pounds polenta,* sliced

Skin, decapitate, and eviscerate the eel or eels; wash and dry them and chop them into 3-inch lengths.

Heat the oil and butter in a pan; add the eel chunks, season with salt and pepper and brown well on all sides. Add the garlic, parsley, and sage leaves mixture, and when the garlic is golden brown, pour in the dry marsala. Reduce the wine appreciably, and add the tomatoes, stirring well, and simmer for 15 minutes.

Fry the polenta and serve with the eel pieces, pouring the pan juices over all. Serves 6 to 8.

CREAMED DRIED COD VICENZA STYLE

(Stoccafisso mantecato alla vicentina)

2 pounds dried cod (stoccafisso)*	Oil
3 cloves garlic	Salt and white pepper
Milk	Pinch of cinnamon
4 tablespoons dry white wine	8 squares of polenta*

Prepare the dried cod according to Note. Having soaked, cleaned, boned, skinned, and flaked it, put it in a fireproof pan, which has been well rubbed with garlic. Cover the fish with milk (add, if you like, a little white wine) and put on a low heat; cook slowly, stirring often, until the fish is pulped. As soon as the liquids are reduced, begin pouring in, a tablespoon at a time and alternately, oil and warm milk, stirring constantly. Slowly a creamy purée will be obtained; at this point the cooking is complete. Season with a little salt (if necessary), white pepper, and cinnamon. Serve immediately with polenta squares either fried or heated in the oven. Serves 8.

DRIED COD VICENZA STYLE

(Stoccafisso alla vicentina)

2 pounds dried cod (stoccafisso)*	8 fillets desalted anchovy,* mashed
Salt and pepper	1 tablespoon chopped parsley
Flour	½ cup dry white wine
½ cup grated Parmesan	2 pints hot milk
Pinch of cinnamon	2 tablespoons butter
½ cup oil	8 slices of polenta*
1 small onion chopped with 1 clove garlic	

Prepare the dried cod. Having soaked, cleaned, boned, flaked, and dried it, season with a little salt and pepper. Dust with flour and transfer to a large pan; sprinkle over the grated Parmesan and the cinnamon and reserve.

Pour the oil into a saucepan and sauté the onion and garlic mixture; add the anchovy, the parsley and, immediately, the wine. Reduce the liquids almost completely over a low heat, then slowly add the hot milk and the butter. Cook for a few moments together until the mixture is combined; then pour it over the dried cod in the large pan. Bring this to the boil on the stove and then pass to a preheated moderate oven and simmer until the pan liquids are almost completely absorbed. Transfer to a serving dish. Fry the polenta slices or heat them in the oven, and serve hot. Serves 8.

MUSSELS IN THE PAN

(Peoci in tecia alla veneta)

3 pounds mussels	*2 tablespoons vinegar*
½ cup oil	*Salt and pepper*
A mixture of:	
3 cloves garlic, chopped	
3 tablespoons chopped parsley	
2 tablespoons bread crumbs	

Scrub and beard the mussels and wash them in plenty of water; put 2 tablespoons oil in a pan along with the mussels and sauté them over a brisk heat until the shells open. Then remove them from the stove; discard the empty shells and remove the top shell from each. Lay the bottom shells, with the mussels in them, in a pan—2 pans may be necessary—and distribute over each a pinch of the garlic, parsley, bread-crumb mixture. Combine the remaining oil with 2 tablespoons of vinegar and sprinkle over all, seasoning also with salt and pepper.

Preheat a moderate oven and put the pan (or pans) in it; remove when the bread crumbs begin to brown. Serves 6.

SKEWERED SWEETBREADS MOSIANA

(Stecchi alla mosiana)

12 slices Italian sausage (dry salame-type)	*12 gherkin halves*
	12 slices Gruyère cheese
12 slices sweetbreads	*24 slices sweet red peppers*
Butter	*(in oil)*
Salt	*12 black olives, pitted*
24 slices sweet yellow peppers (in oil)	*12 green olives, pitted*

Cook the sausage slices in boiling water for 5 minutes. Blanch, peel, and slice the sweetbreads; sauté them lightly in a little butter and a pinch of salt. Put on a wooden skewer, in the following order, a slice of sweetbread, a slice of yellow pepper, half a gherkin, a slice of Gruyère, a slice of red pepper, a black olive, another slice of red pepper, a slice of sausage, another slice of yellow pepper and, finally, a green olive. Plainly the rules for this are not strict; but it is an excellent entremets snack which may vary with circumstances. Corned beef may be substituted for the sweetbreads. Serves 6.

GRILLED VEAL HEART TRENTINO STYLE

(Cuore di vitello ai ferri alla trentina)

1 veal heart	*¼ cup melted butter*
Marinade:	*Salt and pepper*
3 cloves garlic, chopped (or onion)	*Juice of ½ lemon*

Clean the heart and cut into slices ½-inch thick, discarding unattractive parts. Marinate for three to four hours, turning the slices from time to time.

Place on a hot grill and brown on both sides: lower the heat and continue cooking for about 20 minutes, brushing the slices of veal heart with the marinade sufficiently to keep the meat moist. Serve hot. Serves 4 to 6.

OX TONGUE BRAISED IN RED WINE

(Lingua di bue brasata al vino rosso)

1 ox tongue (4 pounds)	*3 cups stock*
1 onion, sliced	*1 teaspoon chopped thyme*
1 carrot, sliced	*and bay leaf*
1 stalk celery, chopped	*2 teaspoons chopped parsley*
¼ cup oil	*Salt and freshly ground pepper*
3 tablespoons flour	*1 sheet greaseproof paper,*
1 pint dry red wine	*buttered*
1 tablespoon brandy	

Pass the tongue over a flame, scrub it, and allow it to stand in cold well-salted water for twenty-four hours. Simmer it for one hour in plenty of water with slices of onion, carrot, and the chopped celery; drain and dry well with a cloth.

Take a heavy fireproof casserole, pour in the oil, heat well and brown the tongue on all sides; remove tongue and reserve. Sprinkle in, a little at a time, the flour, and combine with the pan juices over a very low heat, taking care that the flour does not stick to the pan. As soon as it begins to color, add the wine, the brandy, and the stock, stirring constantly. Bring the liquids slowly to the boil, replace the tongue adding also the thyme and bay leaf mixture, the parsley, and a tablespoon of salt and a pinch of pepper. Bring to the boil again, turn down heat, and lay the buttered greaseproof paper over the top of the pan and cover both greaseproof paper and casserole with a lid. Simmer for three hours. Fifteen minutes before the three hours are up, remove, drain, and reserve the tongue. Pass the pan juices through a fine strainer and pour back into the casserole. Replace, also, the tongue in the casserole. Meanwhile, preheat a moderate oven and place the casserole in it for the remaining cooking time.

Slice the tongue, transfer slices to a serving dish, and pour the pan juices over all. This dish should be accompanied by a vegetable purée or with fresh vegetables sautéed in butter. Serves 6 to 8.

CALF'S LIVER VENETIAN STYLE

(Fegato alla veneziana)

½ cup oil	Salt and freshly ground pepper
½ pound onion, thickly sliced	6 lemons, halved
1¼ pounds calf's liver slices,	
not too thick	

Heat the oil in a pan until smoking; sauté the onions until golden and crisp. Add the liver seasoned with 1 tablespoon of salt and a pinch of pepper; mix together over a lively heat until the liver is cooked on the outside (about 2 minutes), but still pink and tender and underdone inside. Serve hot with lemon halves. Serves 6.

DUCK AND HORSE-RADISH SAUCE

(Anitra al rafano)

1 duck (from the spaghetti	1 cup bread crumbs
with duck sauce recipe)*	Pinch of salt
Horse-radish sauce:	½ teaspoon sugar
¼ pound grated horse-radish	3 tablespoons thick cream
	2 tablespoons vinegar

This recipe uses the duck from which the duck sauce of the earlier recipe is made. The horse-radish sauce is made by combining the grated horse-radish with the bread crumbs (these should be soaked in milk and drained well), salt, sugar, cream, and vinegar. Serves 4 to 6.

RABBIT SAUTÉ

(Coniglio fritto dorato alla veneta)

1 plump rabbit	*½ cup flour*
Marinade:	*3 eggs, beaten*
½ cup oil	*Salt*
Juice of 1 lemon	*1½ cups lard*
2 tablespoons chopped onion	*¾ cup oil*
1½ tablespoons salt	*4 lemons, halved*
Pinch of pepper	

Prepare the rabbit as follows: skin it by first making an incision at the top of the hind legs near the abdomen; remove the skin from the hindquarters. Then, holding the rabbit's hind legs, strip off the rest of the skin. Lay it on its back; open the abdomen and eviscerate. Cut off the feet at the joint: cut the rabbit, then, in half lengthwise and continue cutting it into smaller pieces. Wash well.

Prepare the marinade; put the rabbit chunks in a pan and pour the marinade over them. Leave for two hours, turning the chunks occasionally. Then drain and dry the meat with a cloth. Dip the rabbit chunks in flour and then in the beaten egg seasoned with a teaspoon of salt.

Heat the fats—the lard and the oil together—in a large pan till they smoke; toss in the rabbit pieces, a few at a time, and sauté well till golden and crisp. Drain and transfer to a serving dish, sprinkling with a little salt. Serve with lemon halves. Serves 4 to 6.

PORK AND BEANS ZERMEGAI

(Fagioli Zermegai)

¾ pound dried cranberry or black-eyed beans	*Salt*
	Olive oil
6 ounces pork rind	*White pepper*

Soak the beans overnight; wash well. Pass the pork rind over a flame to remove bristles and blanch for 10 minutes in boiling water; transfer to another pot with plenty of lightly salted water and bring to the boil. Add the beans, turn down heat and cook over a moderate heat till the beans are tender (the time will vary according to the variety of bean). Drain and serve hot, seasoning with olive oil, salt, and freshly ground pepper. Serves 4 to 6.

FRIED ZUCCHINI

(Zucchine alla veneta)

2 pounds small zucchini	*1 tablespoon chopped parsley*
3 tablespoons butter	*2 eggs*
3 tablespoons oil	*1 egg yolk*
Salt and pepper	*4 tablespoons grated Parmesan*

Cut off hard ends of the zucchini; wash and slice them. Heat the butter and oil in a frying pan until smoking; toss in the zucchini, sprinkling with salt, pepper, and chopped parsley. Sauté the zucchini until their liquid has evaporated and the slices begin to crisp.

Meantime, pour the 2 eggs and egg yolk into a bowl and beat them, adding the 4 tablespoons of Parmesan. Two minutes before the zucchini are fully cooked, pour the beaten egg mixture into the frying pan and mix with a wooden spoon. As soon as the eggs begin to set, remove from the heat and serve hot. Serves 6 to 8.

FRIED CUSTARD SQUARES

(Crema fritta alla veneta)

1 pint milk	3 small dried, grated
1 teaspoon vanilla extract	macaroons (amaretti)
1 cup sifted flour	2 eggs, beaten
1 cup superfine sugar	1 cup bread crumbs
1 teaspoon salt	Oil and lard (equal quantities)
2 eggs	for deep-frying
6 egg yolks	Vanilla-flavored confectioners'
5 tablespoons butter	sugar

Bring the milk to the boil in a saucepan, add the vanilla extract, and simmer for 15 minutes.

Put the flour, the superfine sugar, and the salt into a mixing bowl and—one at a time—combine the eggs and egg yolks, using a wooden spoon; then mix in, very slowly, as though making mayonnaise, the milk.

Put on a low heat and, stirring constantly, bring the mixture slowly to the boil; then boil briskly for 1 minute and remove from heat. Stir in 2 tablespoons of butter and the grated macaroons.

Pour this custard cream over a buttered table and spread out until less than 1 inch thick: melt the remaining butter and pour over, spreading it with a knife. Allow to cool.

When the custard cream has cooled completely, cut it first into 1½-inch-wide strips and then into 1½-inch squares.

Dip each square first in beaten egg and then in bread crumbs; at this point, they can be reserved.

When required, prepare a large frying pan for deep-frying with smoking oil and lard; drop in the squares and sauté them till golden brown and crisp. Drain them and transfer to a serving dish. Sprinkle over vanilla-flavored confectioners' sugar (this is made by putting vanilla beans and confectioners' sugar in a screw-top jar) and serve either hot or cold.

Friuli–Venezia Giulia

Friuli-Venezia Giulia is a border province which, like the Veneto proper, was for over a century under the domination of the Austro-Hungarian Empire. The port of Trieste was—and still is—the geopolitical hinge on which the economies of Austria and Yugoslavia turn. Italy finally won back the province after World War I, only to lose half of it to Yugoslavia after World War II.

These vicissitudes inevitably have had their effect not only on the people but on the gastronomy; there is, in fact, always something of Mittel-europa about Trieste as one can learn from the writings of James Joyce and the even more fascinating tales of Italo Svevo. There is always something of the wry humor of Prague, Vienna, and Budapest in the Triestino's spirit; and there is often goulash, Wiener Schnitzel, or boeuf Voronoff on his plate.

But the Triestino has Italianized all these subtly and also has a whole range of seafood which landlocked Mittel-europa could never have. The Adriatic Sea has some of the finest fish in the world and, in Trieste, one finds not only fine fresh fish, but local seafood, which seem unknown elsewhere in the Mediterranean.

For centuries before becoming part of the Austro-Hungarian Empire—along with the whole Yugoslav coast down to Corfu—Friuli-Venezia Giulia was part of the Venetian Republic; and before that it was part of the Roman and Byzantine Empires. Its real traditions, therefore, are Italian, with Greek overtones, rather than Germanic. The northern overtones, however, which one finds so often, are a pleasant surprise. After all, one does not expect to find rollmops in Italy and when one finds them in Friuli (marinated fresh herrings),* they are discreetly Italianized and more subtle than their northern cousins.

An interesting marriage of central and southern Europe is exemplified by roast mussels with bacon and tomato sauce Trieste style; this is an improbable gastronomic juxtaposition—seafood and bacon—which is not to be found in any other part of Italy, but its improbability in no way detracts from its effectiveness as a gastronomic idea.

The vicissitudes of Friuli-Venezia Giulia have included having their vineyards destroyed during both world wars; on both occasions, they were quickly replanted and on a larger scale. Today, the regional wines have again won a very high reputation in Italy. In particular, the Tocai whites and the magnificent Merlot and Cabernet reds are to be noted. Friuli-Venezia Giulia is not the best of farmland, which usually means that it is very good vineyard land. This fact, in the past, has led the people to look to the sea for their living—to fishing and to manning the ocean-going liners which sail from Trieste port. More recently, the shipbuilding industry has again grown large (supertankers are built there) and, quite exotically, in the little country town of Pordenone, the largest factory in all Europe making household appliances has grown out of nothing but the determination of the people to overcome their times of trouble and the expatriation of their men in search of work.

Friuli-Venezia Giulia, therefore, lives on its industry and industriousness, and, gastronomically, on its fine wines and its world-famous hams. The San Daniele air-cured raw ham is often considered to be Italy's best; like Parma ham, it is also available in cans, which in no way diminish its delicate qualities. There is one essential rule to follow with this sort of Italian prosciutto crudo: it must be cut paper-thin with a very sharp knife (or better, use a slicing machine), and, once cut, it must be eaten immediately, as it dries out quickly and loses its charm. Moist and delicate San Daniele ham, with slices of mature cantaloupe or ripe figs, is for most Italians the simplest and most tempting of hors d'oeuvres.

Antipasti
> MARINATED FRESH HERRINGS   104
> (Aringhe fresche marinate alla friulana)

Soups
> RICE SOUP   104
> (Minestra di riso alla friulana)

Pastas and other farinaceous dishes
> FRIULI RAVIOLI   105
> (Ofelle alla friulana)

> CORN-MEAL POLENTA   106
> (Polenta al forno alla friulana)

Fish
> ROAST MUSSELS WITH BACON
> AND TOMATO SAUCE TRIESTE STYLE   107
> (Cozze in spiedini con lardo affumicato e salsa di pomodoro triestina)

Entrées
> FRIED CHEESE SAVORY   107
> (Crema al formaggio fritta)

Meats
> BEEF STEW UDINE STYLE   108
> (Ciar in padiele)

> CHICKEN RAGOUT   109
> (Intingolo di pollo alla friulana)

Vegetables
> STUFFED ARTICHOKES   109
> (Carciofi al tegame alla maniera della Venezia Giulia)

MARINATED FRESH HERRINGS

(Aringhe fresche marinate alla friulana)

2 *medium-sized onions,*	1 *bay leaf*
chopped	1 *sprig thyme*
1 *clove garlic, chopped*	1 *teaspoon salt*
1 *tablespoon chopped carrot*	3 *peppercorns, bruised*
1 *sprig parsley*	1 *pound small fresh herrings*
3 *cups white wine*	*Olive oil*
¼ *cup vinegar*	

Simmer the onions, garlic, carrot, and parsley in the white wine and vinegar, along with the bay leaf, the thyme, salt, and peppercorns for 20 minutes, adding some water if necessary.

Fillet the herrings, discarding bones, head, etc., and place in a fireproof pan.

Strain the simmered stock through a damp cheesecloth, replace in a saucepan and bring to the boil. Pour this liquid over the herring fillets boiling hot: cover the fireproof pan with greaseproof paper and put into a moderate oven for 20 minutes. Remove and allow to cool. When cold pour a generous cup of oil over the herrings. Serve cold. Serves 4 to 6.

RICE SOUP

(Minestra di riso alla friulana)

4 *pints beef stock*	5 *egg yolks*
1 *pound rice, cleaned but not*	*Juice of ½ lemon*
washed	6 *tablespoons grated Parmesan*

Bring the stock to the boil and toss in the rice. Meanwhile put the egg yolks in a soup tureen and beat, adding the lemon juice and a tablespoon or so of grated Parmesan.

When the rice is cooked al dente, allow it to rest a little; then pour the stock and rice slowly into the soup tureen, whisking briskly so that the egg incorporates with the rice but does not set. Serve the remaining Parmesan at table. Serves 6 to 8.

FRIULI RAVIOLI

(Ofelle alla friulana)

Filling:
1½ pounds spinach
Salt
½ pound butter
2 tablespoons chopped onion
½ pound lean veal, chopped
6 ounces raw pork sausage, skinned and chopped

Dough:
3 pounds potatoes, boiled
2 cups sifted flour
3 tablespoons baking powder
Salt
2 eggs
1 cup grated Parmesan

Filling: Wash the spinach and boil it for 5 minutes with a little salt. Chop it and squeeze it in a colander to remove all excess liquid and reserve.

Heat 1 tablespoon butter in a pan and sauté the onion. When browned, add the spinach and allow to cook a little to dry out and then add the chopped veal and sausage, stirring and cooking for about 12 minutes over a medium heat, being careful not to let the ingredients stick to the pan. Remove the mixture from the pan, allow to cool, and reserve.

Dough: Pass the boiled potatoes through a sieve and heap the purée in a mound on the tabletop; add the flour. Scoop out a hole in the center of the mound and add the baking powder, dissolved in a little warm water, a pinch of salt, and 2 beaten eggs; knead the mixture until a smooth dough is obtained. Reserve.

To combine: Roll out the dough into very thin sheets—as thin as possible. Lay out on one sheet little Lima-bean-sized balls of the meat filling 3 or 4 inches apart; cover with another sheet.

Press down around the filling and cut out squares with a cooky cutter.

Bring a pot of lightly salted water to the boil, toss in the ofelle and cook till al dente; drain and pass to a warmed serving dish.

Warm the remaining butter in a little saucepan, meanwhile sprinkling over the ofelle a little Parmesan and mixing it in. As the butter begins to turn golden brown, remove from the stove and pour over the pasta. Mix in and serve with the remaining Parmesan immediately. Serves 8.

CORN-MEAL POLENTA

(Polenta al forno alla friulana)

*1 pound yellow corn-meal polenta**	*6 ounces lean salt pork, chopped*
½ cup oil	*4 eggs, well beaten*
1¼ pounds sausage meat	*Salt*

While the corn-meal polenta is cooking (it should be, when finished, on the thin side), heat the oil in a frying pan and, when smoking, sauté the sausage meat and salt pork till golden brown. Remove meat with slotted spoon and mix with the beaten eggs and a little salt; stir this mixture into the polenta. Reserve the frying-pan fats.

Grease a fairly large fireproof dish with some of the fats in which the sausage meat and salt pork were cooked in and pour the polenta mixture into it. Level off with a spoon, frequently dipped into boiling water to prevent polenta sticking to it. Pour over the remaining cooking fats and pass the fireproof dish into a moderate oven. Remove from oven after a few minutes when the surface is browned. Grated cheese may be served with this. Serves 6 to 8.

ROAST MUSSELS WITH BACON AND TOMATO SAUCE TRIESTE STYLE

(Cozze in spiedini con lardo affumicato e salsa di pomodoro triestina)

48 very large mussels or clams	4 metal or wooden skewers
	¼ cup butter, softened
4 slices of bacon, very thin	1 cup tomato sauce*

Scrub and beard the mussels, shuck them with a knife, remove from shell; dry each of them with a cloth and put a dozen on each skewer. Wrap the skewers in a slice of bacon and cover with softened butter.

Place these loaded skewers in a pan in a hot oven until the bacon is crisped. Serve hot immediately with tomato sauce. Serves 4.

FRIED CHEESE SAVORY

(Crema al formaggio fritta)

1 cup flour	1¼ cups Gruyère or Parmesan, grated
½ cup rice flour	
3 whole eggs	3 tablespoons butter
4 egg yolks	3 eggs, beaten
Salt and pepper	1 cup bread crumbs
Grating of nutmeg	1 cup oil
1 pint milk	

Mix both the flours, the 3 whole eggs and the 4 egg yolks together with ½ teaspoon of salt, a pinch of pepper, and a grating of nutmeg. Transfer this dough to a large saucepan; warm the milk and pour it, stirring constantly, into the flour mixture. Bring to the boil for 5 minutes stirring vigorously. Remove from heat, add the grated cheese mixing in well and pour into a flat dish that has been well smeared with 3 tablespoons of butter and leave to cool.

When cold, cut the paste into squares or diamonds; dip them in beaten egg, dust in bread crumbs and deep-fry in smoking oil. When golden brown, remove and drain. Serves 8.

BEEF STEW UDINE STYLE

(Ciar in padiele)

2 pounds lean sirloin beef,
    boned and tied
¼ pound salt pork, cut in strips
    and peppered
2 tablespoons oil
A mixture of:
    ¼ pound prosciutto fat,
        diced
    2 tablespoons chopped onion
    1 tablespoon chopped carrot
    1 tablespoon chopped celery
    1 tablespoon chopped parsley

6 peppercorns, bruised
2 tablespoons freshly grated
    horse-radish
1 clove
¼ teaspoon ground cumin seed
Pinch of orégano
2 cups beef stock
2 cups peeled tomatoes,
    drained and sieved
Salt
12 slices polenta,* browned in
    oven

Preheat a moderate oven. Lard the beef with the peppered salt pork strips. Heat the oil in a large pan and, over a very low flame, lightly sauté the prosciutto fat, the onions, carrots, celery, and parsley. Add the beef and brown it on all sides; then remove from pan.

Mix the peppercorns, the horse-radish, the clove, the cumin, and the orégano with the pan juices. Replace the beef in the pan, add the stock and place in the oven. Cook for 45 minutes, basting frequently and turning the meat occasionally.

Remove from oven, add the tomatoes, and adjust for salt. Finish cooking over a moderate heat on top of the stove—45 minutes or more, adding stock or water if the gravy becomes too thick.

Transfer the beef to a serving dish, slice and keep warm. Strain the sauce and pour it over the sliced beef and serve with hot polenta straight from the oven. Serves 6 to 8.

CHICKEN RAGOUT

(Intingolo di pollo alla friulana)

2 spring chickens (1½ pounds
   each) ready to cook*
2 tablespoons onion, chopped
1 clove garlic, crushed
½ cup oil
4 tablespoons butter
Salt and pepper
1 cup dry white wine

A mixture of:
   ½ pound salame, chopped
   2 tablespoons chopped
    dried mushrooms,
    soaked for 30 minutes
   ½ pound prosciutto, chopped
   2 tablespoons chopped parsley
   8 slices polenta*

Cut the chickens into medium-sized pieces. Sauté the onion and garlic in oil and butter till golden; add the chicken pieces with 1 tablespoon salt and a good pinch of pepper and sauté them until golden also. Pour in the dry white wine and add the chopped mixture of salame, mushrooms, and ham, and simmer for 30 minutes. Five minutes before removing from heat, add the chopped parsley. Heat and brown the polenta in the oven and serve hot with the ragout. Serves 6 to 8.

STUFFED ARTICHOKES

(Carciofi al tegame alla maniera della Venezia Giulia)

12 artichokes
Juice of ½ lemon
A mixture of:
   3 sprigs parsley, chopped
   2 cloves garlic, chopped

2 tablespoons bread crumbs
Salt and pepper
2 tablespoons oil
½ cup oil
Salt and pepper

Trim the artichokes, removing hard outer leaves and the choke. Cut the stems short and to equal lengths; chop the remaining stem pieces and reserve all in water with lemon juice.

Prepare the parsley, garlic, bread crumb, and oil mixture: and spoon into each of the artichoke centers a portion of this paste.

Transfer the artichokes and the chopped artichoke stems to a pan, sprinkle generously with oil, and pour in sufficient cold water to half cover the artichokes. Season with salt and pepper. Pass the pan to a moderate preheated oven and cook for one hour, basting now and then with the pan juices. Transfer to a serving dish and pour the pan juices including the chopped stems over the artichokes. Serves 6.

FRIED FENNEL HEARTS WITH ARTICHOKES

(Fritole de fenoci e fondi di carciofi)

1 pound fennel hearts	*Oil for deep-frying*
Juice of 1 lemon	*Salt*
Flour	*2 artichoke hearts, chopped*
2 eggs, beaten with a pinch	
of salt	

Strip off the outer skin of the fennel, leaving the white hearts; dice them and reserve in a casserole containing water and lemon juice.

To prepare for cooking, dry the diced fennel with a cloth, dip first in flour, then in beaten egg and deep-fry in smoking oil. Drain when crisp and golden: sprinkle with salt and serve immediately mixed with chopped raw artichoke hearts. Serves 6.

SWEET FRITTERS

(Fritole alla Venezia Giulia)

2 tablespoons baking powder	*Pinch of cinnamon*
2 cups milk	*1 tablespoon rum*
1 egg	*Pinch of salt*
1 egg yolk	*3 tablespoons raisins*
4 tablespoons superfine sugar	*3 tablespoons pine nuts*
¾ pound flour, sifted	*Oil for deep-frying*
Peel of 1 lemon, grated (no	*Vanilla-flavored sugar*
pith)	

Dissolve the baking powder with warm milk in a mixing bowl; whisk in first the egg, then the egg yolk and sugar, followed by the flour, the grated lemon peel, the pinch of cinnamon, the rum, and the salt. This mixture should be fairly soft. Work it with a wooden spoon and allow to rest for one hour in a warm place. Then mix in the raisins and pine nuts.

Smoke plenty of oil in a frying pan and toss the mixture into the pan, a tablespoon at a time (dip the spoon in boiling water continuously so that the mixture does not stick to the spoon). When golden and crisp, remove these little fritters with a slotted spoon; drain, put on a serving dish and sprinkle with vanilla-flavored sugar. Serves 6.

Liguria

Liguria is a strip of mountain, which runs from Monte Carlo down to Tuscany. It is a land of great beauty with a mild sunny climate, which has required all the sweat and brains of the Genoese to make a living out of. It is almost completely without natural resources; not even Genoa is a natural harbor—it is all man-made.

The climate is the only really favorable element, since the coast is protected from the east winds by the mountains. What does grow in Liguria, as long as it is artificially irrigated on man-made terraces on the hillsides, grows luxuriantly.

In the past, these disadvantages spurred the Ligurians to investigate the Indes and the Western Hemisphere. One noted Genoese, who stayed on in the latter, founded the Bank of America. The Ligurians are an enterprising people because they have been forced to be by circumstances. Today, they are not attempting commercial rivalry at which they cannot win—they are specializing. They cannot, broadly, produce fruit as cheaply as Sicily so they have settled for a few special peach and apricot varieties. They cannot produce wine at, say, the price obtaining in the Romagna, so they have turned their vineyards over to growing carnations, long-stem roses, and ornamental plants with a success which is now Europe-wide. There are almost no cattle, consequently no local cheeses; no wheat, since you cannot grow wheat profitably on a three-yard-wide terrace.

The Ligurians were the first to bring the tomato and the potato from the New World to Italy, but even these crops have given way to a great extent to more valuable ones such as asparagus, artichokes, mushrooms, basil, and other aromatic herbs and market gardening of a specialized nature.

The enterprise of the Genoese is such that their city has become the third corner of the Italian industrial triangle (Turin-Milan-Genoa) and, along with regular heavy industry, there is a huge food-processing industry of raw products from all Italy. Particularly important in this sector is olive-oil refining and bottling: much comes from the olive groves of Liguria, but much more comes from other regions.

The Ligurian cuisine is, with some notable exceptions, light and delicate as are the winds. It is based almost exclusively on pasta, fish, vegetables, and fruit. Ravioli needs no introduction: it is Liguria's major offering to world gastronomy. The pesto sauce, however, is one of the exceptions: it is made of basil, garlic, oil, and Pecorino (sometimes with the addition of chopped pine nuts and walnuts) and is an overpowering mixture. Those who cannot take it straight as a pasta sauce would be wise to add a little to a vegetable soup or minestrone to observe the miraculous effect.

One Ligurian specialty, frivolously called cappon magro (lean capon)* is the piquant salad of seafood and vegetables to end all salads. The recipe is given in the text, but it is plainly one of those dishes which is as flexible as the fancy of the cook, particularly in the decoration with the shrimps, lobsters, and seafood.

Fried fish, of course—particularly mullet and whitebait—is most popular; but the fish is not comparable to nor as plentiful as that of the Adriatic. There is a fair amount of shellfish, among which the datteri di mare (sea dates) are most prized; they are clamlike shellfish, brown and shaped like the palm date.

Though naturally meat is imported into Liguria nowadays, the traditional recipes deal chiefly with rabbits, kid, and game birds, all of which are treated with gentle loving care. Ligurian cooking is simple but thoughtful, and rarely does it become complex.

The recipe which leaps to mind as being complicated is rolled veal cima Genoa style*; it is a highly seasoned, light galantine of a completely original and delightful nature: though, to read the recipe, it sounds as heavy as lead. It is in fact only an egg mixture cooked in rolled veal in which the meat makes up a minimal part.

The wines are few and with a modest production. But Liguria

is by no means without fine wines. The best known is the Cinqueterre which comes from five villages west of La Spezia which are so difficult to reach by land that it is easier to reach them by boat. The Cinqueterre is a good full-flavored 14° dry wine made from the vernaccia grape. There is also a passito variety of the same name which has a 16° alcoholic content. The passito process requires that the grapes be left in the sun for a week or two after being picked and before being pressed; they then produce a strong, sweet wine.

There is also the golden Coronada from above Genoa and the better-known Dolceacqua ruby red from near the French frontier at Ventimiglia; this ages well and is an excellent dinner wine at four years old. Dolceacqua was imported by Napoleon Buonaparte for his own table; it is a curiosity that, by a trick of twelve months, Napoleon was not an Italian and a citizen of the Republic of Genoa. He was born in 1769, less than a year after Genoa sold the island of Corsica to France.

Sauces

Antipasti

Soups

Entrées

SAUSAGE FRITTERS   130
(Frittelle di salsiccia alla ligure)

Meats

SAUTÉ OF VEAL   131
(Vitello all'uccelletto)

ROLLED VEAL CIMA GENOA STYLE   131
(Cima alla genovese)

BRAISED BEEF WITH ANCHOVIES   132
(Brasato di manzo con acciughe alla genovese)

BRAISED DUCK WITH GREEN OLIVES   133
(Anitra brasata con olive verdi)

RABBIT HOME-COOKING STYLE   134
(Coniglio alla casalinga)

Desserts

FRIED MILK SWEET AND SOUR   134
(Latte brusco alla ligure)

TRADITIONAL GENOESE PESTO

(Pesto alla genovese)

¼ pound basil, cleaned not washed	*1 scant cup Pecorino (substitute Parmesan)*
3 cloves garlic	*½ cup oil*
Salt	*2 tablespoons hot water*

Having cleaned the basil leaves with a cloth, remove the hard stems, etc., put them in a mortar a few at a time, and pound. Add, a little at a time, the garlic and salt.

Continue pounding lightly, turning the mixture every now and then, until it is reduced to a pulp. Finally add the cup of Pecorino (or Parmesan) and begin pouring in the oil as though making mayonnaise, adding also a tablespoon or two of hot water, preferably taken from a pot of cooking pasta. When a smooth paste is obtained, the pesto is ready. Yields scant 1½ cups.

PESTO SAUCE GENOA STYLE (NON-TRADITIONAL)

(Pesto alla genovese)

¼ pound basil leaves, cleaned, not washed	½ cup grated Parmesan
4 spinach leaves	¾ cup grated Pecorino
3 sprigs parsley	3 tablespoons butter
3 sprigs marjoram	½ cup oil
3 cloves garlic	Salt

Pound the ingredients in a mortar until the whole is reduced to a smooth paste. Yields scant 1½ cups.

LIGURIAN CAPONATA

(Caponata alla ligure)

24 hard, dry "gallette" biscuits (made with bread dough*)	¼ pound olives, pitted
	2 tablespoons capers
Vinegar	Olive oil
¼ pound fillets desalted anchovy*	Table salt

Soak the biscuits in a mixture of water and vinegar to flavor them; do not let them become soggy. Place these biscuits on a serving dish and decorate with fillets of desalted anchovy, pitted olives, and well-washed, small (or chopped) capers. Season with plenty of olive oil and a pinch of table salt. Serves 6.

CAPPON MAGRO FISH SALAD GENOA STYLE

(Cappon Magro alla genovese)

½ pound "gallette" biscuits,
   made with bread dough*
   with little or no yeast
½ pound salsify, scorzonera
   or oyster plant, boiled
   and diced
½ pound beets, boiled and
   quartered
½ pound carrots, boiled and
   chopped in 2-inch lengths
½ pound string beans, boiled
½ pound cauliflower, boiled,
   broken into single flowerets
1 cup oil
½ cup vinegar
2 tablespoons salt
3 pounds mixed fish, boiled
   and sliced
1 pound shellfish, boiled,
   shelled, sliced
Green sauce:
   1 cup parsley, chopped
   6 fillets desalted anchovy,*
   chopped

4 gherkins, chopped
1 boiled potato, chopped
1 clove garlic, chopped
1 small onion, chopped
Pinch of salt
½ cup oil
1 tablespoon vinegar
1 bay leaf, crushed
12 mazzancolle (like large
   shrimps), boiled
6 olives
¼ pound fillets desalted
   anchovy*
   lengthwise
6 lettuce hearts, quartered
6 hard-cooked eggs, quartered
   lengthwise
3 salad tomatoes, sliced

Prepare the little round "gallette" biscuits (rub them with garlic, if desired); lay them on a large serving dish. Put all the vegetables in a large mixing bowl (i.e. salsify, beets, carrots, string beans, cauliflower) and toss with a dressing of oil, vinegar, and salt. Spoon out this mixture onto the biscuits.

Around the perimeter of the dish, lay out slices of boiled fish and shellfish. Prepare the green sauce by pounding all the ingredients in a mortar—i.e. parsley, anchovy, gherkins, potato, garlic, onion, salt, oil, vinegar, and bay leaf. Pour this sauce over the fish.

Further garnish the dish with little skewers loaded with mazzan-colle (use large shrimps), with olives, desalted anchovy fillets, quarters of hard-cooked eggs, little lettuce hearts, and slices of salad tomato. Serves 12.

RICE AND VEGETABLE SOUP GENOA STYLE

(Minestra di riso con erbaggi alla genovese)

½ pound white cabbage	2½ cups rice
½ pound beet tops	2 tablespoons pesto sauce
Salt	Genoese* (more if
2 quarts water	desired)

Put the cabbage and beet tops in a pot, season with salt, cover with 2 quarts of cold water, and bring to the boil. Simmer for 30 minutes, cool and reserve.

When preparing for the meal, bring the cabbage and beet soup to the boil, add the rice, and cook for 12 minutes; add half the pesto, and simmer for a further 8 minutes. Put the remaining pesto in the soup tureen and pour the soup over it. Serves 6 to 8.

PASTA AND CIMA BROTH

(Minestra di bavette alla ligure)

4 pints meat stock*	2 eggs, beaten with ½ cup
½ pound pasta, broken into	grated Parmesan
short lengths	Salt and pepper
2 sprigs parsley or marjoram,	3 tablespoons stock
chopped	½ cup grated Parmesan
A mixture of:	

Bring the stock (traditionally, this stock is the liquid obtained from rolled veal cima Genoa style*) to the boil, toss in the pasta and the parsley (or marjoram). Combine the egg, Parmesan mixture and pour in and bring back to the boil. Serve immediately, passing the Parmesan at table. Serves 6 to 8.

BASIL AND GARLIC MINESTRONE

(Minestrone con battuto d'aglio e basilico)

A mixture of:
  3 ounces ham fat, chopped
  3 cloves garlic, chopped
1 scant cup oil
¼ pound peeled tomatoes,
    drained
1½ tablespoons salt

Pinch of pepper
10 ounces spaghetti (or
    linguine), broken
3 tablespoons coarsely
    chopped basil
1 scant cup grated Parmesan

Sauté the ham fat and garlic in a large saucepan with oil; when browned, add the tomatoes and allow all to cook together gently, stirring. Pour in 3 pints cold water and season with salt and pepper: bring to the boil and sprinkle in the broken pasta (or substitute with rice). When the pasta is cooked al dente, remove from heat, add the basil and some of the grated cheese. Serve hot. Serve remaining Parmesan at the table. Serves 6.

MINESTRONE WITH PESTO SAUCE

(Minestrone di pasta, verdura e pesto)

5 pints water
2 tablespoons salt
6 ounces fresh beans, shelled
    (substitute dried beans,
    soaked and parboiled)
½ cabbage, parboiled and
    chopped fine
¼ pound spinach, chopped
¼ pound green beet tops,
    chopped
4 large potatoes, peeled
½ pound in-season vegetables
    —squash, string beans,
    etc., chopped

A mixture of:
  2 cloves garlic, chopped
  1 stalk celery, chopped
  1 small onion, chopped
  2 sprigs parsley, chopped
  1 tomato, peeled, seeded,
    drained, chopped
½ cup oil
10 ounces of small or
    broken pasta
Traditional Genoese pesto*
    (1 or 2 tablespoons, more
    if desired)

Pour into a large fireproof pot 5 pints of water with 2 tablespoons of salt and bring to the boil. Add all the vegetables—beans, cabbage, spinach, beet tops, potatoes, string beans, etc.; as well as the chopped mixture and the ½ cup of oil. Bring to the boil again: after one hour's simmering, remove the potatoes, mash them with a fork, and put the resultant purée back into the minestrone. Bring to the boil and toss in the pasta (preferably homemade pasta) and cook till al dente. Two minutes before taking the minestrone from the stove, add Genoese pesto to taste, mixing in well. Serves 6 to 8.

FORTIFIED BROTH GENOA STYLE

(Sbira genovese)

3 tablespoons butter	1 pound peeled tomatoes,
10 ounces beef or veal	drained
A mixture of:	Salt and pepper
4 cloves garlic, chopped	4 pints beef stock*
1 tablespoon chopped	12 slices day-old bread,
rosemary	toasted
½ cup dry white wine	1 scant cup grated Parmesan

Melt the butter in a pan and brown the meat on all sides over a lively heat; remove meat and reserve. Add the mixture of garlic and rosemary to the pan juices and, when browned, replace the meat. Pour in the wine and reduce by over half on a low heat; add the peeled tomatoes, a little hot water, a tablespoon of salt and a pinch of pepper and bring to the boil; turn down heat to a simmer. Simmer, adding a little water if required, until meat is cooked: remove meat, and chop it. Pass the sauce through a fine sieve, then replace both the chopped meat and the sauce in the pan and reserve.

At mealtime, bring the stock to the boil in a fireproof pot, add the meat and the sauce, and combine for a few moments. Prepare the soup plates with slices of toast in each, sprinkle with Parmesan and pour over all the broth, offering the remaining Parmesan at table. Serves 6 to 8.

PASTA WITH WILD MUSHROOMS

(Tagliarini con funghi porcini alla ligure)

5 tablespoons butter
¼ cup oil
3 cloves garlic, crushed
1 tablespoon chopped sage
2 tablespoons chopped parsley
1¼ pounds peeled tomatoes, drained

1 pound porcini (large field mushrooms) or substitute dried mushrooms*
Salt and freshly ground pepper
1½ pounds tagliarini pasta (substitute spaghetti)
½ cup grated Parmesan

Put the butter and half the oil in a pan and brown the garlic and the sage; then add the parsley and immediately afterward the tomatoes. Allow the mixture to cook gently for 30 minutes, adding a little water if the sauce becomes too thick.

In another pan, heat the remaining oil and sauté the mushrooms, seasoned with a little salt and a pinch of pepper for 10 minutes; pour this mixture into the other pan and combine.

Meanwhile, prepare the pasta in the customary manner; toss into boiling, lightly salted water and drain when al dente. Transfer the pasta to a warmed serving dish, mix in half the Parmesan and then half the sauce and serve: the remaining cheese and sauce are served at table. Serves 6.

LINGUINE WITH PESTO SAUCE

(Linguine con pesto)

2 potatoes, sliced
1½ pounds linguine, trenette, or spaghetti
½ cup grated Parmesan (or Pecorino)

Traditional Genoese pesto sauce* (quantity to taste: 1 or more tablespoons)

Put the slices of potato into a large pot with plenty of lightly salted water and bring to the boil. When the potatoes are ¾ cooked, add the pasta and cook till al dente. Drain the spaghetti and potato slices and transfer to a warmed serving dish. Immediately add the ½ cup of grated cheese and a few tablespoons of the pasta's cooking water and mix. Add the traditional Genoese pesto, allow the pesto time to soften from the heat of the pasta, and mix well. Serves 6.

PASTA WITH SEAFOOD

(Pasta con frutti di mare)

Sauce:
  2 *cloves garlic, crushed*
  3 *tablespoons oil*
  Salt and pepper
  1 *pound peeled tomatoes,*
    drained
  2 *tablespoons chopped basil*
    and parsley

3 *pounds mixed shellfish*
  (mussels, clams, etc.)
2 *tablespoons butter*
½ *cup dry white wine*
1½ *pounds pasta—spaghetti*
  or other

Sauce: Sauté the crushed garlic in 3 tablespoons of oil and a pinch of pepper; then discard it. Add the tomatoes, the basil, the parsley, and a little salt. Bring to the boil and simmer for 30 minutes.

Shellfish: Meanwhile the shellfish should have been cleaned and washed, put in a pan, sautéed over a lively heat until open. Drain in a colander, reserving the pan liquids. As they cool, remove from shell; filter the pan liquids through a fine sieve and reduce over a lively heat to a cupful.

Melt 2 tablespoons of butter in a pan, add the shellfish, and sauté gently; after a minute or two, add the wine and the reduced and sieved pan liquid. After a few minutes, remove from heat and combine with the tomato sauce and simmer for a few minutes all together.

Pasta: Cook the pasta with plenty of boiling, lightly salted water, drain it when al dente and transfer to a warmed serving dish: cover with the sauce, mix well. Serves 6.

FRIED POLENTA WITH CABBAGE

(Polenta con cavoli alla ligure)

1 large red cabbage   *2 cups grated Parmesan*
Salt   *Flour*
½ cup oil   *¼ pound lard*
2½ cups yellow corn-meal
  *polenta**

Remove the core and hard outer leaves from the red cabbage; wash and coarsely chop the remainder. Boil in lightly salted water until tender, but not limp; drain the leaves of excess water. Sauté them lightly in oil and a little salt and allow to cool.

Meanwhile, according to the Note on polenta cooking, the corn meal should have been prepared—a little on the stiff side rather than liquid—and poured into a large casserole, followed immediately by the cabbage and grated Parmesan. Mix these ingredients together well, allow to cool and reserve.

When required, the polenta-cabbage mixture is cut into medium-sized cubes and dusted in flour. Sauté them in lard in a frying pan over a brisk flame and serve when hot, golden, and crisp. Serves 6 to 8.

SAVORY CHICK-PEA CAKES

(Panisetti di farina di ceci alla ligure)

2 pounds chick-pea flour   *Vinegar*
1½ cups oil   *Freshly ground pepper*
Salt

Bring 3 quarts of lightly salted water to the boil and sprinkle into it the chick-pea flour, stirring to prevent lumps forming. Skim the surface of any residues and keep simmering for three hours, stirring assiduously. When cooked, pour the water and the cooked flour through a fine sieve. Transfer the cooked chick-pea flour to a bowl and mix with 1½ cups of oil.

Pour this paste onto a lightly oiled surface and, with a large knife or other suitable instrument, smooth out the paste (dipping the knife in boiling water so the paste does not stick to it), until it is ½ inch thick; allow to cool completely.

When cooking time comes, cut the cake into 3- by 1-inch strips; drop them into abundant smoking oil in a frying pan. When well browned on both sides and crisped, remove and drain. Serve hot, sprinkled with vinegar and freshly ground pepper. Serves 6.

RAVIOLI GENOA STYLE

(Ravioli alla genovese)

Dough:
  4 generous cups sifted flour
  2 eggs beaten with a little
    warm water
  1 teaspoon oil
  Pinch of salt
Filling:
  1 pound lean veal, chopped
  3 tablespoons butter
  ½ pound calf brains
  ½ pound sweetbreads
  ½ pound green beet tops,
    cleaned, trimmed
  ¼ pound borage (or
    spinach) cleaned, trimmed
  1 scant cup bread crumbs
    dipped in stock and drained

1 scant cup grated
  Parmesan
1 teaspoon salt
Grating of nutmeg
6 eggs
4 egg yolks
Flour
1 egg beaten with few
  drops warm water
1 scant cup grated
  Parmesan
Salt
2½ cups Italian meat sauce*
  or traditional Genoese
  pesto

Dough: Make the dough as explained in the Note and let it rest for 30 minutes; roll it out very thin.

Filling: Brown the veal in a pan with a little butter. Blanch, in boiling water, both the calf brains and sweetbreads and mince all three together and pound in a mortar. Having boiled the beet tops and the borage (or substitute spinach for both), chop well and remove all excess water. Put both the pounded meat and the chopped green vegetables in a casserole together along with the bread crumbs, the Parmesan, the salt, the nutmeg, and, with the aid of the eggs and egg yolks, work them all into a smooth paste.

Sprinkle some flour onto a tabletop and, with hands dusted with flour, make little nut-sized balls of the above filling; reserve.

To combine: Lay out the sheets of dough on a flour-dusted tabletop, brush them with the mixture of the egg beaten with a little water. Place the little balls of filling at geometrically regular intervals, about 2 inches apart, on half of the dough sheets. Place the other sheets on top of those on which the filling has been placed and press down lightly with the fingers all around the filling. Then, with a cooky cutter, cut out little squares; reserve these on a lightly dusted kitchen cloth.

Cook the ravioli a few at a time in plenty of lightly salted boiling water. After about 5 minutes, perhaps longer, they will begin coming to the surface; remove them with a slotted spoon, drain them well, and transfer to a warmed serving dish. Season with Parmesan, adjust for salt, and pour over the Italian meat sauce (or some pesto). Serves 6 to 8.

FISH SOUP GENOA STYLE

(Zuppa di pesce alla genovese)

2 quarts fish fumet*:
    2 pounds raw fish, heads, bones, and trimmings
    1 carrot, chopped
    1 onion, chopped
    1 stalk celery, chopped
    Salt and pepper
3½ pounds mixed fish—sole, mullet, bass, cuttlefish, squid, eel, mussels, etc.
¾ cup oil
1 tablespoon chopped leek
1 tablespoon chopped onion

2 lettuce hearts, chopped
Bouquet garni:
    2 sprigs thyme
    2 sprigs parsley
    1 bay leaf
Salt and pepper
½ cup dry white wine
4 fillets desalted anchovy,* mashed
2 cloves garlic
8 slices day-old bread, browned in oven
1 tablespoon chopped parsley

Prepare the fish fumet, cooking the ingredients for 20 minutes; filter through damp cheesecloth and reserve. Clean and wash all the fish and seafood, dividing the hard-fleshed from the soft-fleshed—i.e., the cuttlefish and squids from the fish and mussels. Having bearded and scrubbed the mussels and clams, put them in a pan with a little oil, sauté them till they open; remove from shells and reserve. Filter the liquid and reserve.

Pour almost all the oil in a pan and when it begins to smoke, add the cuttlefish, squids (hard-fleshed), etc., cut into strips. Stir in the chopped leek and onion with the lettuce hearts and the bouquet garni. Season with salt, freshly ground pepper and simmer for 15 minutes or so. Pour in the wine, little by little, and reduce almost completely. Mix in the anchovy and then the soft-fleshed fish, whole if small, cut into pieces if large. Allow these to gather flavor from the pan juices for a few minutes, then pour in the fish fumet (hot) and simmer for a further 10 minutes. Finally add the mussels and their filtered cooking liquid.

Brown the garlic cloves in a little pan with the remaining oil, remove from heat and discard the garlic, pouring the garlic-flavored oil into the soup. Adjust for salt. Place the toast in the bottom of soup plates, distribute the fish and the soup in each plate and sprinkle with chopped parsley. Serves 6 to 8.

GRAND FISH SOUP GENOA STYLE

(Zuppa di pesce alla ricca)

3 pounds fish—porgy, bass,
    mullet
1 pound lobster, shrimps
1 pound mussels, scrubbed and
    bearded
2 quarts fish fumet*
A mixture of:
    1 onion, chopped
    3 leeks, chopped
    1 clove garlic, chopped
    4 lettuce hearts, chopped

Bouquet garni:
    1 sprig parsley
    1 sprig basil
    1 bay leaf
    1 sprig thyme
1 cup oil
¼ pound butter
Salt and pepper
½ cup dry white wine
8 slices day-old bread,
    browned in oven
1 tablespoon chopped parsley

Clean, wash, and cut the fish into pieces; clean and devein the shrimps, chop the lobster into slices; sauté the mussels in a pan, remove the shells, and filter the liquid. Prepare the fish fumet with fishbones, shrimp shells, etc., along with a carrot, onion, celery stalk, a pinch of pepper and salt and the necessary water; 20 minutes' cooking is sufficient to produce 4 pints of fumet. Filter and reserve.

First put the chopped mixture of onion, leeks, garlic and lettuce hearts, with the bouquet garni, the oil, and the butter, seasoned with salt and pepper, in a pan and cook together for a few minutes on a low heat to color lightly and flavor; then pour in the wine.

Add the fish to the pan, followed by the lobster slices, the shrimps and the mussels; bring to the boil and reduce the wine. Add the fish fumet and the pan juices of the mussels. Bring to the boil again, turn down heat and continue cooking.

Prepare a large, warmed serving dish and begin removing the various seafood and fish as they reach doneness. Brown the bread slices in the oven and place them in deep soup plates. Distribute the fish in the soup plates, pour over the fish soup and sprinkle each plate with parsley. Serves 6 to 8.

BABY OCTOPUSES GENOA STYLE

(Moscardini alla genovese)

3 pounds baby octopuses
1 onion, chopped
½ cup oil
A mixture of:
  2 cloves garlic, chopped
  3 sprigs rosemary, chopped
  3 sprigs parsley, chopped
2 tomatoes, peeled, drained
  and chopped

4 tablespoons chopped dried
  *mushrooms**
1 cup cold water
Salt and freshly ground pepper
2 cups diced day-old bread,
  browned in oven

Clean the baby octopuses and cut them into strips. Sauté the chopped onion in a pan with a little oil till golden: add the chopped mixture of garlic, rosemary, and parsley and simmer together for a few seconds. Add the chopped tomatoes, the dried and chopped mushroom and the cup of water: allow to combine and then add the octopus strips, a little salt and a pinch of pepper. Cover the pan and simmer for one and a half hours until the octopus strips are tender. Serve with browned bread cubes. Serves 6 to 8.

SAUSAGE FRITTERS

(Frittelle di salsiccia alla ligure)

3 cups flour	*1½ cups water*
2½ tablespoons baking powder	*¾ pound dry (salame-type)*
½ cup butter	*sausage, crumbled*
2 tablespoons salt	*1 cup oil*

Make a mound of 1 scant cup sifted flour on the tabletop; scoop out the center and pour in the baking powder dissolved in warm water and mix well. Wrap the dough in a clean cloth and allow to rise for 15 minutes in a warm place.

Make another mound of the remaining flour on the tabletop and put the previously prepared dough in its center, along with the butter, the salt, and the water. Knead until a smooth dough is obtained; wrap in a cloth and keep in a cool place for several hours.

Before using this dough, a further kneading is required on a freshly floured working surface. Divide the dough then into 1-ounce balls and flatten them with a rolling pin. Lay these out on the table and put in the middle of each a little of the crumbled sausage; dampen the edges of each with a little water and turn the dough rounds into little balls in such a way that the filling is sealed inside.

Heat plenty of oil in a frying pan; when it is smoking, put in the fritters, a few at a time, and sauté till golden and crisp. Scoop out each with a slotted spoon as soon as it is cooked and reserve in a warm place. Serves 6.

NOTE: Sausage is just one of many fillings which may be used; others include dried mushroom, salsify (oyster plant), brains, sweetbreads, cauliflower, squash, and artichokes.

Also sweet fritters of apple, pineapple, banana, and raisins can be made; the only difference is that sugar instead of salt is used in the dough.

SAUTÉ OF VEAL

(Vitello all'uccelletto)

2 pounds veal, fillet or noisette
¼ cup butter
1 tablespoon oil

2 bay leaves
Salt and pepper
½ cup dry white wine

Cut the veal into very thin slices. Melt the butter and heat the oil in a pan with the bay leaves, and add the veal slices, seasoned with salt and pepper; sauté them lightly on both sides.

Reduce the heat and continue cooking for another 2 minutes until done. Lay out the veal slices on a hot serving dish, meanwhile pouring the wine into the pan. Reduce the wine almost completely and pour the pan juices over the meat in the serving dish.

This is usually accompanied by vegetables in season, but is best with artichokes. Serves 6 to 8.

ROLLED VEAL CIMA GENOA STYLE

(Cima alla genovese)

2½ pounds lean breast of veal
Stuffing:
  ¾ pound lean pork or veal,
    minced
  5 ounces salt pork, minced
  6 ounces sweetbreads, diced
  ¼ pound calf brains, finely
    chopped
  2 cups bread crumbs, soaked
    in milk, drained
  ½ cup grated Parmesan
  ¼ pound shelled peas

2 ounces shelled pistachio
  nuts
Salt
Freshly ground pepper
Grating of nutmeg
5 eggs
1 small onion, chopped
1 small carrot, chopped
2 tablespoons chopped
  marjoram
2 peppercorns, bruised
1 bay leaf

Prepare the breast of veal for stuffing by cutting a deep pocket in it, leaving a 1-inch border.

Stuffing: Combine, in a bowl, the mixture of pork or veal, salt pork, sweetbreads, brains, bread crumbs, Parmesan, peas, pistachio nuts, salt, pepper, nutmeg, and eggs until a smooth mixture is obtained.

To combine: Fill the "pocket" in the meat so that a pillow effect is obtained; sew up the opening with a white thread so that the stuffing is firmly enclosed; tie the whole with string so that it keeps its shape during cooking.

Put this prepared veal roll in a fireproof pot and cover with plenty of water: add the slices of onion, carrot, the marjoram, the peppercorns, and the bay leaf, and bring to the boil. Turn down heat, and simmer for about two hours. Remove the veal cima roll and put it on the kitchen table; press it into an oval shape with the aid of a breadboard—or, traditionally, with iron weights. This pressure amalgamates the stuffing in the correct manner as well as giving the cima its traditional shape. Serve either hot or cold. Reserve the cooking liquids for stock. Serves 8 to 10.

BRAISED BEEF WITH ANCHOVIES

(Brasato di manzo con acciughe alla genovese)

8 fillets desalted anchovy*	½ cup oil
Juice of 1 lemon	½ cup dry white wine, mixed
Grating of nutmeg	with ½ cup water
2 pounds sirloin tips, well hung	Salt

Chop 4 of the anchovy fillets into small pieces and, in a bowl, season them with ¼ of the lemon juice and a grating of nutmeg; pierce the meat with a larding needle and insert these pieces of anchovy.

Pour the oil into a fireproof pan, add the remaining 4 anchovy fillets and lemon juice, and heat for a few seconds before adding the beef. Cook slowly, basting the meat now and then with the wine-and-water mixture. Adjust for salt. Simmer for three hours, checking now and then that the pan juices are sufficient. Serves 6 to 8.

BRAISED DUCK WITH GREEN OLIVES

(Anitra brasata con olive verdi)

2-pound duck, ready to cook
2 tablespoons salt
Pinch of pepper
2½ tablespoons butter
1½ tablespoons oil
1 tablespoon flour
A mixture of:
  2 tablespoons chopped onion
  1½ tablespoons chopped
    carrot

1 tablespoon chopped celery
1 tablespoon chopped parsley
Bouquet garni:
  1 sprig thyme
  1 sprig rosemary
  1 bay leaf
1½ cups dry white wine
1 pint stock
½ pound green pitted olives,
  parboiled

Remove the wings from the duck. Sprinkle with salt and a pinch of pepper. Melt the butter and oil in a casserole and lightly brown the duck on all sides. Then add the flour, the mixture of onion, carrot, celery, and parsley, and the bouquet garni; mix well and cook together for a few seconds. Pour in the wine and reduce by half. Turn down the heat and simmer, adding stock as required, until the duck is cooked.

Five minutes before finally removing the casserole from the stove, remove the duck. Pass the pan juices through a fine sieve or damp cheesecloth and replace both the duck and sauce in the casserole. Add the parboiled and pitted green olives; simmer for a few minutes and serve hot in the same casserole in which the duck has been cooked. Serves 6 to 8.

RABBIT HOME-COOKING STYLE

(Coniglio alla casalinga)

½ cup oil	Salt and pepper
3 cloves garlic, chopped	¼ pound peeled tomatoes,
4-pound rabbit, chopped into	drained
chunks	4 tablespoons stock
1 sprig rosemary	¼ pound pitted olives
½ bottle dry red wine	

Smoke the oil in a pan and add the garlic and the rabbit pieces which have been well washed and dried. Sauté them on all sides till golden brown; remove and reserve.

Add the rosemary, pour in the dry red wine, and reduce by half. Replace the rabbit pieces, season with salt and pepper, and simmer for 15 minutes. Then add the tomatoes and a few tablespoons of stock (or water). Continue simmering, add the pitted olives, and after 15 minutes the meat is cooked. Discard the rosemary sprig and serve hot. Serves 6.

FRIED MILK SWEET AND SOUR

(Latte brusco alla ligure)

2 eggs	Pinch of salt
6 egg yolks	1 egg, beaten
½ scant cup superfine sugar	Bread crumbs
1 pint milk	Oil and lard (half and half)
1 cup flour, sifted	for deep-frying
1 teaspoon cinnamon powder	Confectioners' sugar
Grated peel of ½ lemon (no	
pith)	

Put the eggs and egg yolks and the superfine sugar in a bowl and beat together; pour in the milk and combine. Sprinkle into the mixture, a little at a time and beating vigorously, the flour, the cinnamon, the grated lemon peel and a pinch of salt. Pass this mixture through a fine sieve and transfer to a casserole; put the casserole on a moderate heat and cook, stirring constantly, until done. Pour the mixture onto a suitably sized tray or baking dish so that the mixture is 1 inch thick; allow to cool.

When cold and set, cut the mixture into 1-inch cubes, dip first in beaten egg and then in bread crumbs. Heat plenty of oil and lard in a frying pan until smoking and toss in the fried milk cubes, sautéing till crisp and golden. Transfer to serving dish, sprinkle with confectioners' sugar, and serve hot. Serves 4 to 6.

Emilia-Romagna

There is something rambunctious about Emilia-Romagna. It is Italy's major food-producing area and the inhabitants are, in consequence, hearty eaters. Bologna, famous for its nine-centuries-old university, was nicknamed "the fat and the learned"; since the Middle Ages, the people of Bologna have been thinking up new ways of adding something extra to a dish; anything *alla bolognese* or *alla petroniana* (after Bologna's patron saint, St. Petronius) involves an extra stuffing, a richer sauce or added slices of ham and cheese. Centuries ago, they specialized in stuffing a calf with a sheep, the sheep with a suckling pig and the suckling pig with some game birds and roasting the lot together over a slow fire.

Nowadays, they settle for magnificent pasta dishes and those extra slices of cheese and ham and for rich meat sauces.

When traveling in those parts, they say that the quickest way to find out if one is in Emilia is to knock on any door and say you are thirsty; if you are given a glass of wine, you are in Emilia.

Emilia-Romagna is the heartland of Italy, the elbow of the Rome-Bologna-Milan Sun Highway; but it has not been blessed by nature, except for its fertile alluvial soil. For the rest, it has a long harsh winter, often there are disastrous floods when the river Po spills over its banks and mist-in-the-Po-Valley is a joke to all Italy; it is a daily fixture on the TV and radio weather bulletins all winter. Yet Emilia-Romagna produces over $600 million of agricultural products annually with the most modern methods, mechanization, and automation in Europe. The particular energy and enterprise of the people have made that land of plenty which was one of Napoleon's goals when he looked over the Italian frontier with his hungry army.

However, the postwar period has produced an even more florid situation: one need only mention a few of the famous products of the region such as Parmesan (Parmigiana-Reggiana grana cheese), and "Bologna" sausages (mortadella, Modena zampone, and cotechino) to realize the wealth that has accrued. Emilia-Romagna has also become the biggest fruit-growing area of Italy (apples, peaches, pears, plums, strawberries, apricots, and cherries); it also has 1 million pigs, big canning industries, and a huge production of controlled denomination wine.

Lambrusco is perhaps the best-known wine—a sparkling red. It is a regional wine that is perfect with regional food and particularly with the zampones and other rich, fatty and spiced dishes of Modena. It has the effect of breaking down the fats, clearing the palate and giving one the appetite for another sausage. However, the Sangiovese of Emilia is more acceptable to all palates and goes with a far wider variety of dishes (it even goes well with seafood); Sangiovese is a rich, dry, ruby-red, full-bodied, smooth wine with a satisfying and tangy aftertaste. There are also excellent Albana and Trebbiano whites, but the Sangiovese reds win all the laurels as fine all-round table wines.

The major delight of Emilia-Romagna's cooking is the imaginative way in which pasta is prepared; they are masters of the art. In the recipes which follow for tortellini, cappelletti, lasagna, fettuccine and spaghetti *alla bolognese,* you can glimpse the magnificent panorama of pasta dishes that they have invented. If you lose heart at the thought of making cappelletti, for example, at home and settle for the factory-produced article, at least make the meat sauce with as close an approximation to the recipe as possible.

The food of Emilia-Romagna is perhaps the most difficult of all Italian regions, but this is proof of the people's love of the table and perhaps also the source of their exceptional vigor and vivacity. Emilia-Romagna's cuisine—with its savory sauces, its pastas, and its meats, sausages, and cheeses—has without doubt provided Italian gastronomy with some of its finest dishes.

Desserts

EMILIAN MEAT SAUCE

(Sugo di carne all'emiliana)

*2 pounds lean meat (mixture
    of beef, veal and pork
    or only one of these)*
Meat seasoning:
    2 cloves garlic
    1 tablespoon orégano
    2 ounces salt pork strips
    *1 tablespoon salt and pinch
    of pepper*
Marinade:
    1 cup dry red wine
    2 tablespoons chopped onion
    2 tablespoons chopped carrot
    1 clove garlic, chopped
    *1½ tablespoons chopped
    celery*
    1 clove
    1 small bay leaf

3 sprigs parsley, crushed
Flour
1 tablespoon lard
2 tablespoons butter
1½ tablespoons oil
*2 tablespoons chopped salt
    pork*
*1 tablespoon chopped dried
    mushrooms, soaked*
1 tablespoon salt
Pinch of freshly ground pepper
*½ inch hot red pepper
    (peperoncino) or ½
    tablespoon red pepper*
*1 pound peeled tomatoes,
    drained*
1 tablespoon flour
3 pints cold water

Rub the meat with garlic, sprinkle with orégano, and tie with string, affixing the salt pork strips firmly. Season with salt and pepper.

Prepare the marinade and leave the meat in it for an hour or two, turning it occasionally.

Remove the meat from the marinade, dry it, and dust it lightly in flour. Heat the lard in a pan and brown the meat well on all sides.

Remove the meat from the pan and place in a large casserole

with the butter and oil, the chopped pork and mushrooms, seasoned with 1 tablespoon salt, a pinch of freshly ground pepper and ½ inch of hot peperoncino or substitute ½ tablespoon red pepper. Heat this mixture and cook over medium heat, stirring with a wooden spoon, for 5 minutes. Then pour in the complete marinade, simmering—and stirring—until the wine is mostly evaporated. Add the tomatoes, the flour (mixed with a little liquid) and the 3 pints of cold water. Bring to the boil, turn down heat and simmer for two and a half hours.

Remove the meat and reserve; this is not required for the Emilian meat sauce. Pass the sauce through a sieve and simmer in the casserole until the quantity is reduced to 2 pints. Pour a little over the reserved meat to savor it; the remainder serves to flavor risottos, gnocchi, and pastas of all descriptions. Makes 1½ pints.

EMILIAN BÉCHAMEL

(Besciamella all'emiliana)

2 tablespoons chopped onion	Pinch of pepper
4 tablespoons butter	Grating of nutmeg
5 tablespoons sifted flour	Bouquet garni:
1 pint milk	2 bay leaves
1 teaspoon salt	2 sprigs thyme

Put the 2 tablespoons of onion with the butter in a casserole and cook, over a very low heat, till the onion is translucent but not browned. Add, a little at a time, the flour and allow to cook for a few seconds, stirring well. Pour in, a little at a time, the milk, and dissolve the flour-onion paste. Sprinkle in a teaspoon of salt, a pinch of pepper, and a grating of nutmeg, and add the bouquet garni, tied with a white thread. Bring to the boil and simmer for 15 minutes, stirring constantly; the sauce is ready when it is decidedly thick. Discard bouquet garni. Makes 2 cups.

FAMILY MEAT SAUCE

(Ragù di carne romagnola casalinga)

A mixture of:
  2 ounces salt pork, chopped
  1½ tablespoons chopped
    onion
  1 tablespoon chopped carrot
  ½ tablespoon chopped celery
3 tablespoons butter
½ pound lean beef, chopped

Salt and pepper
Grating of nutmeg
1 bay leaf
½ cup dry red wine
½ pound peeled tomatoes,
  drained

Sauté the chopped mixture with butter in a pan till browned; add the meat seasoned with salt, pepper, the nutmeg, and the bay leaf. As soon as the meat is well impregnated with the fats, pour in the red wine and turn up the heat until the wine evaporates. Then add the tomatoes, bring to the boil again, turn down heat, and simmer till a smooth sauce is obtained. Makes 1 cup.

SHRIMP HORS D'OEUVRES

(Antipasto di cannochie)

24 very large shrimps
  (cannochie)
4 lettuce leaves
4 eggs, hard-cooked
1 cup mayonnaise*

1 tablespoon oil
1 teaspoon vinegar
Pinch of salt
Pinch of pepper

Clean, devein, shell, and cook the shrimps; chop the shrimp meat. Prepare individual plates, each with a lettuce leaf, on which the shrimp meat is distributed, surrounded by wedges of hard-cooked eggs.

Prepare mayonnaise, combine into it a little oil, vinegar, salt, and a grinding of fresh pepper; distribute over each dish. Serves 4.

SARDINES, SWEET PEPPERS AND EGG HORS D'OEUVRES

(Sardine sott'olio alla romagnola)

24 sardines in oil	Pinch of sage
3 hard-cooked eggs	1 peeled tomato, seeded,
1 sweet pepper	drained, chopped
Sauce:	½ tablespoon butter
1 clove garlic, crushed	Salt

Skin and bone 24 sardines; lay them out fanwise on a serving dish. Cut each egg into 6 wedges, and lay out decoratively between the sardine fillets.

Roast 1 large sweet pepper, plunge into cold water, peel, seed, and cut in strips. Decorate the serving dish with these strips.

Prepare a little sauce, mixing a crushed garlic clove (or better, the juice of garlic only; with a little sage, a tomato, a ½ tablespoon of butter, and some salt. Simmer for a few minutes to combine and gain consistency and flavor. Spoon on each of the sardines a little of this sauce. Serves 6 to 8.

PASTA AND BEAN SOUP

(Minestra di fagioli con quadretti di pasta all'uovo)

10 ounces white navy beans,	A mixture of:
soaked overnight	2 ounces salt pork, chopped
Salt	1 tablespoon chopped onion
Dough*:	1 tablespoon chopped celery
2 cups sifted flour	1 tablespoon chopped carrot
3 eggs	3 ounces peeled tomatoes,
Few drops oil	drained
Pinch of salt	1½ tablespoons salt and
¼ cup oil	generous pinch of pepper

Wash the beans in running water and boil them in plenty of lightly salted water; drain and reserve both beans and cooking water.

Knead the dough and allow to rest; then roll out into sheets and cut into ¾-inch squares.

Heat the oil in a pan and gently brown the chopped mixture; then add the tomatoes, season with salt and pepper and simmer for 30 minutes.

Put the beans in a casserole, pour in the tomato sauce and a generous 2 pints of water, in which the beans were cooked. Bring to the boil, toss in the pasta squares, and cook for about 12 minutes, till the pasta is al dente. Serves 6 to 8.

RAVIOLI IN BROTH

(Anolini in brodo)

Dough*:
  1 pound flour
  4 eggs
  1 teaspoon oil
  1 tablespoon salt
A mixture of:
  1 tablespoon chopped carrot
  1 tablespoon chopped celery
  1 tablespoon chopped onion
5 tablespoons butter
10 ounces lean beef

3 ounces dry, spiced
  salame-type sausage,
  skinned
5 pints chicken-and-beef stock*
1½ cups bread crumbs
1 cup grated Parmesan
Salt and pepper
Grating of nutmeg
4 eggs
Flour

Knead the pasta dough; allow it to rest, then roll it out into very thin sheets.

Sauté the chopped mixture of carrot, celery, and onion in a deep casserole in butter; when lightly browned, add the beef and sausage. Pour in sufficient stock to cover the meat, cover casserole with lid, and simmer for about three hours.

When the meat is cooked and the sauce thickened, remove the casserole from the heat, chop the meat and put the chopped meat back in the casserole with the pan juices. Allow to cool completely. Then combine, in the casserole, the bread crumbs, 2 tablespoons of Parmesan, a dash of salt and pepper, a grating of nutmeg, and 3 eggs, until a smooth paste is obtained.

Line up the sheets of pasta on the table top; dust them well with flour. Beat an egg with a little water and brush this mixture over the sheets of pasta. On one of the sheets, at geometrically regular distances, put a meatball of filling; cover this first sheet of pasta with another, press down with the fingers around the filling and, with a cooky cutter or suitably sized glass, obtain ravioli.

Bring the remaining stock to the boil, toss in the ravioli and cook till al dente. Serve hot with the remaining grated Parmesan. Serves 6 to 8.

CAPPELLETTI IN BROTH

(Cappelletti in brodo)

Dough*:
  3 generous cups sifted flour
  4 eggs
  2 tablespoons water
Filling:
  ¼ pound pork fillet
  1 slice mortadella
  1 slice prosciutto
  3 ounces chicken or
    turkey meat
  2 ounces lamb brains

1 tablespoon grated
  Parmesan
Grating of nutmeg
1 scant tablespoon salt
1 teaspoon pepper
1 small glass sweet
  marsala wine
1 egg
6 pints stock*
1 cup grated Parmesan

Dough: Prepare the dough; allow to rest, and reserve.

Filling: Pass the filling ingredients, the pork, the mortadella, the ham, chicken, and brains, through the mincer together, and season with Parmesan, nutmeg, salt, pepper, and combine together with the sweet marsala wine and the egg until a smooth paste is obtained.

To combine: Roll out the dough into thin sheets and, with a cooky cutter or glass, cut out 2½-inch-diameter rounds. Lay these on a flour-dusted table and put in each of them a Lima-bean-sized ball of filling; fold these rounds so as to make half-moons, and press down around the edges. Knead again and roll out the remaining dough and carry out the same operation until there is neither dough nor filling left.

Place these little cappelletti on a floured cloth and allow to rest for a full twenty-four hours before cooking.

Bring the stock to the boil, toss in the cappelletti and cook for about 20 minutes. Serve broth and cappelletti in soup bowls with a sprinkling of Parmesan on each. Serves 8 to 10.

TORTELLINI IN BROTH

(Tortellini in brodo)

Dough*:
   3 generous cups sifted flour
   4 eggs
   2 tablespoons water
Filling:
   ½ turkey or capon breast,
     roasted
   ½ pound ricotta

½ cup grated Parmesan
Pinch of salt
Grating of nutmeg
Grated peel of 1 lemon
2 egg yolks
6 pints of stock*
1 cup grated Parmesan

Proceed precisely as with cappelletti in broth*: these tortellini, however, should be somewhat smaller than cappelletti. Serves 8.

POTATO GNOCCHI AND MEAT SAUCE

(Gnocchi di patate alla romagnola casalinga)

2½ pounds mealy potatoes
1 pound sifted flour
Salt

½ cup butter
1 cup grated Parmesan
2½ cups family meat sauce*

First boil the potatoes al dente, drain, peel, and pass them through a sieve. Then prepare the gnocchi dough; this should be left till the last moment, as it can spoil if it becomes damp. Knead the potatoes and the flour together on a slightly floured tabletop till a firm yet soft dough is obtained. With hands dusted with flour, divide this dough (preferably while the potato flour is still warm) into pieces and roll into cylinders ½ inch in diameter. Cut these into 1-inch lengths and press each of them lightly between forefinger and thumb so that they take the traditional gnocchi shape. Lay them out on a floured cloth, taking care that they do not touch each other.

Bring a pot of lightly salted water to the boil and drop the gnocchi in, a few at a time, and remove them with a slotted skimmer as they come to the top. Drain on a cloth. When they are all cooked, put into a fireproof dish, distribute lumps of softened butter, ½ the Parmesan and ½ the meat sauce and heat in oven for a few moments. Serve remaining sauce and Parmesan at table. Serves 6 to 8.

BAKED LASAGNA MODENA STYLE

(Lasagna pasticciata alla modenese)

1 pound lasagna (or a pasta	*½ cup butter*
dough* made from 1 pound	*1½ cups Italian meat sauce**
flour, 5 eggs, 1 teaspoon oil	*1 cup grated Parmesan*
and a pinch of salt)	*1 cup béchamel,* very thick*
Salt	

Cook the lasagna, a few at a time, in a low, large casserole in plenty of lightly salted boiling water. Drain and allow to cool on a damp cloth.

Butter a pan and, in layers, put first lasagna, then Italian meat sauce, then grated Parmesan. Continue with these layers until a last layer of lasagna; cover this with béchamel, grated cheese, and melted butter. Put in a hot oven until the surface is browned: serve hot with the remaining Parmesan. Serves 6.

FETTUCCINE WITH CREAM AND TOMATO SAUCE

(Fettuccine ricche alla emiliana)

Dough*:	*Salt and pepper*
1 pound sifted flour	*2 ounces green peas, boiled*
5 eggs	*2 ounces sweet peppers,*
1 teaspoon oil	*roasted, peeled, cut in*
Pinch of salt	*strips*
1½ cups butter	*¼ pound prosciutto (fat and*
6 ounces peeled tomatoes,	*lean), chopped*
drained	*½ cup cream*
	1 cup of grated Parmesan

Prepare the dough and allow to rest; roll and cut it into ½-inch-wide strips; or substitute a similar dry egg pasta. Melt half the butter in a pan, add the tomatoes seasoned with a little salt and pepper, and simmer for 8 minutes. Add the peas, the sweet pepper strips, and the ham, and cook together for two minutes; remove from heat and keep warm.

Cook the pasta in lightly salted boiling water, drain when al dente and transfer to a warmed serving dish. Then, in layers, pour over the cream, half the Parmesan, the remaining butter in softened lumps, and, finally, the tomato sauce. Allow to stand a few moments, mix, and serve in warmed plates; pass the remaining Parmesan at the table. A few slices of truffle (black or white) combined in the sauce is an added pleasure. Serves 6 to 8.

SPAGHETTI WITH BOLOGNESE SAUCE

(Spaghetti alla bolognese)

¼ cup oil
A mixture of:
  2 ounces salt pork, chopped
  1½ tablespoons chopped
    onion
  1 tablespoon chopped carrot
  1 tablespoon chopped parsley
  1 clove garlic, chopped
6 ounces lean beef, minced
2 tablespoons chopped cooked
  ham

1 tablespoon chopped dried
  mushrooms
1 small bay leaf
½ cup dry white wine
1¾ pounds peeled tomatoes,
  drained
1 tablespoon salt
Pinch of pepper
1½ pounds spaghetti
1 cup grated Parmesan

Heat the oil in a pan and add the mixture of salt pork, onion, carrot, parsley, and garlic; when browned, add the minced beef, ham, the mushrooms, and bay leaf and cook together gently stirring with a wooden spoon. When the meat is well browned, pour in the wine and reduce it: add the tomatoes, season with salt and pepper, and stir for 2 minutes. Pour in a scant cup of water and simmer for one and a half hours, stirring often, until a light yet thick sauce is obtained.

Cook the spaghetti in plenty of lightly salted boiling water; drain when al dente, pour into a warmed serving dish, sprinkle in half the Parmesan, mix, then pour in half the sauce. Mix well and serve the remaining sauce and Parmesan at table. Serves 6 to 8.

BASS IN WHITE WINE CATTOLICA STYLE

(Cernia al burro e vino bianco alla maniera di Cattolica)

3-pound bass
Marinade:
  ½ cup oil
  Juice of 2 lemons
  1 clove garlic, sliced
  1 sprig parsley, crushed
  Salt
  Freshly ground pepper

Flour
½ cup butter
1 tablespoon chopped onion
Salt and white pepper
½ cup dry white wine
Juice of ½ lemon

Scale, eviscerate, and clean the fish; cut into 6 slices. Prepare the marinade of oil, lemon juice, garlic, parsley, salt and pepper, and marinate the fish slices for two hours, turning them now and then.

Remove the fish from the marinade, dry with a cloth and dust with flour. Melt the butter in a fireproof dish, brown the chopped onion lightly, and add the fish, seasoned with salt and pepper. Brown the slices on both sides and pour in the wine and the juice of ½ lemon. Cook for 35 to 40 minutes in a medium oven. Serve in fireproof dish, preferably accompanied by boiled potatoes. Serves 6.

FISH FRITTERS MODENA STYLE

(Bignè di pesce alla modenese)

½ pound roast or boiled fish*
5 ounces shrimp meat, cooked
1 cup grated Parmesan
A little salt and pepper

3 egg yolks
Frying batter*
Plenty of vegetable oil

Chop the fish and shrimp meat into very small pieces and put in a mixing bowl with the Parmesan, a little salt and pepper and the egg yolks; combine until a smooth paste is obtained.

Make nut-sized balls of this mixture, dip them in frying batter and sauté them, a few at a time, in plenty of smoking oil in a frying pan; drain when golden and crisp. Serves 4 to 6.

STUFFED PIG'S FOOT WITH BRAISED LENTILS MODENA STYLE

(Zampone con lenticchie brasate alla modenese)

2-pound zampone* (stuffed
   pig's foot—a Modena
   specialty)
A mixture of:
   1 large onion, sliced
   1 carrot, sliced
   1 small stalk celery, chopped
  10 ounces lentils, soaked
    overnight, washed

A mixture of:
  1½ tablespoons chopped
    onion
  1 tablespoon chopped celery
2 ounces prosciutto, chopped
1½ tablespoons oil
Salt and pepper

Prepare the zampone by soaking it overnight in cold water; drain and dry. Scrape the skin carefully with a knife, making two incisions in the lower part of the foot to facilitate cooking. Wrap in a cheesecloth and tie with string.

Put the zampone in a large pot covered with plenty of water; bring slowly to the boil and skim off the scum with care. Turn down heat, add the onion, carrot, celery mixture, and simmer over a very low heat (to prevent zampone's bursting), adding a little boiling water as required. Remove pot from heat after about 3 hours, leaving the zampone in it. Reserve.

While the zampone is cooking, braise the lentils. First boil the lentils in lightly salted water, flavored with the chopped mixture of onion and celery, for about one hour. Drain (reserving the cooking liquid), and transfer to a pan. Sauté the prosciutto in oil and transfer to the pan with the lentils and season with salt and pepper; cook together for a minute or two, adding a little water from the zampone pot. Then simmer for 10 minutes.

Bring the zampone pot to the boil again; remove the zampone, slice it, and transfer to a serving dish. Transfer the braised lentils to a serving dish and serve both hot. Serves 6 to 8.

VEAL KIDNEYS WITH VINEGAR

(Rognone all'aceto alla romagnola)

2 veal kidneys (½ pound each)	2 tablespoons chopped parsley
1 tablespoon flour	2 tablespoons vinegar
Salt and pepper	6 slices day-old bread, sautéed
4 tablespoons butter	in oil and butter

Skin the kidneys, remove the fat, and slice them, discarding the gristle and hard fatty core. Dust the slices in flour, sprinkle with salt and pepper.

Heat the butter in a pan and toss in the kidney slices. Sauté them over a lively flame for 5 minutes. Transfer them to a warmed serving dish and add the parsley and vinegar to the pan; turn down heat and reduce liquids.

At the same time, sauté the bread slices in oil and butter; decorate the serving dish with them and pour the sauce over both the fried bread and the kidney slices. Serves 4 to 6.

VEAL CUTLETS BOLOGNA STYLE

(Costolette di vitello alla bolognese)

6 veal cutlets (or slices of noisette)	½ cup butter
	6 small slices prosciutto
Salt and pepper	1 scant cup grated Parmesan
4 tablespoons flour	2 tablespoons butter
2 eggs, beaten	3 tablespoons Italian meat
⅔ cup bread crumbs	sauce*

Trim the meat, removing any skin and gristle, break bone with a cleaver, and flatten a little. Season with salt and pepper and pass first in flour, then in beaten eggs, and finally in bread crumbs; reserve.

Fifteen minutes before serving time, heat the butter in a frying pan; sauté the cutlets for 5 minutes on each side till a golden brown. As they are cooked, put them in a pan and, on each, place a slice of ham, sprinkle some Parmesan and distribute a lump of softened butter. Before serving, put the pan in a warm oven for a minute, transfer the cutlets to a warm serving dish and pour over each a spoonful of Italian meat sauce. Serves 6.

PORK "BIRDS" REGGIO-EMILIA STYLE

(Uccelletti scappati alla reggiana)

2 pounds slices lean pork	1 tablespoon salt
¼ pound lean salt pork, sliced very thin	Generous pinch of freshly ground pepper
½ cup butter	
½ cup dry white wine and water	

Shape up 18 little slices of pork and 18 slivers of salt pork; on each slice of pork lay a sliver of salt pork. Roll them into tubes, and impale them, three at a time, on short wood or metal skewers.

Heat the butter in a pan; sauté the "birds" well till golden on all sides. Then add the mixture of wine and water, salt and pepper.

Turn down the heat, cover the pan, and simmer until the wine and water have completely evaporated. Serve hot with the pan liquids as the sauce, preferably accompanied by boiled potatoes. Serves 6.

STEAMED STEAK TARTARE

(Bistecca fra due piatti alla emiliana)

½ scant cup softened butter	Juice of ½ lemon
1½ pounds beef fillet steak, chopped	1 tablespoon salt
	Pinch of pepper
3 eggs, beaten with 2 tablespoons grated Parmesan	

Smear a fairly large oval serving dish with ½ the softened butter. Mix the chopped meat with the beaten eggs, the Parmesan, and the lemon juice in a bowl: transfer this mixture to the serving dish and spread the remaining butter over all, seasoning with salt and pepper.

Cover the serving dish with another of the same size and place them both securely over a pot of boiling water; allow to steam for 15 to 20 minutes. Serves 6.

STUFFED CAPON

(Cappone ripieno alla romagnola)

Stuffing:
10 ounces lean veal
10 ounces calf brains, blanched
10 ounces sweetbreads, blanched
1 capon liver
2 tablespoons butter
1 scant tablespoon salt
Pinch of pepper

1 bay leaf
1 cup chopped prosciutto
2 tablespoons grated Parmesan
½ cup cream
2 eggs
3½-pound capon ready to cook, boned
Salt and pepper
1 shot brandy
2 tablespoons butter

Dice the veal, the calf brains, sweetbreads, and the capon liver. Heat the butter in a pan and sauté this mixture along with the salt, the pepper, and the bay leaf. When well browned, pass through the mincer and transfer to a large casserole. Add the chopped prosciutto, the Parmesan, the cream and the eggs to the same casserole, and combine well.

Sprinkle the inside of the boned capon with salt and pepper and brandy; fill the capon with the stuffing, sewing up the incisions and trussing it with string to regain its correct shape. Wrap the bird in well-buttered (double) greaseproof paper and lay in a pan; bake for two hours in a medium oven. Serve with green vegetables sautéed in butter. Serves 6 to 8.

STUFFED ZUCCHINI

(Zucchine ripiene della nonna)

3½ pounds small zucchini,
   (about 3 ounces each)
A mixture of:
   10 ounces lean beef, chopped
   3 tablespoons chopped
     prosciutto (fat and lean)
   3 tablespoons chopped
     mortadella
   2 tablespoons bread
     crumbs, soaked in water,
     drained
   3 tablespoons grated
     Parmesan

2 eggs, beaten
Grating of nutmeg
Salt and pepper
2 tablespoons lard
A mixture of:
   4 tablespoons chopped
     prosciutto
   3 tablespoons chopped onion
   3 sprigs parsley, chopped
   ½ cup tomato sauce*
Salt and pepper

Wash and dry the zucchini. Using an apple corer or other suitable instrument, remove the pulp from the zucchini without damaging the outer skin.

Combine the first mixture of beef, ham, mortadella, bread crumbs, Parmesan, and beaten eggs in a bowl with a grating of nutmeg and some salt and pepper. Stuff the zucchini with this filling, using a pastry bag.

Put the lard and the chopped mixture of ham fat, onion, and parsley in a suitable pan, sufficiently large to accommodate the zucchini; heat and, when the onion browns, add the tomato sauce. Cook together for a few minutes, seasoning with salt and pepper and adding some water. Lay the stuffed zucchini in the pan; add more water, if necessary, so that they are just covered. Bring to the boil and simmer, covered, for about one hour. Add more water if the sauce becomes too thick. These are served either hot or cold. Serves 6.

BENSONE CAKE

(Bensone)

2¼ pounds sifted flour
1⅓ cups softened butter
5 eggs, beaten
½ pound superfine sugar
Grated peel of 1 lemon (no pith)

Pinch of salt
1 egg, beaten with few drops of water
4 tablespoons granulated sugar
Oil

Make a mound of the flour, and work in the butter, the beaten eggs, the sugar, the lemon peel, and the salt. Knead this mixture well and reserve in a cool place.

Then knead the dough into any imaginative shape that you wish; brush it with the egg beaten with a few drops of water, and sprinkle the surface with granulated sugar. Oil a pan and put the bensone in a moderate oven till cooked. Serves 8.

Tuscany

Just as in the distant past the Tuscan dialect became the Italian language, so, if any regional style of cooking were ever to become the Italian national cuisine, it would certainly be the Tuscan cuisine. It is by far the most acceptable to all Italians, and, over recent years, it has been spreading its prestige throughout northern Italy. Even in Rome there is no lack of Tuscan restaurants and no lack of customers to fill them.

Tuscan food is at one and the same time of a very high culinary standard, yet rustic in character; they love to use the spit. This reflects the Italian's distaste for the pretentious, the overrefined, and the dainty and, at the same time answers his demand for high quality. The Italian distaste for the fancy is deep-rooted and, in the culinary field, may go back to the Council of Trent in the seventeenth century at which it was stressed that it was a venial sin to insist on overly recherché dishes.

Tuscany, which with Umbria once made up most of ancient Etruria, is in many ways becoming non-viable and outdated as an agricultural region. Tuscany is 90 per cent hills—beautiful hills covered with olive trees, vines, and cypresses, and dotted with handsome villas and secluded monasteries. But today, mechanized agriculture requires flat land; anything in the hills costs twice as much to produce. There is, therefore, a general exodus of the Tuscans from their beautiful hills to the plains, to the seacoast, and to other regions. The only branch of farming which manages to turn the hills to advantage (they are green and cool in summer in contrast to the sun-baked rest of Italy) is cattle raising. Tuscany, therefore, is still producing fine beef and its well-known T-bone Florentine steaks show no sign of disappearing from the menu.

Tuscany also produces fine wines: Chianti needs no introduction to the world. Names like Antinori and Ricasoli's Brolio are household words; but there are other fine wines, made on a much more modest scale which are equally famous in Italy—the Brunello of Montalcino and the Vin Nobile of Montepulciano. These two great wines, like the fine Reserve Chiantis, are not sold in raffia-covered flasks, but in conventional burgundy-style bottles. Chianti in the flask is in the spirit of Italian anti-pretentiousness: the wine is good, young and vigorous and the flask is the essence of rusticity. But the aged and matured Chianti's, like the Brunello and Vin Nobile, are another story altogether.

The Tuscans have a passion for beans, and they season them with warm Tuscan olive oil which really tastes of olives; this, too, is in true rustic spirit. But the Tuscans also have a penchant for fine living and, accordingly, often add a tablespoon of caviar to the dish. The result is exquisite, but it is not dainty.

Tuscan cooking is not so aggressively masculine as Piedmont's, but with T-bone steaks, jugged hare, minestrones which are a meal in themselves, and braised duck and olives, it is something of a rival. Among Tuscany's pasta dishes, one of the most welcome is pappardelle with jugged hare sauce; pappardelle are thin, 2-inch-wide strips of pasta and the hare sauce is both historic and delicious.

Often people talk of white Chianti: but technically this does not exist. There are, however, a few dry white wines produced in Tuscany of great distinction. The finest of these—and they are very fine—are the Pomino and the Nipozzano, followed closely by the Arbia and the dry Vernaccia of San Gimignano. There are also sweet white vin santos, which are heavy dessert wines of great character and do not lack a following.

Italy had the satisfaction of seeing the hungry, conquering Napoleon being held in forced residence in the Tuscan isle of Elba (he escaped to fight the battle of Waterloo three months later), where he no doubt enjoyed the Tuscan seacoast's specialties such as Caciucco fish soup, and Elba's fine wines.

In the last decade, after two millennia of efforts which always lost their momentum, the malarial plains of the Maremma in the south of Tuscany by Grosseto at last have been reclaimed, irrigated and put into useful production, thus giving Tuscany, the flat land it needed for its agriculture. As a by-product, the beautiful Argentario peninsula by Orbetello has become the most elegant summer resort in all Italy where, also, the delights of Tuscany's wholehearted and savory cuisine can be enjoyed.

Vegetables

Desserts

TUSCAN SAUCE FOR GAME DISHES

(Salsa per selvaggina)

1½ cups vinegar
1½ cups dry white wine
6 tablespoons chopped onion
1 bay leaf
1 sprig thyme
3 sprigs parsley
A mixture of:
   1½ tablespoons softened
     butter
   1½ tablespoons flour

1 pint of Italian meat sauce*
2 tablespoons pickled chopped
   gherkins
1 tablespoon capers
1 tablespoon chopped parsley
1 tablespoon chopped marjoram
Salt
½ inch red pepper (or
   teaspoon ground
   peperoncino)

Heat the wine and vinegar over a moderate flame in a saucepan; add the onion, bay leaf, thyme, parsley, and reduce the liquid by half. Pass the contents of the saucepan through a fine sieve and replace in the same saucepan.

Brown the butter and flour lightly in a little saucepan. Add this mixture to the prepared and sieved sauce, followed by the Italian meat sauce, the gherkins, capers, parsley and marjoram, seasoning with a little salt and plenty of red pepper. Bring to the boil, stirring well; turn down heat and simmer for 10 minutes. Note: this is for hare, venison, wild boar, etc., rather than for game birds. Makes 3 to 4 cups.

PANZANELLA COUNTRY HORS D'OEUVRES

(Panzanella toscana)

2 slices bread, or 2 "gallette"
  (dry bread-dough biscuits)
6 fillets desalted anchovy*
6 large slices salad tomato
1 tablespoon chopped onion

½ tablespoon chopped basil
4 tablespoons oil
½ tablespoon vinegar
Salt

Moisten the bread (or dry biscuits) with water (do not soak) and put in a large soup plate. Lay on these the anchovy fillets, the slices of salad tomato, and sprinkle over all the chopped onion and basil. Make a little dressing of oil and vinegar and salt to taste, and mix in. Serves 1.

FLORENTINE MINESTRONE

(Minestrone alla toscana)

½ pound rice
¾ pound small brown dried
  beans
Salt and pepper
1 sprig rosemary
1 small bay leaf
½ cup oil
A mixture of:

3 tablespoons chopped onion
1 tablespoon chopped parsley
2 tablespoons chopped celery
½ pound peeled tomatoes,
  drained
1 pound escarole, washed and
  chopped
½ cup grated Parmesan

Rub the rice with a cloth to clean it; do not wash it. Soak the dried beans overnight and drain. Pour about 4 pints of water into a large casserole and season with salt; add the beans, the rosemary, and the bay leaf. Put over a moderate heat for one and a half hours or more. When the beans are well cooked, discard the bay leaf and pass half of the beans through a sieve and replace this bean purée in the casserole.

Meanwhile, heat the oil in a saucepan and brown the mixture

of onion, parsley, and celery. As soon as this is well colored, pour in the peeled tomatoes and the escarole and simmer for 10 minutes; pour this sauce into the casserole with the beans, mix well, and adjusting for salt and pepper, allow to cook together for a few minutes and reserve.

About 20 minutes before serving time, bring the bean soup to the boil and toss in the rice. When the rice is al dente, remove from heat and allow the minestrone to rest for a minute or two. Serve hot, with grated Parmesan if desired. Serves 6 to 8.

CHICK-PEA AND PASTA SOUP

(Minestra di ceci alla toscana)

1½ pounds chick-peas
1 tablespoon rosemary
Salt
½ cup oil
2 cloves garlic, bruised
4 ounces peeled tomatoes,
  drained

3 fillets desalted anchovy,*
  mashed
10 ounces pasta* (broken or
  small)

Soak the chick-peas overnight, wash and drain them; put them in a covered casserole with plenty of cold water, the rosemary and 1½ tablespoons salt, bring to the boil, and simmer for about two hours, or until the chick-peas are tender. Pass the chick-peas and their cooking water through a sieve and reserve this liquid purée.

Heat the oil in a fireproof pan and brown the crushed garlic cloves; add the tomatoes and cook together for a few minutes before mixing in the mashed anchovy fillets. After two minutes, remove the bruised garlic (and discard) and pour in the chick-pea purée and cooking water; should the water be insufficient for 8 bowls of soup, add more. Bring to the boil, toss in the pasta and cook till al dente. Adjust for salt, transfer to a soup tureen, allow to stand for a minute or two, and serve. This soup should be fairly thick. Serves 8.

PASTA AND BEAN SOUP

(Minestra di fagioli alla toscana)

¾ pound dried beans, soaked
*   overnight*
Salt
2 sprigs rosemary, chopped
4 bay leaves, chopped
1¼ pounds escarole
½ cup oil
A mixture of:
*   1½ tablespoons chopped*
*   onion*

2 tablespoons chopped celery
½ pound peeled tomatoes,
*   drained*
1 tablespoon salt and a pinch
*   of pepper*
½ pound pasta, cannolicchietti
*   (or broken pasta)*

Soak the beans overnight; wash them well in cold water and put them in a fireproof pot with 6 pints of lightly salted water, the rosemary, and bay leaves. Bring to the boil and simmer for about two hours.

Strip off the tough outer leaves from the escarole, wash the rest, blanch in boiling water for a few minutes, drain, chop coarsely, and reserve.

When the beans are tender, pass half of them through a strainer (it is equally correct to pass them all through) and replace in the original pot. Reheat and add extra water if unsufficient for 8 generous bowls of soup.

Heat the oil in a pan and sauté the mixture of onion and celery lightly; as soon as it colors, pour in the tomatoes, blend, and simmer for 10 minutes. Add, then, the chopped escarole and cook together for a few minutes. Pour this mixture into the casserole with the beans, season with 1 tablespoon of salt and a pinch of pepper. Simmer for a few minutes and reserve until mealtime.

Bring the bean soup to the boil, toss in the pasta, turn down heat, and cook till al dente. Remove from heat, allow to stand for a minute or two, and serve. Serves 6 to 8.

REINFORCED PASTA AND BEAN SOUP

(Ribollita toscana)

This is prepared as for pasta and bean soup* but, when cooked, it is allowed to cool. At mealtime, a ½ cup of good olive oil is poured into the pot and the soup is brought to the boil.

PASTA SIENA STYLE

(Pastasciutta alla sienese)

*2 pounds peeled tomatoes,
   drained
A mixture of:
   2 tablespoons chopped carrot
   1½ tablespoons chopped
   celery
   3 tablespoons chopped onion
   1 tablespoon crushed basil*

*Salt and pepper
½ cup oil
3 tablespoons chopped onion
1½ pounds dry pasta
1 cup grated Parmesan*

Put the tomatoes and the carrot, celery, onions and basil mixture with a pinch of salt and a pinch of pepper in a fireproof pot, bring to the boil, and simmer for 30 minutes, stirring often; sieve and reserve.

Heat the oil in a saucepan and brown the other 3 tablespoons of onion; pour in the sieved tomato sauce and cook together slowly, stirring well, and the sauce is ready. Reserve and keep warm.

Cook whatever pasta is preferred in lightly salted boiling water; drain when al dente and transfer to a warmed serving dish. Sprinkle over half the Parmesan and ¾ of the sauce. Mix well and serve, passing the remaining cheese and sauce at table. Serves 6 to 8.

MACARONI WITH WALNUTS COUNTRY STYLE

(Ziti con le noci alla paesana)

5 sprigs basil	½ cup oil
½ pound of shelled walnuts	1½ pounds macaroni
1½ cups grated Parmesan (or Pecorino)	Salt

Pound the basil, the walnuts, and the cheese in a mortar; when these have been brought to a paste, pour in the oil, a little at a time, mixing well; reserve this sauce.

Cook the pasta in plenty of lightly salted boiling water: drain when al dente and transfer to a warmed serving dish. Pour in the sauce, mix well, and serve. Serves 6.

TUSCAN CANNELLONI

(Cannelloni alla toscana)

1¼ pounds extra-wide short macaroni	A mixture of:
	¾ pound lean beef, chopped
Salt	2 ounces mushrooms, chopped
Filling:	
1 cup butter	2 ounces prosciutto, chopped
A mixture of:	Salt and pepper
2 tablespoons chopped onion	A grating of nutmeg
2 tablespoons chopped carrot	1 cup grated Parmesan
1 tablespoon chopped celery	3 egg yolks
1 tablespoon chopped parsley	3½ cups Italian meat sauce*

Cook the macaroni in lightly salted boiling water; when al dente, drain and reserve on a damp cloth.

Filling: Heat ½ cup butter in a pan and sauté the first mixture of onion, carrot, celery, and parsley; when golden brown, add the chopped meat, mushrooms, and ham, and simmer, seasoning with a little salt, pepper, and a grating of nutmeg, for about 30 minutes. Transfer the whole mixture to a bowl, allow to cool and then combine with 2 tablespoons of grated Parmesan and the 3 egg yolks, kneading until a smooth paste is obtained. Using a pastry bag with a round nozzle, fill the macaroni tubes with this paste.

Put ½ of the Italian meat sauce into a casserole, lay the macaroni tubes (cannelloni) on it, and heat over a moderate flame. Distribute, over all, lumps of softened butter, and serve with grated Parmesan and remaining meat sauce at table. Serves 6.

FRIED MULLETS

(Frittura di triglie alla toscana)

2 pounds small mullets	*Flour*
Salt	*Oil for deep-frying*
Milk	*4 lemons*

Prepare the fish for cooking; they need only be scaled lightly and the gills, etc, removed. Make several light incisions on both sides of each mullet to prevent their bursting during cooking. Season with salt, dip one at a time for an instant in a plate of milk, dust lightly in flour, and sauté in a pan of smoking oil. Drain when crisp and golden and serve with lemon quarters. Serves 8.

MULLETS LIVORNO STYLE

(Triglie alla livornese)

6 mullets, approx. ½ pound each	*1 clove garlic, bruised*
¼ cup oil	*Pinch of chopped thyme*
Salt and pepper	*Pinch of crushed bay leaf*
Flour	*1 pound peeled tomatoes, drained*
1 tablespoon chopped onion	*2 tablespoons chopped parsley*

Prepare the mullets for cooking; if they are young, it is not necessary to clean out the interior; one need only scale them and snip off the gills, etc. Wash and dry them with a cloth. Make several light incisions on both sides of each of the mullets, to prevent their bursting during cooking.

Heat 3 tablespoons of oil in a pan. Season the fish with salt and pepper, and lightly dust them in flour; put them in the pan and cook over a medium flame for 5 minutes on each side until golden. Remove from pan, transfer to a serving dish, and keep the mullets warm.

Pour the remaining oil into the pan, and add the chopped onion and the crushed garlic: when the onion colors, discard the garlic and sprinkle in the thyme and bay leaf. Allow to cook together for a moment and then pour in the tomatoes, adjusting for salt and pepper. Bring to the boil and simmer for 12 minutes. Pour this sauce over the mullets, sprinkle with the chopped parsley and serve. Serves 6.

SOLE WITH BUTTER AND LEMON GROSSETO STYLE

(Sogliola con burro e succo di limone alla grossetana)

Flour	*Salt and white pepper*
6 ½-pound soles, readied for	*2 tablespoons chopped parsley*
*cooking**	*Juice of 1 lemon*
¼ pound butter	

Flour the soles lightly and place them in a pan with bubbling butter, seasoned with a little salt and a pinch of pepper; sauté them for 5 minutes on each side. Drain and place in a warmed serving dish, pour over the pan juices, sprinkle with chopped parsley, squeeze over all the juice of a lemon, and serve hot. Serves 6.

BAKED ARTICHOKE FRITTATA

(Tortino di carciofi alla toscana)

3 small artichoke hearts,	1 tablespoon salt
quartered	2 tablespoons butter
Flour	6 fresh eggs
Oil for deep-frying	Pinch of pepper

Dust the wedges of artichoke hearts in flour and sauté in oil till golden brown; drain, and season with salt. Butter a pan and lay the quarters of artichoke in it and keep warm in the oven.

Beat the eggs with salt and pepper. Turn up heat, until oven is very hot; pour the beaten eggs over the artichokes and replace pan in oven; cook till crisp outside but still soft inside. Serves 3.

PORK LIVER AND FENNEL SEEDS

(Fegatelli di maiale con semi di finocchio)

1¼ pounds pork liver	2 tablespoons oil
3 tablespoons fennel seeds	3 tablespoons lard
Salt and pepper	

Clean the pork liver with care, removing skin, core, and gristle and cut into 1-inch cubes. Pound the fennel seeds in a mortar and transfer to a bowl; season with salt, pepper and a little oil and dip the liver cubes in the mixture one by one. Heat the lard in a pan and sauté the liver cubes until golden and crisp (about 5 minutes). Serve immediately, pouring over the pan juices. Serves 6.

VEAL KIDNEYS ON THE SPIT FLORENTINE STYLE

(Spiedini di rognone di vitello alla fiorentina)

3 ¼-pound veal kidneys	3 tablespoons stock*
6 tablespoons butter	1½ tablespoons chopped parsley
Salt and pepper	Juice of ½ lemon

Cut the kidneys in two, removing the hard core and the gristle, but leaving some of the fat. Put the kidney halves on one or more skewers and lay in a fireproof dish. Add the butter and a sprinkle of salt and pepper and put the fireproof dish in a moderate preheated oven for 15 minutes, turning the skewers occasionally. After 12 minutes' cooking, pour in the stock, the parsley and the juice of half a lemon. Remove skewer or skewers and serve kidneys in same fireproof dish with the pan juices. Serves 6.

LAMB CHOPS WITH ARTICHOKES

(Bracioline di agnello con carciofi)

2 pounds leg of lamb, cut into 18 slices	2 tablespoons chopped onion
	Pinch of rosemary
6 young artichokes	1 tablespoon salt
Lemon or vinegar	Pinch of pepper
1½ tablespoons oil	½ cup Chianti
A mixture of:	¾ pound peeled tomatoes,
3 ounces salt pork, chopped	drained
1 clove garlic, chopped	

Trim the lamb, removing skin and gristle, slice, and pound lightly. Remove tough outer leaves, the choke, etc., from the artichokes, and cut the hearts into small wedges, reserving them in lightly salted water with a little lemon juice or vinegar to prevent turning black.

Heat the oil in a pan and add the chopped mixture; as soon as it colors, add the lamb slices seasoned with 1 tablespoon salt and a pinch of pepper. Cover the pan and allow to brown slowly, stirring and turning occasionally.

Pour in the wine and reduce almost completely; add the tomatoes and a few tablespoons of hot water and simmer for 5 minutes. Drain the artichokes, add them to the pan with a pinch of salt, and continue simmering for about 20 minutes more. Serve immediately. Serves 6.

ROAST PORK AND BEANS

(Arista di maiale con fagioli toscanelli)

5-pound rib or loin roast of	*1½ tablespoons salt*
pork	*1 tablespoon pepper*
3 cloves garlic, sliced	*¾ pound Toscanelli beans or*
lengthwise	*substitute black-eyed beans*
5 sprigs rosemary (or 1	*Salt and pepper*
tablespoon dried)	*½ cup oil*

Bone the meat, make little slits in it with a sharp knife, and insert the garlic slices and the rosemary. Rub the meat all over with 1½ tablespoons salt and 1 tablespoon pepper and tie well with string so that the meat maintains its shape during cooking.

Boil the beans in lightly salted water; drain and season with oil, salt, and pepper, and keep warm.

Smear a pan generously with oil, place the pork in it, and pour over the remaining oil.

Roast in a moderate heat for about one hour until the pork is well browned, basting and turning occasionally. Remove string, slice the meat, pour over pan juices, and serve with the beans. This roast is also excellent cold. Serves 6 to 8.

CHICKEN BREASTS TUSCAN STYLE WITH PEAS

(Petti di pollo dorati alla toscana con piselli)

6 chicken breasts	½ cup oil
2 eggs	10 ounces peas
Salt	2 leeks
2 tablespoons flour	Pinch of sugar
3 tablespoons bread crumbs	3 lemons

Clean, pound, and trim the chicken breasts. Beat the 2 eggs, adding a pinch of salt and dip the chicken breasts one at a time; dust them in flour and then in bread crumbs. Sauté these chicken breasts carefully in 4 tablespoons oil till golden brown on both sides.

Shell the peas; strip, and chop the leeks and cook them slowly with a little water and the remaining oil, adding a teaspoon of salt and a pinch of sugar. Serve with the chicken breasts and a half lemon per person. Serves 6.

JUGGED HARE FLORENTINE STYLE

(Lepre in salmi alla fiorentina)

3-pound hare	4 tablespoons butter
Marinade of:	1 medium onion, sliced
½ pint dry red wine	1 medium carrot, sliced
3 tablespoons chopped onion	1 tablespoon flour
2 tablespoons chopped celery	½ pound fresh mushrooms,
1 clove garlic, crushed	quartered
2 peppercorns, bruised	2 tablespoons dry red wine
Pinch powdered thyme	Salt
Pinch crumbled bay leaf	1 shot brandy
Pinch of salt	6 slices polenta,* fried

Prepare the hare, eviscerate, wash, and cut it into pieces. Place in fireproof pot with the marinade; leave for some hours, turning occasionally.

Heat 3 tablespoons of butter in a casserole and sauté the onions and carrot. Reserving the marinade, remove and dry the hare pieces and brown them over a lively heat in the same casserole, seasoning with a little salt. Sprinkle over the flour and mix in well.

As soon as the flour begins to color, pour in the marinade complete. Bring to the boil, cover the casserole; turn down heat and simmer for one and a fourth hours. Transfer the hare pieces to another casserole; pass the pan juices through a fine sieve and pour over the hare.

Sauté the mushrooms with the remaining butter and add the 2 tablespoons wine; pour this mixture into the casserole with the hare. Replace casserole on the stove; adjust for salt and bring to the boil. Heat the brandy in a saucepan, ignite it, and pour over the hare. Serve immediately with hot fried polenta squares. Serves 6.

BEANS IN THE FLASK

(Fagioli nel fiasco alla toscana)

¾ pound small dried beans (toscanelli)	½ tablespoon salt
	½ cup oil
2 tablespoons oil	1 tablespoon salt and pinch of pepper
3 sage leaves	
2 cloves garlic, crushed	

Soak the beans overnight; clean and wash them well. Take a Chianti flask, remove the straw, and put in the beans, the oil, the sage, the garlic, and cover with water. Stopper with a little absorbent cotton, so that the vapor can get out, but the flavor of the garlic remains. Put the flask over a lively wood or charcoal fire and heat for three hours. A few minutes before the end of the cooking period, add ½ tablespoon salt. Pour the beans into a casserole, pour over ½ cup oil, 1 tablespoon salt and, if desired, a pinch of pepper. Serves 4 to 6.

BRIGIDINI WAFERS

(Brigidini)

3½ cups sifted flour
6 eggs, beaten with a little salt
Pinch of salt

8 ounces superfine sugar
2 tablespoons oil
Pinch of powdered aniseed

Heap the flour into a mound on the table, scooping out the center: mix in the beaten eggs, the salt, the sugar, the oil, and the pinch of aniseed. Knead this until a smooth dough is obtained. Allow to stand for a while and then divide into walnut-sized lumps. Roll these out into thin wafers and put in an oiled baking pan and into a moderate oven. Remove when golden and allow to cool. Serves 6.

Umbria

Umbria is not only the smallest region of Italy but an underpopulated one as well. It has only two towns of any size, Perugia its capital, which has a little light industry, and Terni, where there are major steel mills and hydroelectric plants. For the rest, it is rolling hills clad with olives and vines and woods, interspersed with wheat fields.

Though Umbria is an inland region and its weather is not moderated by the sea, the climate is not continental at its worst. However, in 1956, the cold and frosts did enormous damage to the olive trees from which the region is only now recovering. The more profitable forms of agriculture—fruit and market gardening—are not, therefore, easy for the Umbrians. Like the Tuscans, they are looking increasingly to cattle raising and especially to raising large white pigs (on an acorn diet) for their own salvation and to supply their only successful traditional industry, which is sausage-making.

Norcia is a little country town which, for centuries, has had the reputation of making the best charcuterie in Italy. These Norcia sausages are often enhanced with slivers of black truffles, which are almost identical to the famous French Périgord truffles, and which are the region's only natural bonanza.

What then has Umbria other than lovely scenery and excellent sausages? It has small old cities such as Spoleto and Orvieto; the former is the center of the truffle trade and the latter of Umbria's gentle, golden wine, the production of which is not great but which is well recognized as one of Italy's most distinctive table-wines. It comes both dry and amabile; amabile means that it is very slightly sweet, which is much appreciated by those who have no taste for the tangy dryness of most wines.

The cuisine, on the whole, does not differ vastly from that of the Marche and Tuscany; they are the two major influences, but it is more modest and countrified than both. Instead of great T-bone steaks, you will find pork chops; instead of heavy red wine sauces, you will find game birds and rabbit, for example, grilled with plenty of aromatic herbs which grow wild in abundance by the banks of the Tiber River and the shores of Lake Trasimene.

Lake Trasimene is almost as big as Lake Como and offers good fishing—tench, trout, and pike. In the surrounding hills, in winter, there is no lack of deer, hare, and game birds to supply the Umbrians with something inexpensive yet succulent for their table.

The somnolent rusticity of Umbria is little changed since the lifetime of the region's most famous personality, St. Francis of Assisi, and the city of Assisi would appear not to have changed at all. In Umbria, in sum, there still exists the simple life and the simple cuisine of the past.

Pastas and other farinaceous dishes

Fish

Entrées

Meats

Vegetables

Desserts

MUSHROOM SAUCE

(Sugo di funghi)

4 cloves garlic, bruised
3 tablespoons lard
4 tablespoons oil
1 pound fresh mushrooms,*
  ready to cook, chopped

1 tablespoon chopped parsley
Salt
2 pinches red pepper (ground
  peperoncino)
2 peeled tomatoes, drained

Sauté the garlic in the lard and oil and, when golden, discard. Add the mushrooms and parsley, season with salt and red pepper (or substitute black) and simmer till the mushrooms' moisture is evaporated; add the tomatoes and simmer for 10 minutes.

TRUFFLE AND ANCHOVY TOASTS

(Crostini alla maniera dell'Umbria)

A mixture of:
  2 ounces black truffles, finely
    chopped
  4 fillets desalted anchovy,*
    finely chopped
  Olive oil

4 ½-inch-thick slices of bread

Make a paste of the black truffle, the chopped anchovy, and the olive oil. Toast the bread and spread with the truffle and anchovy paste. Serves 4.

LENTEN HORS D'OEUVRES

(Antipasto magro)

14 ounces tuna in oil	*Dressing:*
1 pound potatoes	*4 tablespoons oil*
6 hard-cooked eggs	*1 tablespoon vinegar*
1 large beet, baked	*Salt and pepper*
2 tablespoons salted capers	*1 cup mayonnaise**
	¼ pound green olives, pitted

Slice the tuna. Wash, boil, and peel the potatoes. Cut the hard-cooked eggs in half lengthwise. Slice the baked beet. Wash the salt from the capers and dry them.

Mix the oil, vinegar, salt, and pepper dressing. Dice the potatoes and mix in the dressing, transferring them to a suitable serving dish. On top of the potatoes, lay the tuna slices and egg halves; pour over the mayonnaise. Decorate the edge of the dish with beet slices, olive slices, and capers. Serves 6.

UMBRIAN MINESTRONE

(Minestrone umbro)

½ pound white navy beans	*2 tablespoons onion, carrot,*
½ pound dried chestnuts,	*celery, chopped together*
peeled and diced	*½ tablespoon chopped*
1 tablespoon salt	*parsley*
A mixture of:	*¼ pound broken pasta (or*
¼ pound salt pork, chopped	*small pasta—cannolicchi)*
	Pepper and nutmeg

Soak the beans overnight; wash them and put them in a casserole with the diced chestnuts and salt; bring to the boil and simmer (covered) for about two hours.

Twenty minutes before the two hours are up, sauté the salt pork and the onion, carrot, celery, and parsley mixture in a frying pan;

add this sautéed mixture and the pasta, along with a pinch of pepper and half a pinch of nutmeg to the casserole. Remove from heat when the pasta is al dente; allow to rest for a few minutes and serve hot. Serves 6 to 8.

BREAD AND WATER SOUP

(Acqua cotta [zuppa di fette di pane])

6 thick slices of day-old bread	*1 large onion, sliced*
½ cup oil	*¼ pound peeled tomatoes,*
Freshly ground pepper	*drained*
Salt	*1 sprig mint, chopped*

Put the slices of bread in a tureen with the oil and freshly ground pepper.

Bring to the boil, in a large saucepan, sufficient water for 6 portions of soup, adding salt, sliced onion, the tomato and the chopped mint. Simmer for 20 minutes or so and pour over the bread and oil in the tureen. Allow to stand for a few minutes and serve hot. Serves 6.

SPAGHETTI CASCIA STYLE

(Spaghetti alla maniera di Cascia)

¼ pound black truffles, sliced	*¾ pound peeled tomatoes,*
thin (or raw fresh	*drained*
mushrooms)	*Salt and freshly ground pepper*
½ cup oil	*½ pound spaghetti*
3 cloves garlic, crushed	*2 tablespoons chopped parsley*
6 fillets desalted anchovy,*	
mashed	

To clean the truffles, brush them with a brush dipped in water, then chop them; or substitute 10 ounces of raw chopped mushrooms.

Heat the oil in a pan and add the garlic; as soon as it begins to brown, add the anchovy and almost simultaneously the tomato, seasoned with a little salt and a pinch of freshly ground pepper. Mix well and cook gently for 15 minutes.

Cook the pasta in plenty of lightly salted boiling water; drain when al dente and pass to a warmed serving dish. First sprinkle over the black truffle slices (or chopped mushrooms), then the sauce, and finally the chopped parsley. Mix well and serve immediately. Serves 6 to 8.

PASTA WITH RICOTTA

(Fettuccine secche [o fresche] con la ricotta all'umbra)

1½ pounds dry fettuccine	*½ cup oil*
10 ounces fresh ricotta	*Salt and pepper*

Bring to the boil plenty of lightly salted boiling water and toss in the pasta. Then sieve the ricotta into a mixing bowl and combine with the oil and a few tablespoons of the boiling water from the pasta. When the pasta is al dente, drain, and pass to a warmed serving dish. Pour in the ricotta mixture and a little freshly ground pepper. Carry to table, mix well, and serve. Serves 6 to 8.

BAKED TROUT "NERA"[1]

(Trota della Nera)

2-pound river trout	*1 tablespoon bread crumbs*
A mixture of:	*Salt and pepper*
2 tablespoons chopped	*Juice of 1 lemon*
parsley	*½ cup oil*

Clean, eviscerate, bone, and wash the fish. Mix the parsley, bread crumbs, salt, and pepper with the juice of ½ lemon in a bowl; reserve a tablespoon of this mixture.

Open up the trout and stuff it well with the mixture. Oil an iron pan, lay the trout in it, and spoon the reserved tablespoon of the mixture on top of the trout as well as a tablespoon of oil.

[1] The Nera is a river in Umbria.

Put in a moderate oven for 35 to 40 minutes; serve very hot with a sprinkling of oil and lemon juice mixed. Serves 2.

ANCHOVY FRITTATA

(Frittata con acciuga all'umbra)

3 tablespoons oil	10 ounces peeled tomatoes,
6 fillets desalted anchovy,*	drained
chopped	Salt and pepper
1 tablespoon chopped parsley	10 fresh eggs
1 clove garlic, chopped	

Heat 1 tablespoon of oil in a frying pan till smoking and add the chopped anchovy fillets, the parsley, and the garlic; sauté for a moment before adding the tomatoes, seasoned with a pinch of salt and a pinch of pepper. Turn down heat and simmer for 8 minutes; pour the whole mixture into a mixing bowl and allow to cool.

First beat the eggs, adding a little salt, and then combine them in the mixing bowl with the anchovy and tomato sauce.

Heat the remaining oil in the frying pan till smoking and pour in the mixture, sautéing for a few moments until browned underneath; turn the frittata over (adding more oil if necessary) and brown the other side. Slide into a serving dish and serve hot. Serves 6.

PORK CHOPS IN WINE SAUCE

(Costolette di maiale all'umbra)

6 6-ounce pork chops	½ cup dry white wine
Salt and pepper	¼ cup stock*
1½ tablespoons flour	2 tablespoons butter
½ cup oil	3 tablespoons chopped
2 tablespoons onion and 1	gherkins
garlic clove, chopped	
together	

Lightly pound the cutlets to flatten them; break the bones and trim off any skin and gristle. Season each chop with a pinch of salt and pepper and dust with flour.

Heat the oil in a pan till it smokes. Put the cutlets in the pan and sauté them over a lively heat for 3 minutes on each side; turn down the heat and continue cooking for 5 minutes on each side. Drain the cutlets and keep warm on a serving dish.

Add the mixture of chopped onion and garlic to the pan juices and sauté for a few moments; then add the wine and the stock (or water, if lacking stock) and reduce the liquids by ¾. Before serving, add the butter in little soft lumps and the chopped gherkin; allow to combine but not to cook. Pour the sauce over the pork chops and serve immediately. Serves 6.

BEEF FILLETS SPOLETO STYLE

(Bistecchine di filetto di bue alla spoletina)

1¾ pound beef fillets	*Salt and pepper*
2 tablespoons chopped dried	*¼ cup stock**
mushrooms*	*Juice of ½ lemon*
½ cup oil	*6 or 8 slices of day-old bread,*
3 ounces prosciutto, chopped	*browned in oven*
2 tablespoons chopped parsley	

Lightly pound the beef fillets to flatten them. Soak the dried mushrooms in warm water, wash them, dry them.

Pour the oil into a pan and heat till it begins to smoke; toss in the mushrooms, the ham, and the parsley, followed immediately by the beef fillets, seasoned with a little salt and pepper.

Cook the fillets slowly for 8 to 10 minutes on each side; pour in the stock and the juice of half a lemon and reduce the liquids completely.

Place the fillets on a warmed serving dish, pour the pan juices over them and decorate with bread squares which have been browned in the oven at the last moment. Serves 6 to 8.

RABBIT WITH WHITE WINE

(Coniglio al vino bianco)

*2½-pound rabbit, young and
plump, ready to cook
Flour
2 tablespoons oil
1 cup lard
2 cloves garlic, bruised*

*3 sprigs rosemary, tied with
white thread
Salt and pepper
¾ cup dry white wine
2 tablespoons stock**

First chop the rabbit into 1 ounce chunks and lightly dust in flour. Heat the oil and lard in a pan with the crushed garlic and the rosemary until the garlic browns; then add the rabbit, sprinkled with a little salt and pepper, and allow to brown gently. Pour in the wine and, stirring often, simmer for 25 to 30 minutes, adding, when the pan juices become thick, a tablespoon or two of stock (or water, if lacking stock).

Remove the garlic and rosemary and lay out the pieces of rabbit on a serving dish. Pour the sauce over them. Serves 6.

STRING BEANS AND TOMATO SAUCE

(Fagiolini verdi all'aretina)

*1 pound string beans
¼ cup oil
2 cloves garlic, crushed
2 tablespoons chopped onion
6 sage leaves*

*1 pound peeled tomatoes,
drained
1 tablespoon salt and a pinch
of pepper*

Wash the string beans and chop them into 1-inch lengths. Heat the oil in a pan, and add the garlic, the onion, and the sage and allow to brown together. Then add the tomatoes and the chopped string beans together, season with 1 tablespoon salt and a pinch of pepper and, after a minute, pour in sufficient cold water to cover the contents. Bring slowly to the boil and immediately turn down the heat, covering the pan with a lid and simmering for about 45 minutes, stirring every now and then. Serve in warmed serving dish. Serves 6.

CIARAMICOLA CAKE

(Ciaramicola)

1¼ pounds sifted flour
1 tablespoon baking powder,
    dissolved in warm water
Pinch of salt
¾ cup vanilla-flavored
    superfine sugar
Grated peel of ¼ lemon
2 eggs, beaten

A shot of Mistrà (aniseed-
    based liqueur 85 proof)
    or anisette
Butter
2 egg whites
3½ ounces superfine sugar
1 tablespoon colored
    decorating sugar

Make a dough of 3½ tablespoons of flour with the baking powder and a pinch of salt. Wrap this soft dough in a cloth and reserve in a warm place for 15 minutes.

Make a mound of the remaining flour on the table, scoop out the center and add the prepared dough, the sugar, the grated lemon peel, and the beaten eggs. Knead well, adding the Mistrà. Wrap the dough in a cloth and keep in a cool place for one hour.

Butter a broad, low pan and line the bottom with the dough mixture; beat the egg whites and sugar together and spread over the surface. Put in a moderate oven and remove when the surface is lightly golden. Allow to cool and remove from pan. Sprinkle with gilding or colored decorating sugar. Serves 6.

SWEET RICE FRITTERS

(Frittelle di riso)

3 tablespoons flour	*Pinch of salt*
2 tablespoons baking powder	*2 ounces raisins, soaked in*
3 tablespoons warm milk	*warm water*
1½ pints warm milk	*1½ tablespoons pine nuts*
¼ pound rice, cleaned but not	*Grated peel of ½ lemon*
washed	*1 tablespoon superfine sugar*
4 tablespoons sifted flour	*Oil*
2 egg yolks	*Lard*
1 egg	*Confectioners' sugar*

Make a little mound of 3 tablespoons of flour on a tabletop, add the baking powder and the 3 tablespoons of warm milk; knead this mixture until a smooth paste is obtained. Roll into a ball; cut into 4 pieces crosswise and transfer to a fireproof pot in which a few tablespoons of warm milk have been poured; allow to rise in a warm place for 20 minutes.

Pour 1 pint of milk into a casserole and bring to the boil; toss in the rice, and cook over a moderate heat. When the rice is cooked, in about 20 minutes, pour the milk and rice into a bowl, allow to cool a little and mix in the 4 tablespoons of flour, the egg yolks and the egg, a pinch of salt, the prepared dough (which should have doubled its size), the raisins, the pine nuts, the grated lemon peel, and the superfine sugar. Mix well; if the mixture is too stiff, add a little warm milk.

Heat plenty of oil and lard (half and half) in a frying pan, and dropping the batter in by spoonfuls, sauté the fritters till crisp and golden; remove with a slotted spoon and lay on a cloth to drain. When all are cooked, transfer to a serving dish and sprinkle with confectioners' sugar. Serves 8 to 10.

Marches

The Marches, one of the lesser-known regions of Italy, lie south of the Romagna and overlook the Adriatic. The road and rail communications are not of the best, though the former are being vastly improved now. This region is almost all hills or mountains, which means a hard life for the inhabitants. But the Marchigiani are a very special people—industrious, intelligent, and talented. They have done more than make the best of a bad job, they have—without the aid of industry or investment capital—somehow managed to reach a comfortable though not affluent, standard of living.

Much of this comfort has come through handcrafts, ceramics making, shoe and sandal making (they sell throughout the world), and the production of piano accordions, all of which, to a considerable extent are done by piecework in the homes.

As one drives through the Marches, one sees neat orderly little farms—it is the land of the small holder, par excellence. The climate is unkind in winter and hot and dry in summer; a variety of irrigation systems have, however, made the exploitation of the land, if not easy, at least possible. The aim of the Marches is to feed Rome and this it does not only with market produce but also with meat. The major influence on its gastronomy is its northern neighbor, Emilia, though the Marches tends to be a greater meat-eating region. But, on the whole, the cuisine from the fish soups (brodetti) to the stuffed pastas (the Marches' specialty is vincisgrassi) is much the same in principle, though without that rambunctious spirit which characterizes the people of Emilia-Romagna; the Marchigiani are altogether quieter and more thoughtful. Nor have the Marchigiani been blessed with a great abundance of Sangiovese wine, but they do have Verdicchio dei Castelli di Iesi which is reckoned to be one of the best dry white wines in Italy to accompany fish; it is strong (around 12°), straw-colored, harmonious, and with a very slightly bitter aftertaste. The Marches fortunately have plenty of fish to accompany this wine as the Ancona fishing fleet is the third biggest in Italy, led only by those of Sicily and Puglia.

In the hills of the Marches lies Urbino, the city which, in renaissance times, was the fount of the modern ideal of a civilized way of life. The citizens of this austere and lovely city (which now hosts an international university of art) invented good manners, peaceful relations, and a scholarly appreciation of art, poetry and architecture; needless to say, it did not last. However, a second attempt is now being made to instill those precepts into a new generation which, perhaps, will meet with greater success. Urbino's greatest son was Raphael and the surrounding countryside is reminiscent of the backgrounds of so many of his and other Renaissance painters.

MARCHES' TOMATO SAUCE WITH BASIL

(Salsa di pomodoro al basilico)

3 tablespoons lard	*Salt and red pepper (ground*
2 tablespoons oil	*peperoncino)*
2 tablespoons finely chopped	*Plenty of coarsely chopped*
onion	*basil*
2¼ pounds peeled tomatoes,	
drained, cut in strips	

Heat the lard and oil in a pan; sauté the chopped onion. When the onion is golden, add the tomatoes, seasoning with salt and red pepper. Turn down heat and simmer for a half hour. At the last moment, mix in the chopped basil. Makes 2½ cups.

MARINATED MOREL MUSHROOMS

(Spugnole marinate)

1 pound fresh mushrooms (preferably wild)*	4 peppercorns, bruised
	1 bay leaf, crumbled
4 tablespoons oil	Salt
3 cloves garlic, crushed	½ cup dry white wine
1 sprig rosemary, chopped	Juice of 1 lemon
2 cloves	

Clean and chop the mushroom stems, leaving the caps whole if small. Heat the oil in a pan till smoking, and toss in the mushrooms, the garlic, the rosemary, the cloves, the peppercorns, the bay leaf, and a pinch of salt. Sauté all together for a few minutes before pouring in the wine; turn down heat to a low simmer and reduce the wine by half. Add the lemon juice and continue cooking slowly for another 10 minutes or more with the lid on the pan. Allow to cool and reserve in a cool place. Serves 4 to 6.

PEA SOUP MACERATA STYLE

(Pisellata alla maceratese)

A mixture:	1 tablespoon salt and a pinch of pepper
¼ pound salt pork, chopped	
1 tablespoon chopped onion	5 pints water
1 clove garlic, chopped	1½ pounds shelled peas
1 tablespoon chopped parsley	24 slices bread, browned in oven
½ pound peeled tomatoes, drained	

Put the mixture into a large fireproof pot and allow to cook together for one minute; add the tomatoes, season with 1 tablespoon of salt and a pinch of freshly ground pepper. Pour in the cold water, bring to the boil, and add the shelled peas; turn down heat, simmer over a very low heat for about 20 minutes. Meantime, brown the slices of bread in the oven and distribute 3 each in soup bowl; pour the pea soup over the toast. Serves 6 to 8.

BROTH WITH FRASCARELLI ANCONA STYLE

(Minestra di frascarelli all'anconetana)

Frascarelli:	*A grating of nutmeg*
2 eggs	*3 ounces corn meal*
3½ tablespoons softened	*5 pints light stock**
butter	*½ cup grated Parmesan*
Salt and pepper	

Pour the eggs and the softened butter into a bowl and beat vigorously until a light, foamy cream is obtained; add a little salt and pepper and a grating of nutmeg. Continue beating continuously and sprinkle in the corn meal, a little at a time, until a smooth paste is obtained.

Prepare a low casserole with 4 pints of boiling water; put on the corner of the stove and allow to simmer. With 2 teaspoons, the second being continuously dipped in boiling water so that the paste will not stick to it, use the first to spoon up some of the paste and the second to push it into the simmering water; continue until all the paste is in the simmering water and continue cooking for about 10 minutes until the frascarelli have firmed up. Drain them and distribute them in deep soup bowls.

Heat the stock and pour over the frascarelli. Serve with grated Parmesan, if desired. Serves 6 to 8.

BUCATINI WITH RED WINE SAUCE

(Bucatini alla marchigiana)

2 tablespoons oil or lard
A mixture of:
  2 tablespoons chopped onion
  1 tablespoon chopped celery
  1½ tablespoons chopped
    carrot
¼ pound prosciutto, fat and
  lean (or lean salt pork)

½ cup dry red wine
2 pounds peeled tomatoes,
  drained
Salt and pepper
1¼ pounds bucatini (or thin
  macaroni)
1 cup grated Parmesan

Heat the oil (or lard) in a pan and brown the mixture of onion, celery, and carrot. Cut the ham (or salt pork) into strips, and combine with the mixture for a few moments. Then pour in the wine and reduce almost completely. Add the tomatoes, season with a little salt and pepper, bring to the boil, and simmer for about 30 minutes.

Meanwhile cook the pasta in lightly salted boiling water; drain when al dente, transfer to a warmed serving dish, and pour over ½ the sauce and ½ the Parmesan. Mix and serve, adding the remaining sauce and cheese at the table. Serves 6.

MACARONI STUFFED WITH TURKEY, TRUFFLES, AND CREAM

(Maccheroni grossi alla pescarese)

¾ cup butter
2 tablespoons chopped onion
10 ounces cooked ham, lean
  and fat, chopped
Salt and pepper
10 ounces turkey breasts
½ pound calf's liver

3 ounces lean veal
1 Norcia black truffle[1]
¾ cup cream
1¼ pounds large macaroni
  (suitable for stuffing)
6 ounces grated Gruyère or
  Parmesan

[1] Black Norcia truffles are available in cans and, in a creamed form, in tubes.

Melt 3 tablespoons of butter in a casserole, add the onion and ham; cook for a moment and then add 2 or 3 tablespoons of water. Season with a pinch of salt and brown the mixture very slowly over a low heat until the liquid evaporates. Allow to cool, and reserve.

Chop the turkey breasts, the liver, the veal and the black truffle, and pass through a mincer, reducing the mixture to a paste. Transfer to a mixing bowl and pour in, a little at a time, the cream, and season with a pinch of salt and pepper.

Cook the macaroni in plenty of lightly salted boiling water for 10 minutes; drain and lay out on a table top so that they do not stick together.

Fill a pastry bag with the stuffing and fill the macaroni tubes. Smear a pan with 2 tablespoons of butter and lay the stuffed macaroni in it, adding spoonfuls of the onion-ham mixture and, on top of all, a sprinkling of grated Gruyère or Parmesan; distribute the rest of the butter in little lumps along with any remaining cream. Put into a moderate preheated oven for 15 to 20 minutes until browned. Serves 6 to 8.

VINCISGRASSI BAKED PASTA MACERATA STYLE

(Vincisgrassi alla macetarese)

Dough*:	3 cups Italian meat sauce*
1¼ pounds sifted flour	6 ounces mushrooms*
3 tablespoons semolina	1 cup grated Parmesan
5 eggs	4 tablespoons butter
1 teaspoon oil	1 black truffle
Pinch of salt	3 tablespoons softened butter

Prepare a dough with the sifted flour, semolina, 5 eggs, oil, salt, and a little water, if needed. Roll it out not too thin and cut it into 4-inch squares. Cook these in plenty of lightly salted water—about five at a time—in a broad, low casserole; remove with a slotted spoon when al dente, drain, and put on a damp, warm cloth and reserve.

Prepare Italian meat sauce, but instead of using chicken livers, sauté 6 ounces of sliced mushrooms in 2 tablespoons of butter.

To combine: Butter a pan and distribute the pasta, the Parmesan, and the Italian meat sauce in layers and, if available, a few slices of black truffle; finish with pasta topped off with softened butter and Parmesan.

Put into a moderate preheated oven; as soon as the surface is browned, the pasta is ready. Serve with the remaining Parmesan at table. Serves 6.

ADRIATIC FISH SOUP

(Brodetto delle Coste Adriatiche marchigiana)

2 pounds mixed fish—mullet, bass, porgy, shrimps, etc.
½ cup oil
A mixture of:
   1½ tablespoons chopped onion
   2 cloves garlic, bruised
   1 sprig thyme, chopped
   Pinch of sage
   1 bay leaf, crumbled
   ½ inch hot red peperoncino or teaspoon ground red pepper

½ cup dry white wine
1 pound peeled tomatoes, drained
Salt
½ cup liquid: 4 parts water, 1 part vinegar
1 cup fish fumet*
6–8 slices bread
1½ tablespoons chopped parsley

Clean and eviscerate the fish; chop the larger ones into pieces, leaving the smaller ones whole. Pour the oil into a pan, add mixture of onion, garlic, thyme, sage, bay leaf, and red pepper; as soon as the garlic begins to brown, pour in the wine and let it evaporate almost completely.

Discard the garlic; add the tomatoes, season with salt, and bring to the boil. After a few minutes on the boil, pour in the water-and-vinegar mixture; bring to a fast boil for 10 minutes or so and remove from heat. Pass the pan juices through a sieve into another pan.

Put the pan, with the filtered pan juices, on the stove; begin placing the fish in it, starting with those which require more cooking and ending with the shellfish; turn up heat and, without ever stirring or turning the fish, cook on a high flame. If the pan juices thicken too much, add a few tablespoons of water or better a fish fumet made from onion, carrot, celery and chopped fish bones, etc. Brown the bread in the oven and distribute in deep soup plates; distribute the fish and pour over all the fish soup. Sprinkle with parsley. Serves 6 to 8.

EELS IN WHITE WINE

(Anguilla al vino bianco alla marchigiana)

2-pound eel	3 sprigs parsley
½ cup oil	1 bay leaf
A mixture of:	1 sprig thyme
5 tablespoons chopped onion	Salt and pepper
1½ tablespoons chopped	3 tablespoons butter
garlic	2 tablespoons desalted
4 tablespoons dry white wine	anchovy,* mashed
Bouquet garni:	

Skin the eel (or eels); make an incision around the head, lift the skin, and, holding the head with a cloth, strip off the skin in one swift movement. Cut off the fins, eviscerate, chop into 2- to 3-inch lengths; wash and dry.

Pour the oil into a pan and sauté the onion and garlic mixture;

add 2 tablespoons of wine and the bouquet garni, season with salt and pepper and then add the chopped eel. Simmer for 20 minutes, adding water and remaining wine as required. When cooked, remove eel pieces and reserve in a serving dish.

Discard the bouquet garni; remove pan from heat and stir into the pan juices 3 tablespoons of butter and the anchovy. Combine well and allow to cool. Pour the sauce over the eel pieces and serve cold. Serves 6 to 8.

FISH SOUP SAN GIORGIO PORT STYLE

(Brodetto alla maniera di Porto San Giorgio)

1½ cups oil
A mixture of:
   8 tablespoons chopped onion
   5 cloves garlic, chopped
1½ cups vinegar
6 sprigs parsley, chopped
1 pound peeled tomatoes,
   drained
Salt and freshly ground pepper
1 pound squid, well cleaned
   and chopped

1 pound mullet or perch, ready
   to cook
1 pound cod, ready to cook
1 pound halibut, ready to
   cook
1 pound bass, ready to cook
1 pound mixed shellfish,
   shrimps, etc.
24 slices of day-old bread
2 tablespoons chopped
   marjoram

Heat the oil in a large fireproof casserole and bring the onion-garlic mixture to a golden brown; then pour in the vinegar and reduce by ⅘. Add the parsley and tomatoes and season with salt and pepper; bring to the boil for 5 minutes and pour in 1 pint of water. Bring again to the boil, drop in the squids, and continue boiling for 15 minutes.

According to size and cooking time required of the fish (or pieces of fish), add them to the casserole, finishing with the shrimps, which need less than 10 minutes simmering. Meanwhile, sauté the bread in oil, distribute the slices in deep soup bowls, follow with the fish and shellfish. Pour the fish soup liquid over all, sprinkle with marjoram and serve. Serves 12.

VEAL OLIVES PESCARA STYLE

(Olivette di vitello alla pescarese)

2 pounds veal, fillet or noisette
A mixture of:
  ¼ pound prosciutto fat,
    chopped fine
  6 fillets desalted anchovy,*
    chopped fine
  1½ tablespoons chopped
    capers
  2 cloves garlic, chopped fine

2 tablespoons chopped
  parsley
3 tablespoons peeled tomatoes,
  drained
¼ cup bread crumbs
Salt and pepper
1½ tablespoons butter
½ cup oil

Shape up about 15 little slices of veal, about 2 ounces each and flatten them with a cleaver. Combine, in a bowl, the mixture along with the tomatoes, the bread crumbs, a seasoning of salt and pepper, and, finally, the butter. The resultant filling should be dryish and stiff.

Lay out the little slices of veal on the tabletop, sprinkle a little salt and pepper on each, and put in the middle of each a small portion of the prepared filling. Roll them into little tubes and tie securely with white thread. Heat the oil in a large pan, sauté the veal olives over a medium heat. When browned and crisp, serve immediately. Serves 5.

ROAST SUCKLING PIG ASCOLI-PICENO STYLE

(Porchetta di latte ripiena all'ascolana)

20-pound piglet*	½ cup oil
Pig's liver and heart	3 tablespoons flour
¼ pound salt pork, chopped	2 tablespoons salt and 1
1½ tablespoons oil	tablespoon pepper
A little salt and pepper	Oil
A mixture of:	½ cup red wine
5 cloves garlic, chopped	½ cup stock
½ tablespoon chopped	
rosemary	
½ tablespoon chopped fennel	
seeds	

Having eviscerated, cleaned, and washed the suckling pig, reserve the liver, and heart. Chop these latter and sauté them with the salt pork in a frying pan with 1½ tablespoons oil, a little salt and pepper. Transfer this filling to a bowl and combine with the mixture of garlic, rosemary, and fennel seeds.

Combine ½ cup of oil and 3 tablespoons flour and smear on the inside of the piglet; insert the filling and tie securely with a thin string. Rub 2 tablespoons salt and 1 of pepper on the outside of the piglet and put it in a well-oiled pan in a medium oven.

Cook for three hours, basting often with the pan juices; remove from oven when well browned. Reserve ¾ of the pan juices and pour ½ cup of red wine and ½ cup of stock into the remaining pan juices and reduce by ⅔. The meat should be served either very hot or cold; with the sauce served apart. Serves 18.

STUFFED BRAISED BEEF ROLL

(Brasato marchigiano)

2-pound slice beef rump	*Pinch of rosemary*
1½ tablespoons salt and a	*1 clove garlic, chopped*
pinch of pepper	*Salt and pepper*
A mixture of:	*1½ tablespoons flour*
¼ pound salt pork, chopped	*3 tablespoons butter*
3 tablespoons chopped onion	*2 tablespoons oil*
1½ tablespoons chopped	*½ cup strong dry red wine*
carrot	*½ cup stock**
1 tablespoon chopped celery	*Buttered greaseproof paper*

Pound the meat well, season it with 1½ tablespoons salt and a pinch of pepper; spread on it the mixture of salt pork, onion, carrot, celery, the pinch of rosemary, and garlic. Roll and tie the beef with string in such a way that the filling is securely inside; sprinkle a little salt and pepper and the 1½ tablespoons of flour on the outside.

Heat the butter and oil in a pan and brown the beef roll on all sides; pour in the wine and a few tablespoons of stock; bring to the boil, turn down heat, cover pan with greaseproof paper and a lid, and simmer for about two hours, basting every now and then with the pan juices and adding a little stock or water if needed.

When done, remove the string and slice the beef roll; lay out the slices on a warmed serving dish. Simmer the sauce to thicken a little more and pour over the slices. Serve immediately and with vegetables, as desired. Serves 6 to 8.

CASSEROLED PIGEONS STUFFED WITH CHESTNUTS

(Piccioni ripieni di castagne in casserola)

3 pigeons	1 ounce salt pork, sliced thin
Stuffing:	Salt and pepper
18 medium-sized chestnuts	2½ tablespoons butter
4½ tablespoons butter	
1 egg yolk, beaten with pinch	
of salt	

Pluck, eviscerate, and cut off the feet of 3 pigeons, passing them over a flame to remove residual feathers; dry and clean with a cloth.

Stuffing: Peel the chestnuts and give them 25 minutes in boiling water; drain, skin, and pass them through a wire sieve. Transfer this purée to a bowl, adding 2 tablespoons butter, the egg yolk beaten with a pinch of salt, and combine.

To stuff: Stuff the pigeons with this mixture and truss up with string, at the same time affixing a slice of salt pork to each pigeon breast. Sprinkle the birds with a little salt and pepper and smear with 2½ tablespoons of butter.

Smear a casserole with the remaining butter and cook the pigeons in it for 25 minutes in a moderate preheated oven. Remove from oven; cut each pigeon into two lengthwise and transfer to a serving dish. Pour the pan juices over them and serve. Serves 6.

RABBIT WITH SALAME AND WILD FENNEL

(Coniglio con salame e finocchio selvatico)

1 medium-sized rabbit, young	½ cup oil
and plump	3 tablespoons chopped ham
1½ tablespoons salt	2 ounces lean salt pork,
½ pound fresh green fennel	chopped
4 cloves garlic, bruised	2 ounces salame, chopped

Skin the rabbit, eviscerate (reserve the liver and heart), remove feet and wash well inside and out: dry with a cloth and sprinkle with 1½ tablespoons of salt.

Wash the fennel, discard the flower and seeds, and chop the green leaves. Put the rabbit, the fennel, and the garlic in a casserole with plenty of water; bring to the boil and simmer for one hour.

After the first half hour, discard the garlic; remove the rabbit and reserve. Drain the fennel leaves, transferring the cooking liquid to another casserole; squeeze the fennel leaves in a colander to remove excess liquid and reserve. Replace the rabbit in the cooking liquids and continue simmering for the other half hour. Then drain, cool and reserve. Reserve also the cooking liquid.

Heat ¼ cup of oil in a pan, add the ham, the salt pork, the salame, and the reserved fennel all chopped together; sauté together for a few seconds, mixing with a wooden spoon. Chop the rabbit's liver and heart and add to the mixture. Stuff the abdomen of the rabbit with this mixture and sew up the opening with a white thread.

Put the rabbit in a pan, pour over the remaining oil (more if necessary) and put into a medium oven. Baste as soon as it begins to brown, adding also a little of the rabbit's cooking liquid as required; simmer for about one more hour. Serve when well browned and cooked through. Serves 4 to 6.

QUAILS AND RISOTTO ANCONA STYLE

(Quaglie con risotto all'anconetana)

12 plump quails	Salt and pepper
1½ cups butter	½ cup dry white wine
6 ounces prosciutto fat and	½ cup stock*
lean, chopped	1 generous cup rice, cleaned
2 bay leaves, crumbled	with cloth, not washed
1 sprig thyme, chopped	¼ cup grated Parmesan

Pluck the quails, remove feet and eviscerate; wash and dry them well with a cloth. Heat 6 tablespoons of butter in a large pan and brown the ham. Add the birds, sprinkling with bay leaf, the thyme and a little salt and pepper; turn up heat. Sauté the quails for a minute or two; pour in the wine and reduce it by half. Turn down the heat, cover the pan, and simmer for about 10 minutes. If the pan liquids dry out too much, add a little meat stock. When cooked, reserve and keep warm.

Meanwhile, boil the rice in lightly salted boiling water; drain when al dente (about 20 minutes), season with the remaining butter and the Parmesan. Transfer the rice to a warmed serving dish, lay the quails on top and pour over the pan juices. Serves 6.

SWEET PEPPERS COUNTRY STYLE

(Peperoni casalinghi alla marchigiana)

6 green sweet peppers	*Salt and pepper*
2 tablespoons chopped onion	*5 tablespoons finely chopped*
1 tablespoon lard	*salt pork*

Char the sweet peppers on the grill and plunge them into cold water: peel, seed, and cut into pieces, and wash them well.

Sauté the onion in a pan with the lard; when golden, add the sweet-pepper pieces and season with salt and pepper. Turn down heat, cover the pan, and simmer till done; a few minutes before removing from the heat, add 5 tablespoons of salt pork and mix in well. Remove from heat only when the salt pork is cooked. Serves 6.

SWEET CASTAGNOLE

(Castagnole marchigiane)

¾ pound superfine sugar
1¼ cups oil
1 cup Mistrà (dry aniseed-
based liqueur 85 proof)
or anisette

Salt
Sifted flour
Oil for deep-frying

Mix the sugar, the oil, the liqueur, and the salt in a large bowl. Then add, a little at a time, flour and combine until a light, hard dough is obtained.

Put this dough on a tabletop dusted with flour, and continue kneading it with the palms of the hands, rolling the dough out into little 1-inch-diameter cylinders; cut these into 1-inch lengths. Traditionally, a cross is incised on each castagnola with a knife.

Heat the oil (but not to smoking) and sauté the castagnole over a moderate heat till golden; drain and cool. Serves 8 to 10.

Rome and Lazio

Lazio, the province of Rome, offers a wide variety, not only of dishes, but of styles of cooking; it is, perhaps, the most generous cuisine of all Italy. This is really not surprising; Rome is Rome and the world had knocked on its door for centuries. However, on the whole, the food is simple and even inexpensive provided that olive oil, wine, Pecorino cheese, and young vegetables (such as peas, artichokes, lettuce, and sweet peppers) are reasonably priced.

The traditional Roman cooking tends to rather heavy dishes such as steamed leg of calf with yellow peppers; oxtail cooked with pine nuts and pork rind; tomatoes stuffed with rice; beef stew and lentils; and tripe and other variety meats cooked in all manner of ways, but rarely with a light hand. Though these dishes are to be found in the old Roman quarters, there is also another style born of the cooks (and there are seemingly thousands of them) who hail from the Abruzzi region and chiefly from the town of Amatrice in the hills behind Rome. Though it is almost impossible to find a dividing line between the cooking styles, this Abruzzi-style makes much of lamb, chicken, game birds, and aromatic herbs.

Lamb and chicken are Rome's forte: they are usually roasted (often on the spit) or fricasséed as a spezzatino with wine or vinegar *alla cacciatora* or *alla diavola*. Here, perhaps, are the recipes which are most easy for further cross-pollination with the repertoires of other lands; chicken alla romana (casseroled with red and yellow sweet peppers) should be included, too.

One of the deeper loves of the Romans is for artichokes: these are cooked in many ways from being stuffed and steamed to being deep-fried *alla giudea,* i.e., in Jewish style. Jewish cooking is deeply embedded in Roman culinary tradition and though there has been an inevitable cross-pollination over the centuries, much remains which is apparently unchanged. However they are cooked, Roman artichokes are picked so young that one can eat them in their entirety, or at least there are only a few leaves too tough to eat.

Rome is also a pasta-loving land; *alla carbonara* is the most essentially Roman of all sauces and it is surprising that this recipe has not swept the Western world since it is based on such old favorites as eggs, bacon and pepper. Spaghetti *all'olio e aglio* (oil and garlic), however, is already spreading as an international midnight party snack, while Rome's famous *fettuccine al burro* (egg pasta and butter), as made by an expert chef, is hard to emulate due to its many subtleties—the ripeness of the Parmesan, the freshness of the homemade pasta, the softness of the butter and a perfection of timing; but *fettuccine al burro* even made *alla buona* (just as it comes—even with dried pasta) is always an enjoyable dish.

Rome also has a river, called the Tiber, which used to offer, before pollution set in, little sardinelike fish. But the Tyrrhenian Sea is not far away: Lazio and Rome, therefore, have a range of fish dishes which is extensive. Roast dentex (bass) is the grandest, but for reasons of economy and also fear of tainted fish (an ever-present risk in high summer), the Romans enjoy seafood hors d'oeuvres, which, once chopped, cooked, and preserved in oil are absolutely safe and also inexpensive.

Perhaps the most distinctive characteristic of Lazio dishes is their modesty; the Roman rarely has any taste for pomposity either in his way of life or his food. A real Roman salad, for example, such as any prince or millionaire would go out of his way to eat, is not costly; it consists of local products, some of which even grow wild. One buys, from old crones in the market, a few handfuls of *misticanza* which is a mysterious mixture of the tenderest of lettuce shoots (two days old, perhaps) and edible wild leaves, some of which are bitter and all of which offer new flavors to awaken one's palate: spaghetti-thin wild asparagus also is much loved as is *puntarelle,* a sort of poor man's asparagus which is eaten with a lively sauce of anchovies, garlic and oil.

Equally, using a complicated salad dressing or mayonnaise is frowned on, and with such delicacies as *misticanza* or wild asparagus it would be a desecration. In fact, Romans use only olive oil, with perhaps a squeeze of lemon, on all salads. This penchant for olive oil, preferably not too light from overrefining, is indulged also with all boiled food, whether chicken, beef, fish, vegetables or what you will, either hot or cold, along with a pinch of salt and pepper.

The Frascati white wines of the Alban Hills outside Rome need no introduction to the world; however, Lazio's viticulture has wider and even more rewarding offerings. The Est! Est! Est! from Lake Bolsena is a dry white, which ages well; the Cesanese del Piglio (a Roman favorite) from the Fiuggi area south of the city offers both reds and whites of robust character and high quality (the reds age very well); and there are the Velletri and Viterbo whites which no Roman (or anybody else who appreciates an honest dry white) would spurn.

Sauces

    ROMAN "SUGO FINTO"   210
    (Sugo finto alla romana)

Antipasti

    MOUNTAIN HAM AND FIGS   210
    (Prosciutto crudo di montagna e fichi)

    GARLIC TOAST   211
    (Bruschetta alla laziale)

Soups

    STRACCIATELLA BROTH   211
    (Stracciatella)

Entrées

Meats

Vegetables

Desserts

ROMAN "SUGO FINTO"

(Sugo finto alla romana)

4 tablespoons chopped ham fat
1 clove garlic, crushed
1 tablespoon oil
A mixture of:
    2 sprigs chopped parsley
    2 sprigs chopped marjoram
¼ pound onions, sliced
1 small carrot, chopped

1 stalk celery, chopped
1 tablespoon dried chopped
    mushrooms, soaked*
1 clove
Salt and pepper
½ cup dry white wine
2 pounds peeled tomatoes,
    drained
Salt

Sauté the ham fat and the garlic in a pan with the oil till golden brown. Add the parsley and marjoram, the onions, carrot, celery, and the mushrooms, seasoned with the clove and a pinch of salt and pepper.

Cook together for a few moments to allow the mixture to color and then add the wine; evaporate the wine almost completely and add the tomatoes and season with salt. Cover the pan, and allow to simmer for an hour, adding a little water if necessary. Before serving, pass the sauce through a sieve. Makes 2 cups.

MOUNTAIN HAM AND FIGS

(Prosciutto crudo di montagna e fichi)

¾ pound prosciutto or a strong-flavored country ham
18 ripe figs

Slice the ham very thin and transfer to a serving dish. Peel the figs and transfer to a bowl; place this bowl in another bowl half full of crushed ice. Serve when the figs are chilled. Serves 6.

GARLIC TOAST

(Bruschetta alla laziale)

Italian or French bread	*Freshly ground pepper*
Garlic	*Olive oil (preferably not an*
Salt	*overly refined oil)*

Cut 4 slices of bread, not too thin, and toast them: while still hot, rub them with a peeled and bruised garlic clove to impregnate them well with the garlic flavor. Put them for a minute in a hot oven; then transfer them to a serving dish, season with salt and freshly ground pepper and sprinkle generously with good olive oil. Serves 2.

STRACCIATELLA BROTH

(Stracciatella)

*5 pints meat stock**	*2 tablespoons grated Parmesan*
4 eggs	*2 tablespoons chopped parsley*
4 tablespoons semolina (or	*½ teaspoon salt*
flour)	*Grating of nutmeg*

Having prepared the stock, put aside 1 cup and bring the remainder to the boil. In the meantime, put the eggs into a bowl with the semolina, the Parmesan, the parsley, the salt, and the nutmeg; add the cold stock slowly and combine the mixture with the aid of a wire whisk. Pour the mixture into the boiling stock, reduce to a simmer, and stir well for 4 minutes. More grated Parmesan may be served at table. Serves 6 to 8.

BEAN SOUP WITH BEET TOPS

(Zuppa di fagioli con le bietole)

1 pound white navy beans
1 pound beet tops (the green
leaves of beets) or spinach
A mixture:
½ cup lard
¼ onion
1 clove garlic
3 sprigs parsley

¼ pound peeled tomatoes,
drained
2 tablespoons salt
1 teaspoon freshly ground
pepper
24 slices toast, small

Having soaked the beans for twelve hours and washed them in running water, bring them to the boil in plenty of lightly salted water and then simmer for one and a half hours until tender; drain and reserve both beans and cooking water. Meanwhile, remove the stalks and wash the green vegetables thoroughly. (If the leaves are young, it is sufficient to put them in a pot with a tablespoon of butter and the water that clings to the leaves and cook over a fairly high heat for 5 minutes, tightly covered, turning the green vegetables once or twice to aid the cooking process.) Older spinach or beet tops should be boiled in plenty of lightly salted water for 5 minutes. Drain immediately and press in a colander to remove excess liquid. Reserve 2 quarts of cooking liquid from the vegetables (should they be old).

Brown the mixture of onion, garlic, and parsley in the lard (add a tablespoon of oil, if you like a thick soup), then add the tomato. Stir well for a few minutes and add the beet tops and continue stirring. Add the navy beans and a sufficient quantity of the liquid which was reserved from the cooking of the beans and the beet tops. Season with salt and pepper.

Simmer gently for 10 minutes or so. Place the toast in the soup plates and pour the soup over it. Serves 8.

EASTER BROTH ROMAN STYLE

(Brodetto pasquale alla romana)

2 pounds beef (boned rump or round)
2 pounds breast of lamb (boned)
6 quarts cold water
1 small onion stuck with 2 cloves
1 small carrot
1 stalk celery
3 sprigs parsley
1 tablespoon coarse salt
6 egg yolks
1 cup grated Parmesan
Juice of 1 lemon
1 cup stock
Pinch of white pepper
1 tablespoon chopped marjoram
24 slices of bread, browned in the oven

Put the meat in a large fireproof pot with 6 quarts of water and bring to the boil over a moderate heat. Remove the scum as soon as it comes to the surface. Add the onion, carrot, celery, parsley, and a tablespoon coarse salt and reduce the flame to a simmer for two hours or so. After about one and a half hours the lamb will be cooked; after another half hour (or so) the beef, too. Reserve these meats in a pot with a little of the cooking liquid and keep warm. Pour the rest of the stock into a casserole, straining it at the same time; reduce it quickly to about 2 quarts.

Beat the egg yolks in a bowl with 2 tablespoons of grated Parmesan and the juice of the lemon. Add 1 cup of stock, mix well and—off the heat—pour this mixture into the soup, stirring vigorously. Replace the pot on a low heat and, stirring with a wooden spoon, simmer for 5 minutes till the soup has thickened. Add the white pepper, extra salt to taste, and the marjoram. Serve the soup in bowls, directly, in which the toast has already been distributed. The meat is served as a main course separately. Serves 6 to 8.

SPAGHETTI CARBONARA

(Spaghetti alla carbonara)

1¼ pounds spaghetti	*6 eggs*
Salt	*3½ tablespoons grated*
Sauce:	*Parmesan*
6 ounces lean salt pork,	*Salt and black pepper*
diced	*3 tablespoons heavy cream*
1 tablespoon oil	*3 tablespoons butter*

Cook the spaghetti in plenty of boiling lightly salted water; drain when al dente and transfer to a warmed pan and reserve.

In the meantime, sauté the salt pork in oil in a pan and beat the eggs in a bowl, mixing into the eggs, the cheese, a pinch of salt, plenty of black pepper, and the heavy cream.

Heat the butter in a large pan; as soon as it begins to brown, toss in the egg mixture, and as soon as this begins to show signs of setting, quickly toss in the spaghetti and the sautéed salt pork. Remove from heat: mix well and serve. Serves 6.

NOTE: It is essential to have the spaghetti drained, hot, and ready to pour over the egg mixture at the moment the eggs begin to set.

PASTA WITH GARLIC, OIL, AND HOT RED PEPPERS ROMAN STYLE

(Linguine con aglio, olio e peperoncino alla romana)

1¼ pounds linguine (or	*2 cloves garlic, crushed*
trenette)	*½ inch peperoncino (or*
Salt	*red pepper)*
½ cup oil	*2 tablespoons chopped parsley*

Cook the pasta in lightly salted boiling water until al dente; drain and transfer to a warmed serving dish or bowl.

Meanwhile, put the oil, the garlic, and the peperoncino (or

red pepper) in a little saucepan and heat till the garlic colors golden; pour this mixture over the pasta, sprinkle over the chopped parsley, and mix well. Serves 6.

PASTA WITH HOT RED PEPPER SAUCE

(Penne all'arrabbiata)

1½ pounds penne (short, thick macaroni)	2 cloves garlic, crushed
Salt	Plenty of hot red peppers
Sauce:	1 pound peeled tomatoes, strained
8 ounces lean salt pork, diced	Salt
1 finely chopped onion	1 cup (scant) Parmesan, grated

Cook the pasta in plenty of lightly salted boiling water; drain when al dente. Meantime, sauté together in a pan the salt pork, the onion, the garlic till they are golden. Remove the garlic and throw away. Add the hot red peppers to taste, followed by the tomatoes and a pinch or two of salt. Cook on a high heat for a minute or two, turn down heat, and simmer till the sauce thickens. Remove the pasta from its cooking pot and strain: and pour into the pan with the sauce for ½ a minute, stirring, and mixing in half of the Parmesan. Pass to a serving dish, sprinkle over remaining Parmesan and serve. Serves 6 to 8.

LINGUINE WITH ANCHOVIES AND TOMATO SAUCE

(Linguine con acciughe e pomodoro)

1¼ pounds linguine (or spaghetti)	3 ounces desalted anchovy* fillets, mashed
Salt	1 pound peeled tomatoes, drained
Sauce:	Salt
½ cup oil	2½ tablespoons chopped parsley
2 cloves garlic, crushed	
1 small piece of dried red pepper, or pinch paprika	

Cook the pasta in plenty of lightly salted boiling water until al dente. Drain and put it in a big warmed bowl.

Sauce: While the pasta is cooking, prepare the sauce. Put the oil, the garlic and the pepper in a pan; as soon as the garlic browns, add the anchovy and, immediately afterward, the tomatoes with a little salt. Bring to the boil and simmer for 10 minutes. Pour the sauce over the pasta, sprinkle on the parsley, mix, and serve immediately. Serves 6.

LINGUINE WITH TUNA AND TOMATO SAUCE

(Linguine con tonno)

This recipe, in principle, is identical with that for linguine with anchovies and tomato sauce, except that the anchovies are replaced by 5 ounces of canned tuna in oil.

BUCATINI AMATRICE STYLE

(Bucatini alla matriciana)

Sauce:
  ¼ pound lean salt pork (or bacon), coarsely chopped
  ½ cup oil
  2½ tablespoons finely chopped onion
  Pinch freshly ground red pepper
6 ounces peeled tomatoes, drained
Salt
1¼ pound bucatini (or macaroni)
1 scant cup grated Pecorino cheese (or Parmesan)

Sauce: Sauté the lean salt pork (or bacon) in smoking oil over a lively flame in a frying pan; reserve and keep warm. In the same fat and in the same frying pan, sauté the onion and the pepper; when the onion becomes translucent, add the tomato and a little salt, mix well, and cook for 8 to 10 minutes. Add the salt pork and simmer till sauce thickens.

While the sauce is cooking, sprinkle the bucatini (broken in half—about 4 inches long) into plenty of lightly salted boiling water. Drain when al dente and put in a warmed deep serving bowl; add 3 tablespoons grated Pecorino and mix till melted and then add the sauce. Serve immediately and serve the remaining grated cheese at table. A real matriciana sauce should be only lightly colored with tomato. Serves 6.

BUCATINI GRICIANA STYLE

(Bucatini alla gricia)

(Near Amatrice—from which the adjective "matriciana" is derived—is the town of Griciana, where the bucatini are prepared in the same way as in bucatini Amatrice style, except that the tomato is omitted.)

SQUIDS AND ARTICHOKES ROMAN STYLE

(Calamari con carciofi alla romana)

½ cup oil	Salt and pepper
2 cloves garlic, crushed	6 artichoke hearts
3 pounds squids, ready to cook and cut in strips	

Pour 2 tablespoons of oil into a pan and brown the crushed garlic. Add the squid strips and allow to flavor over a low heat. After 2 or 3 minutes, season with salt and cover them with water and a lid and continue to cook over a low heat.

Meanwhile, having cleaned and quartered the artichoke hearts, put them in a frying pan with the rest of the oil, seasoned with a little salt and pepper; sauté them over a medium heat, turning them often with a wooden spoon. When done, put the artichokes into the pan where the squid strips are cooking; mix together for a few minutes over a low heat and serve hot. Serves 6 to 8.

TUNA FILLETS MARINATED AND FRIED

(Palombo alla laziale)

2 eggs	A mixture of:
Salt	¼ onion, chopped
12 fillets fresh tuna, ½ inch	3 cloves garlic, chopped
thick	1 sprig parsley, chopped
½ cup dry white wine	2 tablespoons bread crumbs
½ cup dry red wine	Pinch of pepper and salt
½ scant cup grated Parmesan	Plenty of oil for frying
	3 lemons, quartered

Beat the two eggs and add some salt; pass the tuna fillets in the beaten egg, place them in a pan and cover with the two wines: marinate for 45 minutes.

Mix the grated Parmesan, the mixture of onion, garlic, parsley, bread crumbs, a pinch of salt and a little pepper in a bowl. Then drain the fillets, one by one, carefully, and dip them in the mixture and sauté in smoking oil. Drain them when they are golden brown and crisp; serve with a quarter lemon each. Serves 6.

SALT COD ROMAN STYLE

(Baccalà in guazzetto alla romana)

2 pounds salt cod (baccalà),*	Salt (if necessary) and pepper
ready to cook and chopped	1 sprig parsley, chopped
into 2 ounce chunks	1 tablespoon seeded raisins,
Flour	well cleaned
Oil for sautéing	1 tablespoon pine nuts
3 cloves garlic	
2 pounds peeled tomatoes,	
drained	

Wash the baccalà well, cut into chunks, dry them and dust them in flour. Then sauté them lightly in smoking oil in a frying pan; reserve and keep hot.

Crush the garlic (this can be replaced with 1 cup chopped onion) and brown with the remaining oil in the frying pan at a moderate heat. Add the tomatoes, plenty of freshly ground pepper, salt if needed, and cook for 10 minutes. Then add the parsley and the raisins and pine nuts (these last two are not essential) and continue cooking slowly for a few minutes. Arrange the pieces of dried cod on a serving dish and pour the sauce over them. Serves 6 to 8.

ARTICHOKE FRITTATA ROMAN STYLE

(Frittata coi carciofi alla romana)

4 tablespoons lard	6 fresh eggs
2 artichoke hearts, quartered	1 tablespoon chopped parsley
1 tablespoon salt and a pinch	
of pepper	

Heat lard in a pan, allow to dissolve; add the artichoke hearts, seasoned with 1 level tablespoon salt, a pinch of pepper and cook till tender, pouring over a little water when necessary to prevent their drying out.

Beat the eggs with the parsley and pour into the pan, mixing the ingredients with a wooden spoon. Serves 3.

OXTAIL VACCINARA

(Coda di bue alla vaccinara con sedano)

3 pounds oxtail
1 tablespoon coarse salt
1 carrot
1 leek
1 bay leaf
1 sprig thyme
A mixture of:
  ¼ pound prosciutto (the fat
    and lean), diced
  1 onion, chopped
  3 sprigs marjoram (or
    parsley)

2 tablespoons oil
1 cup dry white wine
1 pound peeled tomatoes,
  drained
1 tablespoon salt and pinch of
  pepper
Grating of nutmeg
2 pounds celery hearts
1 tablespoon pine nuts
1 tablespoon seeded raisins
Pinch cinnamon

Clean the oxtail well, chop into 8 chunks and soak in plenty of cold water for four hours: then put it in a casserole, covered with water, and bring to the boil for 10 minutes and drain. Clean out the casserole well and replace the oxtail pieces in 2½ quarts of cold water and 1 tablespoon of coarse salt. Bring to the boil, skim off the scum which comes to the top, and add the carrot, the leek, the bay leaf, and the sprig of thyme. Simmer for three hours, and reserve both oxtail and cooking water.

In another casserole put the prosciutto, onion, and marjoram along with the oil, and heat till golden brown. Add to this mixture the pieces of oxtail, which have been well drained and dried, the wine, the tomatoes, 1 tablespoon salt, some pepper and a grating of nutmeg. Continue simmering for another hour, reducing the liquid and until the meat begins to come off the bone.

During this long simmering, if the pan juices become too thick, add a little of the liquid in which the oxtail was boiled.

Meanwhile, boil the celery hearts in lightly salted water for 10 minutes. About 10 minutes before the oxtail is cooked, add these celery hearts (chopped coarsely) along with the pine nuts, the raisins and the cinnamon to the oxtail pot. Pour the whole into a deep tureen and serve very hot. Serves 8.

SALTIMBOCCA ROMAN STYLE

(Saltimbocca alla romana)

1½ pounds veal fillet or
*   noisette*
Salt and pepper
12 sage leaves, preferably fresh
12 slices prosciutto (fat and
*   lean)*

Flour
6 tablespoons butter
½ cup dry white wine

Cut the veal into 12 equal slices and pound each lightly and trim. Lay out on the table and season each slice with a little salt and pepper and place a sage leaf on each. Then put a slice of ham on each and roll them into cylinders, securing each with a wooden toothpick. Dust lightly in flour.

Heat 4 tablespoons of butter in a pan and add the saltimbocca; turn up the heat and sauté till golden. Remove toothpicks and transfer to a warmed serving dish.

Pour the wine into the pan juices and reduce almost completely over a lively heat. Stirring with a wooden spoon, add the remaining butter to make a sauce. Pour this over the saltimbocca and serve immediately. Serves 6.

LAMB CACCIATORA (HUNTERS STYLE)

(Abbacchio all'aceto o alla cacciatora)

3 pounds lamb (either leg or
*   shoulder) in 1-ounce*
*   chunks*
3 cloves garlic
4 fillets desalted anchovy*
1 cup wine vinegar

1 tablespoon oil (or lard, if
*   preferred)*
Flour
3 sprigs rosemary, tied with
*   white thread*
Salt and freshly ground pepper

Wash and dry the chunks of lamb well. Pound the garlic with the anchovy fillets in a mortar and combine with the vinegar.

Heat the oil or lard (or half and half) in a frying pan and, having lightly dusted the chunks of lamb in flour, put them and the rosemary in the pan and sauté on a high flame; remove before they are cooked through. Discard the rosemary and sprinkle the lamb with salt and pepper. Add the garlic, anchovy, and vinegar to the pan mixture and reduce by half over a high heat. Then, dropping the temperature to a simmer, add the lamb for a further 10 to 15 minutes, stirring often. Serve very hot. Serves 6 to 8.

ROAST LAMB TRASTEVERE STYLE

(Agnello arrostito nel forno alla trasteverina)

2½-pound leg of lamb
3 cloves garlic, split lengthwise
4 sprigs rosemary
2½ tablespoons salt and a
   pinch of pepper

½ cup lard
¾ pound potatoes, peeled and
   cut in wedges

Wash and dry the lamb well; pierce it and insert the garlic and rosemary. Truss up the meat so that it keeps its shape, and sprinkle it with salt and pepper. Then, having larded a fireproof dish, lard well also the lamb and the potatoes: put them both in the fireproof dish in a moderate oven for 40 to 50 minutes. Remove from oven, cut string, put on a serving dish and garnish with the roast potatoes. Serves 4 to 6.

CHICKEN CASSEROLE WITH MUSHROOMS AND TOMATOES

(Spezzatino di pollo con funghi e pomodoro alla romana)

2-pound chicken,* ready to cook
2 tablespoons oil
10 ounces chopped fresh
    mushrooms*
Salt
5 tablespoons butter

2 tablespoons chopped onion
Salt and pepper
1 cup dry white wine, mixed
    with a shot of brandy
½ pound peeled tomatoes,
    drained and sieved

Cut chicken into 10 pieces in the following manner. Split the legs in two, cut the breast and wings into three pieces and the carcass into three pieces.

Heat the oil to smoking in a frying pan, toss in the mushrooms, season with a little salt, and cook for 10 minutes; remove with a slotted spoon and reserve.

Heat the butter in a casserole and brown the onion; then add the chicken pieces, seasoned with salt and pepper. Cook over a moderate heat for 20 minutes; remove with a slotted spoon and reserve with the mushrooms.

Pour the wine and brandy mixture into the chicken pan juices and reduce it almost completely; add the tomatoes, a few tablespoons of water, and a pinch of salt. Simmer for a further 20 minutes, then replace the chicken and the mushrooms and cook all together for 5 minutes or so. Serves 4 to 6.

CHICKEN SAUTÉ CACCIATORA (HUNTERS STYLE)

(Spezzatino di pollo alla cacciatora)

2-pound chicken,* ready to cook
2 tablespoons salt and a pinch
    of pepper
1 cup butter
1 cup oil
10 ounces fresh mushrooms,*
    cleaned and sliced

2½ tablespoons finely chopped
    onion
1 tablespoon flour
½ cup dry white wine
½ cup stock*
1 cup peeled tomatoes, drained
2½ tablespoons chopped parsley

Cut the chicken into 1-ounce chunks and sprinkle with 2 table-spoons salt and a pinch of pepper. Heat 3 tablespoons of butter and 3 tablespoons of oil in a pan and sauté the chicken pieces. As soon as they are browned on all sides, remove the wings and the breast, leaving the legs to cook a little more. Reserve the wings and breast in a heated casserole; when the legs are cooked, add them to the same casserole.

Add the remaining oil and butter to the pan juices along with the sliced mushrooms, and sauté them over a lively flame; then add the onion, stirring, followed by a sprinkle of flour to obtain a rich color. Finally, pour in the wine, the stock, and the tomatoes and, stirring, bring to the boil. After 8 to 10 minutes simmering, add the pieces of chicken, which have been reserved, and simmer (covered) for another 7 or 8 minutes.

Put the chicken pieces on a serving dish; quickly reduce the remaining pan juices to a cup of sauce and pour over the chicken, sprinkling the chopped parsley over all. Serves 4 to 6.

TURKEY FILLETS EMPEROR NERO STYLE

(Filetti di tacchino alla nerone)

6 big turkey fillets, trimmed
    and lightly flattened
Salt and pepper
2 cups bread crumbs
5 tablespoons butter

3 bay leaves
½ cup brandy
¾ pound potatoes, peeled and
    cut in wedges
1 cup oil

Sprinkle the turkey fillets with salt and pepper and dip them in bread crumbs; heat the butter in a pan, add the bay leaves, and sauté the turkey fillets till golden on both sides. Turn down the flame, remove the bay leaves, and cook the fillets for 3 minutes more on both sides. Remove the fillets and keep hot. Pour the brandy into the pan and mix with the pan juices, reducing it by half; then, having ignited the brandy, pour the flaming sauce over the turkey fillets; serve instantly.

In the meantime, the potatoes, cut in wedges, should have been fried in oil; serve hot, along with the turkey. Serves 6.

TURKEY "BRODETTATO" ROMAN STYLE

(Gallinaccio brodettato alla romana)

3-pound turkey, cut into regular
    chunks
2 tablespoons salt and a pinch
    of pepper
Flour
1 cup lard
¼ pound prosciutto (the fat
    and the lean), cut in strips

2½ tablespoons chopped onion
½ cup dry white wine
3 egg yolks
2½ tablespoons marjoram and
    parsley, chopped together
Juice of ½ lemon

Wash and dry the chunks of turkey; sprinkle them with 2 tablespoons of salt and a pinch of pepper and dip them lightly in flour.

Heat the lard in a frying pan and add the turkey chunks, moving them around in the pan to prevent the flour sticking to the bottom of the pan. Then add the ham and onion, bringing the mixture to a golden brown.

At this point, pour in the wine and reduce it by ⅔ over a low flame, stirring continuously to prevent sticking; then pour in sufficient water to cover the turkey pieces. Bring to a boil, turn down heat and simmer for about 40 minutes, adding a little water, if required.

Meanwhile, mix the egg yolks, the chopped marjoram and parsley with the lemon juice and, just before serving, mix these into the turkey pan juices and remove immediately from the direct heat, but keeping on the corner of the stove so that the egg yolks reach the necessary condition for binding the sauce. Serves 6 to 8.

SPINACH ROMAN STYLE

(Spinaci alla romana)

2½ pounds spinach	½ cup pine nuts
Salt	½ cup seeded raisins, softened
2 cloves garlic, crushed	in hot water 5 minutes
½ cup oil	
¼ pound prosciutto (fat and	
lean), cut in short strips	

Remove the stalks from the spinach and wash thoroughly in running water. Cook in a little fast-boiling, lightly salted water for 10 minutes, drain, and press spinach in colander to remove excess water.

Brown the crushed garlic in a frying pan with smoking oil, adding the ham, allowing them to cook together for a few seconds. Then add the spinach and mix well together, adding after a few minutes the pine nuts and raisins, which should also be mixed in well. Continue simmering over a low heat for 5 minutes and serve hot. Serves 6 to 8.

RICOTTA CHEESE TART

(Crostata di ricotta)

3½ cups sifted flour
5 tablespoons lard
5 tablespoons butter
1 pound superfine sugar
5 egg yolks
2 eggs
2 tablespoons chopped candied
 fruit
¼ cup brandy
1½ pounds fresh ricotta cheese,
 sieved

Grated peel of ¼ orange (no
 pith)
Grated peel of ¼ lemon (no
 pith)
2 ounces raisins
3 tablespoons pine nuts
Pinch of powdered cinnamon
Lard, melted
1 egg, beaten with a few drops
 warm water
Vanilla-flavored sugar

Make a dough (using as little flour as possible), combining the lard and butter, 5 ounces of superfine sugar, 2 egg yolks, and 1 egg. Allow this dough to rest for a half hour, wrapped in a cloth.

Marinate the candied fruit in brandy and reserve. Combine, in a mixing bowl, the ricotta, the remaining sugar, an egg, 3 egg yolks, the grated orange and lemon peel, the raisins, the pine nuts, the cinnamon, and the candied fruit, discarding the brandy marinade. Work the mixture with a fork until a smooth paste is obtained.

Roll out into dough sheets, cutting one 10-inch (approx.) diameter round for lining a baking pan. Grease the pan with melted lard and lay the dough in it. Add the ricotta-cheese mixture. Cut the remaining dough into strips and decorate the top of the tart with them in the usual criss-cross manner and with the usual border. Lightly brush the border and strips of dough with beaten egg; transfer the pan to a moderate oven. The pastry strips, after a half hour, will begin to brown; at that time remove the pan from the oven and allow to cool. Remove from pan with care and sprinkle with vanilla-flavored sugar.

Abruzzi and Molise

The Abruzzi and Molise region is mountainous and, throughout history, life there has been very hard. Not only has nature been ungenerous but this mountain region has always been an outpost which too often changed governmental hands and always to the detriment of the population which first took comfort in religion and then in emigration.

Only today, with the construction of new autostradas and superhighways and the opening of many winter sports centers (mostly only a few hours drive from Rome) has a hope of the good life reached this long-lost land.

Agriculturally, the Abruzzi and Molise have the poorest and least fertile land of all Italy: in the highlands, there are forests inhabited by brown bears, chamois, and deer. Below that, there is pasture land for cattle and sheep, followed—and particularly in the Molise Adriatic Coast area—by some hard-grain wheat, potato, bean, and maize production. Unlike the Marches, not even tenacious hard work is sufficient to drag a decent living out of this unkind soil.

Its two major cities, however, are something of a surprise. L'Aquila (the Eagle), perched high in the mountains, is a most elegant, historic, and beautiful city full of vivacity and movement, yet one only reaches it after miles and miles of mountain scenery without human habitation.

Pescara, the second city, is a seaport on the Adriatic and a boom town without notable charm, but bursting with energy. This latter's vigor, perhaps is the result of the endemic malaria of the area having been finally disposed of some twenty years ago and the considerable investment made in light industry and in food processing in particular.

For the rest, there are gaunt mountains, soil erosion and wild flowers which incidentally, include large quantities of medicinal herbs such as gentian, arnica, valerian, and belladonna. There is vine growing of a limited nature; the chalky soil is not ideal and the wine is not among the greatest in Italy. However, it is not a wine to ignore and with greater investment and oenological study perhaps the Cerasuola d'Abruzzo may reach national status. There is also a Corfinio white from the Adriatic Coast and a Chieti red, both of which are not without their charms and good qualities.

Gastronomically, one can say that the prospects are sober, simple, yet savory. The meat, whether beef, pork, or chicken, is raised in the open air rather than industrially; it consequently does not lack flavor. There are country cheeses in abundance, especially Pecorino made from ewes' milk. One of the luxuries of the mountain people is roast suckling pig, but more often they settle for stewed mutton, which is less fascinating.

The major contribution in the world of pasta is macaroni *alla chitarra* (guitar)—simple fresh pasta sheets, which have been laid onto a sort of horizontal little harp and passed through it so as to cut the sheets into square instead of round spaghetti. This is usually served with lamb sauce* or with Amatriciana sauce.*

Amatrice, a small hill town, is gastronomically speaking the nub of the Abruzzi; it is the fountainhead of thousands of good cooks. You will find Amatrice cooks in Rome everywhere, on transatlantic liners and in hotels throughout Italy and Europe. The Amatrice chef is no specialist; he is usually quite at home in Tuscan and Umbrian cuisine; Roman cooking he learns at his father's knee and pizza-making soon becomes second nature. After that, it depends on his individual talent whether he stays in a Roman trattoria or climbs the ladder of success; and many do. But the Amatrice cook, for himself, would prefer a menu of say, some *bruschetta*, a light, homemade pasta with a lamb sauce (or perhaps pasta in broth), a few grilled lamb chops (or better a young kid), a game bird sautéed with plenty of aromatic herbs, a Roman *misticanza* salad and a fresh ricotta cheese pie. But he is always open-minded and versatile: if you ask him for a Florentine minestrone, duck and olives, and a gâteau St. Honoré, he will just as happily cook it.

LAMB SAUCE

(Salsa d'agnello)

3 tablespoons lard
3 pounds lamb (shoulder,
    neck, and/or breast),
    chopped into chunks
Salt
1 teaspoon powdered hot red
    pepper (peperoncino)
2 tablespoons oil

¼ pound mushrooms, cleaned
    and chopped*
2½ tablespoons chopped onion
½ cup dry white wine
1 tablespoon flour
2 pounds peeled tomatoes,
    drained
2 tablespoons chopped parsley

Heat the lard in a casserole and add the lamb chunks, seasoned with salt and hot red pepper and cook slowly (without lid) for some 20 minutes; remove the lamb and reserve in another casserole.

In the first casserole, add the oil to the pan juices and allow to smoke slightly; toss in the mushrooms and sauté them over a lively heat for 4 minutes. Remove the chopped mushrooms with a slotted spoon and reserve with the lamb chunks in the other casserole. In the first casserole, sauté also the onion, and when golden brown, pour in the wine and reduce it almost completely.

Remove casserole from heat and add the flour, a little at a time, mixing in well; put back on heat and as soon as it has colored, add the tomatoes and bring to a boil for 5 minutes. Then add sufficient water to make a sauce for the pasta and some extra to serve with the lamb, which makes a main course, garnished with green vegetables. Continue simmering the sauce for 20 minutes and add the meat chunks and the mushrooms to increase the flavor of the sauce and simmer for 10 minutes, adding, at the last moment, the chopped parsley. Remove and strain 2½ cups of sauce to season a dish of pasta; reserve the lamb and remaining sauce. Makes 4 cups.

SHRIMP SALAD

(Gamberi di Vera in insalata)

*1½ pounds shrimps**	*Salt and pepper*
¼ cup oil	*1 tablespoon chopped parsley*
Juice of 1 lemon	

Cook, shell, and devein the shrimps; transfer them to a serving bowl.

Make a dressing with the oil, lemon, salt, and pepper; pour over the shrimps and toss. Sprinkle over all the chopped parsley. Serves 6.

MINESTRONE PESCARA STYLE

(Minestrone alla pescarese)

¾ pound mixed dried beans, chick-peas, lentils, split peas, etc., soaked overnight	*A mixture of:*
	¼ pound ham fat, chopped
2 pounds mixed vegetables, celery, beet tops, fresh fennel, spinach, etc.	*2 ounces onion, carrot, celery, and parsley, chopped together*
1 slice (½-inch thick—6 ounces) raw prosciutto and 1 pig's foot	*Salt and pepper*
	1 pound egg pasta, broken
	¾ cup grated Parmesan

Parboil the vegetables, both dried and fresh; parboil the pig's foot for 30 minutes and put all the ingredients together in a large pot, i.e., the ½-inch-thick slice of ham, the pig's foot, the vegetables, parboiled and chopped, the mixture of ham fat and chopped onion, carrot, etc., and the cooking liquids from the vegetables, well-seasoned with salt and pepper.

Bring to the boil, reduce the heat and simmer till all is cooked.

Bone the pig's foot and dice the meat, dice also the slice of ham, replacing all these pieces in the pot: adjust for salt and bring to the boil again and add the pasta. Cook for about 15 minutes, till the pasta is al dente, and serve. The Parmesan is served separately at table. Serves 6 to 8.

RICE AND BEAN SOUP

(Minestra di riso e fagioli all'abruzzese)

¾ *pound dried beans*
Salt
½ *cup oil*
A mixture of:
  1 onion, chopped
  ½ *stalk celery, chopped*
⅓ *hot red pepper (or*
    paprika)

4 tomatoes, peeled, seeded,
    drained and chopped
1 pound rice, rubbed with a
    clean cloth but not washed
¼ *pound grated Parmesan*

Soak the beans overnight, wash them, drain them, and cook them in plenty of lightly salted water. Remove them from the heat when tender and reserve them in their cooking water.

Heat the oil in a fireproof pan, add the onion-and-celery mixture and the red pepper. Brown. Add the tomatoes, and, after simmering for about 10 minutes, add the beans and their cooking liquid and reserve.

Before mealtime, bring the soup to the boil, toss in the rice, and cook on a lively heat, stirring often, adding some hot water if necessary if the soup becomes too thick. After about 20 minutes, the rice should be cooked; adjust for salt. Serve hot and pass the Parmesan individually. Serves 6 to 8.

MACARONI WITH SHRIMPS PESCARA STYLE

(Maccheroni coi gamberi alla pescarese)

1 sprig of thyme and 1 bay leaf chopped together	*½ inch red pepper (2 pinches of powdered peperoncino)*
1 sprig of parsley, chopped	*1½ pounds peeled tomatoes, drained*
Salt	
1½ pounds shrimps (unshelled)	*1½ pounds macaroni, broken into 4-inch lengths*
3 cloves garlic, crushed	
½ cup oil	*2 tablespoons chopped parsley*

Pour some water into a pan and add to it the thyme and bay leaf, the parsley, and 1 tablespoon of salt. Bring to the boil and drop in the shrimps, well cleaned and deveined. Bring again to the boil and cook for 2 to 3 minutes. Drain the shrimps, remove the tails and shells, dice them and reserve. Pound and chop the shrimp shells and tails and pass them through a metal sieve; reserve this purée.

Brown the garlic in a pan with oil and pieces of hot red pepper, add the tomatoes, some salt, and cook for 10 minutes. Add the shrimps and the reserved purée, mix for a minute and the sauce is ready.

Cook the macaroni in plenty of lightly salted boiling water, drain when al dente and pass to a warmed serving dish; pour over the sauce and sprinkle with chopped parsley. At the table, mix and serve immediately. Serves 6 to 8.

SPAGHETTI WITH FISH SAUCE

(Spaghetti con sugo di pesce)

*3 cloves garlic, chopped
    coarsely
½ cup oil
½ inch hot red peperoncino
    or ¼ tablespoon ground
    red pepper
2 tablespoons chopped onion
2 pounds peeled tomatoes,
    drained*

*Salt
2 pounds ½-inch-thick slices of
    large fish
2 tablespoons flour
1½ pounds spaghetti
2 tablespoons chopped parsley*

Put the garlic cloves in a pan with half the oil, the red pepper, and the onion. Sauté them together and then add the tomatoes and some salt, and simmer for 30 minutes.

At the same time, pour the remaining oil into a frying pan and heat, adding the fish slices lightly salted and floured. Sauté the fish on both sides over a lively heat. Take the fish slices from the frying pan and add them to the tomato mixture, pouring in also the frying-pan fats. Bring to a boil and simmer for 15 minutes, basting now and then with the sauce. Remove fish slices and reserve.

Cook the spaghetti in plenty of lightly salted boiling water and drain when al dente; transfer to a warmed dish and pour in the fish sauce and sprinkle with chopped parsley. The fish slices are served separately as a main course with a little sauce. Serves 6 to 8.

PASTA WITH LAMB SAUCE

(Fusilli alla molisana)

Dough:
  1¼ pounds flour
  5 eggs
  1 teaspoon oil

Pinch of salt
Salt
½ cup grated Parmesan
*2½ cups lamb sauce**

Knead the dough as for pasta,* and allow to rest for 30 minutes. Roll out thickish sheets and cut them into ½-inch-wide strips (or substitute standard dry fusilli or fettuccine). If using fresh pasta, flour a thickish knitting needle and twist the pasta around it, thus you will obtain "fusilli"; flour the needle again and twist pasta around, and so on.

At cooking time, bring a large pot of lightly salted water to the boil, toss in the pasta and cook till al dente (10 minutes at the most for fresh pasta—longer for dry). Drain, transfer to a warmed serving bowl and mix in the Parmesan and half the lamb sauce. Serve the remaining Parmesan and sauce at table. Serves 6.

POACHED SQUIDS CHIETI STYLE

(Calamari in umido alla chietina)

½ cup oil
1 onion, chopped
2 cloves garlic, crushed
*3 pounds squids, ready to
    cook and cut in strips*
Salt

*8 fillets desalted anchovy,**
    chopped
½ cup dry white wine
½ cup peeled tomatoes, drained
½ tablespoon tomato paste
The squids' yellow deposit

Heat the oil in a pan and brown the onion and garlic. Add the squid strips and allow to flavor over a low heat. Season with salt and, after 2 to 3 minutes, add the anchovy, the dry white wine, the tomatoes and the tomato paste. Allow to combine, cooking together for a few moments. Pour in sufficient water to cover the squids; cook slowly, adding after awhile the "yellow deposits" of the squids. Simmer, covered, until the squids are tender, adding water as required. Serves 6 to 8.

ONION FRITTATA AMATRICE STYLE

(Frittata con le cipolle all'amatriciana)

6 ounces white onion	1 tablespoon salt and a pinch
3 tablespoons butter	of pepper
6 fresh eggs	

Chop the onion and boil for 6 minutes: drain well and transfer to a pan. Cook gently for a few minutes without letting it brown in 3 tablespoons of butter.

Put the eggs, 1 tablespoon salt and a pinch of pepper in a bowl and beat well. Add the onion-butter mixture to the eggs and continue beating until a light froth is obtained, and then pour into the hot pan according to Note on frittatas.* Serves 3.

POTATO AND BACON FRITTATA

(Frittata all'abruzzese)

2 ounces lard (or oil)	2 ounces boiled potatoes,
1 small onion, sliced	sliced thin
5 tablespoons lean salt pork,	6 fresh eggs
diced (or bacon)	Salt

Heat the lard (or oil) in a frying pan with the sliced onion; as soon as the onion begins to brown, add the salt pork and potato slices. Sauté so that none of the ingredients stick to the bottom of the pan and, after 2 minutes cooking together, pour in the eggs beaten with a little salt. Cook on both sides, according to frittata* Note, slide onto a dish, and serve. Serves 3.

SPINACH FRITTATA

(Frittata con spinaci)

2 ounces spinach, cleaned   6 fresh eggs
4 tablespoon butter   Pinch of pepper
1 tablespoon salt

Steam the spinach with very little water and drain thoroughly of excess liquid; chop coarsely and sauté in a pan with 1 tablespoon of butter and a pinch of salt.

Heat the remaining butter in a frying pan and brown it; then pour in the eggs, beaten together with the spinach, the remaining salt, a pinch of pepper, mixing the ingredients with a wooden spoon.

As soon as the frittata begins to set, shake the pan, turn the frittata with the aid of a plate, and cook it on the other side always over a lively flame. Pass to a dish and serve immediately. Serves 3.

SQUASH FRITTATA

(Frittata con zucchini)

¼ pound small squash   6 fresh eggs
    (zucchini)   1 pinch pepper
1 tablespoon oil   2 tablespoons chopped parsley
Salt   4 tablespoons lard

Slice the zucchini; remove skin only if not young. Cook them very gently in a little water with the oil and a little salt.

Put the eggs, 1 tablespoon salt, a pinch of pepper, and the parsley in a bowl then add the warm zucchini and sauté in the frying pan with the lard. Continue cooking according to frittata* Note. Serves 3.

SWEET PEPPER FRITTATA

(Frittata con peperoni dolci)

2 sweet peppers (green, yellow, or red)
½ cup oil

1 clove garlic, bruised
6 fresh eggs
1 teaspoon salt

Char the sweet peppers, plunge in water, peel, seed, clean, and cut into strips.

Heat the oil and the garlic in a pan; sauté the garlic till browned and discard. Put the sweet pepper strips in the pan and cook them, turning them with a wooden spoon, for a couple of minutes. Beat the eggs with salt and pour into the pan and proceed with the frittata* according to Note. Serves 3.

LAMB WITH BLACK OLIVES

(Agnello con olive nere all'abruzzese)

Salt
2½ pounds leg of lamb, cut in slices
Flour
½ cup oil
6 ounces black olives, pitted and chopped

Pinch of orégano
2 pinches ground hot red pepper or ½ inch peperoncino
Juice of 1 lemon

Lightly salt and dust the slices of lamb in flour and sauté them in oil on both sides. Remove ⅓ of the cooking oil from the pan and reduce the flame. Add the chopped olives and season with a pinch of orégano and a piece of red peperoncino (or 2 pinches red pepper). After a few moments, squeeze in the juice of a lemon, mix well and after 20 seconds transfer the whole to a warmed dish and serve. Serves 6 to 8.

STUFFED VEAL BREAST

(Petto di vitello ripieno)

3½ pounds veal breast	Ground hot red pepper (or
A mixture of:	paprika)
½ pound lean pork, minced	2 eggs
3 ounces of ham fat, minced	8 ounces ham, sliced thin
1 clove garlic, chopped	½ cup oil
2 tablespoons chopped	Salt
parsley	1 cup white wine
1 teaspoon salt	1 cup stock

Remove the breastbone, taking care not to damage the meat tissue. Wash the meat and dry it, and then, starting with an incision in the middle, make two pockets (with a joint central opening) and closed at the two ends.

Put the pork, ham fat, garlic, and parsley in a mixing bowl, season with 1 teaspoon salt and plenty of hot pepper, and combine with the eggs until a smooth paste is obtained.

Put a layer of this filling inside the pockets in the veal breast and lay slices of ham on these; repeat if filling and ham remains. Sew up the opening with a coarse white thread so that the filling is well secured and then roll the meat and tie with string diagonally.

Pour a little oil into a casserole and heat well. Meantime, oil and salt the meat and, turning down the heat, put the meat in the pot with ½ cup wine and ½ cup stock; cover and simmer slowly, adding every now and then a tablespoon of half stock and half wine (or water) if needed.

When cooked, drain the meat, remove the string and the thread, and slice it and serve with the pan juices passed through a strainer. Best with fresh vegetables. Serves 6 to 8.

BEEF STEW WITH POTATOES

(Spezzatino di manzo con patate)

A mixture of:
2½ ounces lean salt pork,
    chopped
2 tablespoons chopped onion
1 tablespoon chopped celery
2½ pounds stewing beef,
    chopped into 1-ounce
    chunks
2 tablespoons salt and a
    pinch of pepper

½ cup dry white wine
A mixture of:
1 clove garlic, chopped
2 tablespoons chopped
    parsley
1 tablespoon lard
¾ pound peeled tomatoes,
    drained
1 pound potatoes, cut into
    wedges and parboiled

Heat the first mixture, the salt pork, onion, and celery in a fireproof pot; as it browns, add the chunks of meat with 2 tablespoons of salt and a little pepper. Stir and brown the meat; add the wine and reduce before adding the second mixture—garlic, parsley, and lard. Cook together for a few moments and add the tomatoes; continue cooking to combine all the ingredients and then add water sufficient to cover the meat entirely. Cover the pot and simmer for about two hours, adding a little water every now and then if the pan juices become too thick. A few minutes before serving, add the parboiled potatoes, allowing them enough time to cook. Serve hot. Serves 6 to 8.

BONED TURKEY IN ASPIC CANZANO STYLE

(Tacchino in gelatina alla canzanese)

6-pound turkey, plump and
    young
2 tablespoons salt

Freshly ground pepper
White wine gelatin*

Wash turkey and dry with clean cloth. Chop off the wings and the legs (an inch under the joint). With a very sharp knife make an incision from the neck right along the back to the tail, and begin the boning operation.

Using the fingers and the point of the knife, pull the flesh from the wings. Working from inside, lift the flesh from the bones of the legs, thighs, back, and breast. Remove the bones from the legs, thighs, back, breast, and wings. Then remove the complete carcass and entrails. Reserve the liver. Cut off the legs, chopping the meat into cubes.

Sprinkle the inside of the bird with 2 tablespoons salt and plenty of freshly ground pepper, and truss well.

Pound the turkey bones and put them in a pan; put the trussed turkey on top of them with the feet and wings all around: add also the chopped turkey meat and liver, well seasoned with salt and pepper. Cover with water and, allowing a pint for every pound of turkey, put the pan in the oven for four to five hours, basting and turning every now and then.

When cooked, the turkey should be well browned (like a roast) and very little of the liquids should be left. Remove the turkey and drain well; put it in a "close-fitting" oval dish, add the wings. Filter the pan juices and pour them slowly over the turkey so that they penetrate it as much as possible.

Allow to cool and pour over a clear gelatin which has been made with a delicate white wine. Place in a cool place. To serve, slice the turkey and surround with chopped gelatin. Serves 6 to 8.

BEANS IN TOMATO SAUCE

(Fagioli cannellini all'abruzzese)

¾ pound dried beans, soaked
   overnight
6 ounces pork rind
A mixture of:
   3 tablespoons chopped ham
   fat
   2 tablespoons chopped onion
   1 clove garlic, chopped

½ tablespoon chopped basil
½ tablespoon chopped parsley
1 tablespoon oil
¾ pound peeled tomatoes,
   drained
Salt and pinch red pepper
   (ground peperoncino)

Boil the beans till tender. Pass the pork rind over a flame to remove bristles, clean and wash well; blanch for 10 minutes in boiling water, drain and cut into 2-inch squares. Then cook the pork-rind squares in plenty of water over a moderate heat till tender.

Brown the mixture of ham fat, onion, garlic, basil, and parsley in a pan with the oil; pour in the tomatoes and season with salt and a pinch of red pepper. Turn down the heat and simmer for 20 minutes.

Drain the beans and add them to the tomato sauce: drain also the pork rind squares and add them to the tomato sauce. Add a little of the water from the bean-cooking liquid if required and allow all the ingredients to cook together slowly for a few minutes. Serves 6.

STUFFED SWEET PEPPERS

(Peperoni imbottiti alla molisana)

6 fleshy sweet peppers	1 tablespoon chopped parsley
Oil	Salt and ground peperoncino
½ pound bread crumbs, sauté	(diavolillo)
in oil for 2 seconds	6 ounces peeled tomatoes,
9 fillets desalted anchovy,*	drained
chopped	

Char the sweet peppers on the grill and plunge them into cold water; peel, seed, and wash them and lay them out, cut in halves, in a large oiled pan.

Mix the sautéed bread crumbs, the anchovy, and a tablespoon of parsley (add also a sprinkling of basil, if any is at hand), seasoned with salt and pepper (preferably red pepper) in a large bowl with plenty of oil. Cool and reserve.

Stuff the peppers with this mixture and season again with a little salt, pepper, and oil. Pour a diluted mixture of tomatoes and water into the pan till the sweet peppers are half covered and place in a moderate oven. Remove after 50 minutes, basting often, and serve hot. Serves 6.

FRIED SWEET CRÈPES

(Crespelle alla molisana)

3½ cups sifted flour
3 eggs
3 tablespoons butter
3 tablespoons sugar
*Grated peel of ½ lemon (no
    pith)*

Pinch of salt
Oil for deep-frying
Vanilla-flavored sugar

Knead the flour, the eggs, the butter, the sugar, the lemon peel, and a pinch of salt together. Roll out the mixture into a thickish sheet; cut into a variety of shapes, rounds, squares, rectangles, etc.

Heat the oil in a frying pan till smoking; toss in the crespelle and sauté each for a few seconds only. Remove with slotted spoon and drain. Transfer to a serving dish; sprinkle with vanilla-flavored sugar.

Campania

God, in an offhand way, was kind to the Neapolitans. Visiting the food markets you will find melons, figs, plums, peaches, oranges, cheeses, sausages, a riotous choice of vegetables, oil and a magnificent selection of fish, seafood, and shellfish. And perhaps the most important for the Neapolitans, there is always a plentiful supply of buffalo-milk mozzarella cheese which is the basis of so much of their cuisine.

The beef and veal, however, leave much to be desired and there is a surprising lack of lamb and pork. The Pompeii area is one big vegetable market garden and the zone south of Salerno is now becoming one, too. Sorrento supplies oranges and walnuts, Amalfi lemons, and wonderful new potatoes at Christmas time. Then God somehow forgot to give the Neapolitans the art of cooking—or perhaps it was the harsh years of scarcity during World War II which got them out of the habit. However, it is good to be able to report that there is a renaissance of the art also in the Campania; a new generation of cooks are expressing true Neapolitan fantasy in the kitchen, thus removing the major lacuna in that land of visual, cultural, and sensual delights.

The Campania was called Campania Felix (Happy Campania) by the Romans. When the name was changed a millennium or so later to Terra del Lavoro (the Land of Work), it would seem that emigration started as it was brought home to all that it was a land without work. For centuries the Campania has been and still is overpopulated and undercapitalized and, since it is mostly hill country, incapable of giving its people a living.

The Spaniards, when they ruled, probably did the most damage as they milked southern Italy with their taxes to pay for their adventures in the Americas. The Bourbons who followed were not as bad as they were painted. In 1767, they began turning land over to small holders, organized education for promising children of the poor, and introduced adult education for farmers; despite a considerable lack of perfection, Bourbon Naples became powerful and economically sound. This was upset by the brief rule of Napoleonic France and was never continued with the restoration of the Bourbons. With the Unity of Italy, most of Naples' industries were pushed off the market by the factories of Milan, Turin, and Genoa. Again, emigration began—this time mostly to the United States.

In the last decade, even the Campania standards are improving with better communications, land reclamation, irrigation, industrialization, and an ever-lively movement of tourists both Italian and from abroad; though some areas are still being ignored, as they are too difficult to improve.

Though Naples was the capital of the Bourbon Kingdom, its kings were not all stuffed shirts. One of them used his royal yacht to go trawling and used to sell the catch himself in the fish market. This easygoing tradition of the Neapolitans and their equally free-wheeling cuisine spread widely throughout Italy and the world. There must be few people in the West who, having never set foot in Naples, have never eaten a pizza with anchovy, cheese, and tomato. So widely is Neapolitan cooking known throughout the world that it is often thought to be Italian cooking, though anyone, who has riffled through this book, will know that this is far from true. But it is the cuisine of the Bourbon Kingdom of the Two Sicilies, which was no mere principality but an important state in western Europe.

Seafood and shellfish are inevitably—along with pasta—major items of Neapolitan cooking. Baby octopuses, as can be seen from the recipes, are a special delicacy enjoyed by rich and poor, and a good *red* wine is recommended to accompany them. In the case of seafood and shellfish, the traditional rule of white wine with fish can always be broken with equanimity and complete self-assurance.

Surprisingly, however, there are few fine red wines in the Campania; the most robust is the Gragnano from the Sorrento peninsula and there is a most pleasing Solopaco from near Benevento and the Ravello rosés and reds have a delicate charm most suited for accompanying seafood. The only wine with a nationwide gourmet reputation is the Taurasi from Avellino. For the rest, there is a wide swath of whites from Capri, Ischia and Vesuvius which have delicate bouquets and, often, an unexpectedly high alcoholic content.

Sauces

TOMATO SAUCE   252
(Salsa di pomodoro)

Antipasti

TOMATO SALAD PARTENOPEA   253
(Insalata di pomodoro alla partenopea)

RINFORZO SALAD PARTENOPEA   253
(Insalata di rinforzo alla partenopea)

HOMEMADE PIZZAS NEAPOLITAN STYLE   254
(Pizzelle casalinghe napoletane)

PIZZA NEAPOLITAN STYLE   255
(Pizza alla napoletana)

CALZONE NEAPOLITAN STYLE   255
(Calzone napoletana)

Soups

MEAT AND VEGETABLE SOUP NEAPOLITAN STYLE   256
(Minestra maritata also called "O Pignato Grasso")

TOMATO SAUCE
(Salsa di pomodoro)

4 tablespoons lard	1 small carrot, chopped
3 tablespoons chopped ham fat	1 stalk celery, chopped
1 clove garlic, chopped	1 clove
A mixture of:	½ cup dry white wine
2 sprigs parsley, chopped	2 pounds peeled tomatoes,
1 sprig marjoram, chopped	drained
¼ pound onion, chopped	Salt and pepper

Heat the lard in a pan and add the ham fat and garlic clove; sauté this for a moment before adding the mixture of parsley, marjoram, onion, carrot, and celery and the clove. Mix and brown lightly; pour in the wine and reduce almost completely. Add the tomatoes, seasoned with salt and pepper, cover the pan, and simmer for one hour, adding if necessary a little water. Before serving, pass through a sieve. Makes 2½ cups.

TOMATO SALAD PARTENOPEA

(Insalata di pomodoro alla partenopea)

*2 pounds salad tomatoes, large
    and slightly green
Dressing:
    1 cup oil
    2 cloves garlic, bruised*

*2 tablespoons chopped basil
1 tablespoon chopped
    orégano (or dried)
Salt and pepper*

Wash the tomatoes and leave them in very cold water to firm up.
Drain them, dry them, cut them in half; remove the seeds and
excess moisture and cut them into wedges. Put the wedges in a
salad bowl and pour over a dressing made of oil, garlic (discard
before adding to salad), basil, orégano, pepper, and generous salt.
Serves 6 to 8.

RINFORZO SALAD PARTENOPEA

(Insalata di rinforzo alla partenopea)

*1 pound cauliflower
12 fillets desalted anchovy*
2 ounces black olives, pitted
2 tablespoons pickled capers
6 hard-cooked eggs, cut in
    wedges*

*Dressing:
    ½ cup oil
    3 tablespoons vinegar
    1 teaspoon salt
    Pinch of pepper*

Boil the cauliflower, drain it, and allow to cool. Break it up
into flowerets and heap them in the center of a serving dish.
Decorate this with the fillets of anchovy, the black olives, and the
capers. Around the dish, lay out the wedges of hard-cooked egg.
Make a simple dressing of oil, vinegar, salt, and pepper and pour
over all. Serves 6.

HOMEMADE PIZZAS NEAPOLITAN STYLE

(Pizzelle casalinghe napoletane)

Dough:
  ¾ pound sifted flour
  4 tablespoons lard (or oil)
  1 tablespoon baking powder,
    dissolved in water
  Pinch of salt
Filling:
  2 small escaroles, Boston
    lettuce, or endive
  1 clove garlic, bruised
  2 tablespoons oil

Salt
12 fillets desalted anchovy*
2 tablespoons capers
2 tablespoons black olives,
  pitted and sliced
1 tablespoon raisins, seeded,
  cleaned, chopped
1 egg yolk
A pinch of pepper
Some extra flour
Oil for deep-frying

Dough: Make a dough from the flour, the lard (or oil), the baking powder, the salt, and a few tablespoons of warm water as with Pizza Neapolitan style.*

Filling: Boil the escarole (or substitute lettuce) in lightly salted water, drain, and chop fine; sauté the clove of garlic in a frying pan with 2 tablespoons of oil and a pinch of salt till it is browned, and discard. Add the escarole, sauté lightly, and when it has taken flavor from the oil, remove and put in a mixing bowl along with the anchovy, the capers, the olives, and the raisins. Combine all these with the egg yolk and a pinch of pepper.

To combine: When beginning to prepare the "pizzelle," dust the tabletop with flour, knead the dough a little more and divide it into 2-ounce balls; roll these in the hands and, with floured fingers, press them so that they take the form of 6-inch-diameter disks. Line up these disks on the table and put in the center of each of them some of the filling. Fold each of them into half-moons and press the edges with fingers dipped in water so that the filling remains firmly in place. Fry the "pizzelle" in plenty of smoking oil, drain them when crisp and golden and serve immediately. Serves 6.

PIZZA NEAPOLITAN STYLE

(Pizza alla napoletana)

Dough:
  ¾ pound sifted flour
  1 tablespoon baking powder,
    dissolved in warm water
  ½ cup oil
  Pinch salt
  Some extra flour
Filling:

1½ pounds peeled tomatoes,
  drained
½ pound mozzarella cheese
8 fillets desalted anchovy,*
  chopped
Salt and pepper
1 teaspoon orégano
Oil

Dough: Make a mound of the flour on a tabletop and put the baking powder in the scooped out center, along with half the oil and a pinch of salt; knead this mixture with a little water (or milk, if preferred) until a smooth dough is obtained. Reserve in a warm place for three hours to allow it to rise. From this dough, make discs 8 inches in diameter and ½ inch thick.

Filling: On each round, pour a little oil and scatter little mounds of tomato all over, garnishing with slivers of mozzarella and anchovy and seasoning with a pinch of salt, pepper, and orégano and another dribble of oil; put into a hot oven for 15 to 20 minutes. Serves 6 to 8.

CALZONE NEAPOLITAN STYLE

(Calzone napoletana)

1 pound sifted flour
2 tablespoons oil
1 tablespoon baking powder,
  dissolved in tablespoon
  warm water
Salt
Flour
½ cup lard

10 ounces mozzarella cheese,
  chopped
6 ounces salame or ham
  (either raw or cooked),
  sliced
1 egg, beaten with a few drops
  water

Make a mound with the flour on a tabletop: scoop out the middle and pour in the oil, the dissolved baking powder and a pinch of salt. Knead well, adding as required tablespoons of warm water until the dough is smooth and soft. Make a ball of it, dust it with flour and place in a covered casserole in a warm place for about three hours to rise. Dust the tabletop with a little flour and knead the dough for another two minutes and then shape it into as many ¼-inch-thick by 10-inch-diameter rounds as can be obtained, 6 or more.

Brush the rounds with melted lard and, in the center of each, put some mozzarella and some sliced salame. Moisten the edges of these rounds with egg beaten with a few drops of water, and fold them over on themselves, making half-moons, and press the edges so that the filling is firmly enclosed. Brush each of the calzone with melted lard and place on a lightly larded baking sheet and put in a hot oven for about 10 to 15 minutes. Serve immediately and hot. Serves 6.

MEAT AND VEGETABLE SOUP NEAPOLITAN STYLE

(Minestra maritata also called "O Pignato Grasso")

1 3-pound boiling pullet, ready to cook	*1 onion, stuck with a clove*
1 pound beef, rump or other suitable cut	*1 small carrot*
	1 stalk celery
6-ounce slice of lean salt pork	*1 small Savoy cabbage*
6-ounce slice of salame	*1½ pounds chicory (or spinach)*
6-ounce slice of prosciutto	*1½ pounds escarole (or endive)*
6 ounces of pork rind, cleaned, parboiled, and passed over a flame to remove remaining bristles, etc.	*Salt*
	A mixture of:
	¼ pound chopped ham fat
1½ tablespoons coarse salt	*2 cloves garlic, chopped*

Put the chicken and the various meats in a large fireproof pot and cover well with water, adding the salt. Bring to the boil and skim off the foam which comes to the surface. Add the onion stuck with a clove, the carrot, and the celery. When the chicken is cooked (after about 50 minutes) put it aside in a casserole and cover with some of its own stock; after about two hours, the beef will be cooked and this, too, should be reserved in the same way. Strain the stock through a damp cheesecloth and place in same casserole.

Select the tender leaves of the cabbage and chop each leaf in two; wash them along with the chicory and escarole, cutting these latter two in four lengthwise. Parboil these green vegetables in lightly salted water for 5 minutes, drain and press them to remove excess liquid.

Put these green vegetables along with the mixture of ham fat and garlic, the lean salt pork and the slices salame and ham and the pork rind in the casserole with chicken and beef. Bring to the boil, turn down the heat and simmer for two hours, or more if necessary.

Scoop the salame, the salt pork, the ham, and the pork rind out of the soup, drain them, slice them, and replace them in the casserole. Remove then the chicken and beef and reserve. Heat up the minestra and serve. The chicken and beef can serve as a second course with a side dish of fresh vegetables sautéed in oil and garlic. Serves 10 to 12.

MINESTRONE NEAPOLITAN STYLE

(Minestrone alla napoletana)

½ pound shelled fresh beans
  (or dried, out of season)
6 ounces shelled peas
2 carrots, chopped
1 stalk celery, chopped
2 turnips, medium-sized,
  chopped
6 pints cold water, or more
1 cup oil
½ pound peeled tomatoes,
  drained

6 ounces potato, sliced
A mixture of:
  1 onion, chopped
  1 clove garlic, chopped
  1 tablespoon chopped parsley
Salt and pepper
½ pound rice, rubbed with a
  cloth to clean, not washed
¼ cup grated Parmesan

Place the beans, the peas, the carrots, the celery, and the turnips in a fairly large pot and add the water and the oil; bring to the boil, turn down heat and simmer for an hour. At this point, add the tomatoes, the potato slices, and the mixture of onion, garlic, and parsley along with a seasoning of a little salt and pepper. Bring again to the boil, simmer for another 45 minutes, and re-serve.

When mealtime comes, bring to a fast boil and add the rice and cook for about 20 minutes. Pour into a soup tureen and serve with grated Parmesan. Serves 6 to 8.

PASTA AND POTATO SOUP

(Minestra di pasta e patate)

A mixture of:
  5 tablespoons chopped salt
    pork (or ham fat)
  2 tablespoons chopped onion
  1 tablespoon chopped carrot
  1 tablespoon chopped parsley
¼ cup oil
1½ pounds potatoes, peeled
  and sliced

¼ pound peeled tomatoes,
  drained
Salt and pepper
4 pints water or (better) light
  stock, hot
1 pound of pasta (use any
  broken dry pastas)
1 cup grated Parmesan

Put the chopped mixture in a fireproof pot or casserole, heat the oil and brown over a moderate flame. Add the potatoes, the tomatoes, 1 tablespoon salt (omit if using stock rather than water), and a little pepper and cook slowly, stirring, for 30 minutes. Add either stock or water and bring to a boil; toss in the pasta and cook till al dente. Add extra stock or water, should this be necessary. When the pasta is cooked, allow the soup to rest for a minute on the corner of the stove, then serve it with the Parmesan passed apart. Serves 6 to 8.

NOTE: Peas, squash, spinach, zucchini, or cabbage can be used in place of the potatoes.

STRING-BEAN SOUP SALERNO STYLE

(Zuppa di fagiolini alla salernitana)

½ cup oil	1 pound string beans, chopped
2 cloves garlic, sliced	coarsely
½ tablespoon powdered	Salt
peperoncino or other red	24 cubes day-old bread,
pepper	browned in oven
1 pound peeled tomatoes,	2 tablespoons chopped basil
drained	(or substitute parsley)

Heat the oil in a pan and add the sliced garlic and red pepper; as soon as the garlic browns, pour in the tomatoes and cook together for 15 minutes. Add the chopped string beans, sufficient water for 6 plates of soup, and some salt. Simmer, stirring every now and then until the beans are tender. This soup should be fairly thick.

Prepare the soup plates with the bread cubes and, at the last minute before serving, add the chopped basil (or parsley) to the soup. Serves 6.

PASTA AND MEAT BALLS PARTENOPEA

(Maccheroncelli con polpettine di carne alla partenopea)

A mixture of:
  1 ounce prosciutto (fat and lean), chopped
  1 small onion, chopped
  1 tablespoon oil
1 pound lean beef
1 cup dry white wine
2 pounds peeled tomatoes, drained
Salt and pepper
2 tablespoons raw beef marrow
1 clove garlic

3 sprigs parsley
1 cup bread crumbs, soaked in milk and drained
Grated peel of 1 lemon
2 egg yolks
¼ cup flour
1½ pounds maccheroncelli, broken (or other thick, short macaroni)
2 tablespoons butter
1 scant cup grated Parmesan
A generous pinch of fresh orégano

Put the ham and onion mixture in a pan; sauté lightly in oil and add the pound of lean beef. As the onion and the beef brown, pour in the wine and reduce it almost completely; then add the tomatoes, 1 tablespoon salt, and a pinch of freshly ground pepper, with sufficient water to cover the meat completely.

Cover the pan and bring to the boil, turn down heat and simmer for two hours, adding a little water if needed.

When the meat is cooked, reserve and allow to cool. Pass the pan juices through a sieve and reserve as the sauce. Mince the meat and place in a casserole; mince also the beef marrow, the garlic, the parsley, and the bread crumbs and put them in the same casserole as the minced beef; add a little grated lemon peel and salt and pepper. Toss in the 2 egg yolks and combine all the ingredients, kneading with the fingers and the palms of the hands, to make nut-sized meat balls. Roll them in flour and let them cook in a small quantity of lightly salted water on the lowest possible heat for 5 minutes and then keep warm on a corner of the stove.

Cook the maccheroncelli (or other thick, short macaroni) according to rule, drain when al dente, and pour into a warmed serving dish. Add the butter in little lumps and 2 tablespoons of grated Parmesan and mix; pour in, then, half of the sauce, distribute meat balls and sprinkle orégano over all. Serve remaining Parmesan and sauce at table. Serves 6 to 8.

LASAGNA AND RICOTTA WITH BRAISED PORK SAUCE

(Lasagne di giovedì grasso)

1½ pounds dry-egg lasagna	*1 onion, chopped*
Salt	*1 stick celery, chopped*
6 ounces ricotta	*1 clove garlic, chopped*
1 cup grated Parmesan	*2 sprigs parsley, chopped*
Braised pork sauce:	*Salt and hot red pepper*
1 pound lean pork	*¾ cup dry white wine*
¼ pound lard	*3 pounds peeled tomatoes,*
A mixture:	*drained*
1 small carrot, chopped	

Begin cooking the lasagna in lightly salted boiling water, drain when al dente, and place in a big warmed serving dish. Meanwhile, put the ricotta in a casserole diluted with a few tablespoons of warm water to make a thick cream (use the water from the cooking pasta).

Pour the creamy ricotta over the lasagna, add half the Parmesan and half the braised pork sauce, and serve. The remaining Parmesan and meat sauce are served at the table.

Braised pork sauce: Chop the pork; heat the lard in a pan till smoking well; sauté gently the pork and the mixture of carrot, onion, celery, garlic, and parsley in the pan and mix well, seasoning with a little salt and red pepper. Add the wine and reduce entirely. Then add the tomatoes, pour in 2 pints of water, and bring to the boil; turn down heat and simmer for an hour, or more if necessary. Remove the pork pieces and reserve as a second course. Pass the pan juices through a fine sieve and the braised pork sauce is complete. N.B. A pork liver sausage or two can be added to this recipe to good effect. Serves 8.

SPAGHETTI WITH TOMATO SAUCE AND FRESH BASIL NEAPOLITAN STYLE

(Spaghetti con filetti di pomodoro alla napoletana)

Sauce:
- 5 *tablespoons butter*
- 3 *ounces ham fat, chopped*
- 2 *tablespoons chopped onion*
- *White pepper*
- 2 *pounds peeled tomatoes, drained*

Salt
1½ *pounds spaghetti (or vermicelli, which is slightly thinner)*
1 *cup grated Parmesan*
4 *tablespoons coarsely chopped basil leaves*

Sauce: Heat 2 tablespoons of butter in a pan, along with the ham fat, the onion, and plenty of freshly ground white pepper; sauté till the onions are golden brown. Add the tomatoes and some salt and simmer for 15 minutes.

Meanwhile, begin cooking the spaghetti in plenty of lightly salted boiling water; drain when al dente and pass into a warmed serving dish. Add ⅓ of the Parmesan to the pasta and mix in well along with the rest of the butter in small lumps, the basil, and, finally, the sauce. Take to the table, mix well and serve with the remaining Parmesan. Serves 6.

PASTA WITH FRESH ANCHOVY SAUCE

(Farfalline con le alicine fresche)

Sauce:
- 1½ *pounds small fresh anchovy* (or whitebait)*
- 3 *cloves garlic, crushed*
- 1 *cup oil*
- ¼ *pound peeled tomatoes, drained*
- 2 *tablespoons chopped parsley*

Salt and freshly ground pepper
½ *cup bread crumbs sautéed for 2 seconds in a little oil*
1½ *pound farfalline, vermicelli, or other small pasta*

Decapitate, fillet, and wash the anchovy. Fresh anchovy can be replaced by salted anchovy which must be well desalted, filleted, and pounded to a paste.

Lightly brown the garlic in the oil, add the fish, chopped coarsely, and sauté together for a minute; add the tomatoes and simmer for a few minutes, adding 3 or 4 tablespoons of water, the parsley, and a little salt and pepper. Turn up the heat and, stirring, cook for 5 minutes, sprinkling in the bread crumbs.

Cook the pasta, drain it, and transfer to a warmed serving dish; pour the fish sauce over all, carry to the table, mix and serve immediately. Serves 6.

PASTA WITH CLAM SAUCE

(Vermicelli con le vongole)

Sauce:	*1½ pounds peeled tomatoes,*
½ *cup oil*	*drained*
Salt	*Salt and pepper*
2 pounds clams, cleaned and	*1½ pounds vermicelli (or*
scrubbed	*spaghetti)*
3 cloves garlic, bruised	*2 tablespoons chopped parsley*

Sauce: Heat the oil with a little salt in a frying pan and sauté the clams; as soon as they open, drain them into a colander over a pan. Remove from their shells and pass the pan liquids through a sieve.

Lightly brown the garlic in the pan in oil, add the strained clam liquid and reduce to 2 or 3 tablespoons. Then add the tomatoes, a little salt and pepper (or preferably red pepper—peperoncino) and cook over a lively heat for 10 minutes. Turn down heat and simmer till the sauce reaches a normal consistency; then add the clams. To sharpen the flavor of this sauce, a few fillets of desalted anchovy (mashed) can be added before the tomato, i.e., when the strained clam liquid is being reduced.

The pasta, traditionally vermicelli (thin spaghetti) is cooked in the classic manner in lightly salted boiling water and drained when al dente; pass into a warmed serving dish, pour in the sauce, and sprinkle on chopped parsley. Take to the table, mix, and serve. Serves 6.

MACARONI TIMBALES

(Timballi di maccheroni)

2 pastry timbales and 2 lids:
  1½ pounds sifted flour
  ½ cup softened butter
  ½ cup lard
  2 eggs
  2 tablespoons sugar
  Pinch of salt
Flour
¼ cup butter
1 pound macaroni, broken into
  3-inch lengths
Butter
Salt
2 cups braised pork sauce (see
  lasagna and ricotta with

braised pork sauce*). (In
this sauce, beef can be
substituted for the pork,
but only with the addition
of 6 ounces of chopped
mushrooms sautéed in
butter.)
1 cup grated Parmesan
6 ounces finely sliced
  mozzarella
¼ pound ricotta
24 wedges (quarters) hard-
  cooked eggs

Prepare the two pastry timbales and lids in the following manner: heap 1½ pounds sifted flour in a mound on a tabletop, scoop out the middle and put in ½ cup butter, ½ cup lard, 2 eggs, 2 table-spoons of sugar, and a pinch of salt; knead well, adding, when necessary, up to ½ cup of water. The dough should be rather coarse and should, therefore, be kneaded as little as possible. Therefore, as soon as all the ingredients are combined well, wrap the dough in a cloth and put it aside in a cool place for an hour— this will make the dough lose its elasticity.

Then put the dough on the tabletop, lightly dusted with flour, and roll out sheets which are not more than ½ inch thick. Line the bottom and sides of 2 timbale molds with some of the dough, having first buttered the molds well. With the remaining dough, cut 2 suitably sized circles to serve as lids for the timbales and put them (on a lightly greased baking dish) along with the timbales in a hot oven for 12 to 15 minutes. Remove from oven, cool and remove timbales from molds.

Prepare the macaroni in plenty of boiling, lightly salted water; drain when al dente, and transfer to a mixing bowl; add half the meat sauce and half the Parmesan.

Butter the insides of the timbale molds again and replace the timbales; fill them with layers of macaroni, slices of mozzarella, ricotta, and hard-cooked egg wedges, and replace the pastry covers. Put in a warm oven for sufficient time for the timbales to warm up. Remove from the oven, allow to rest for a few minutes. Remove the timbales from the molds and put on serving dishes. Serve the remaining grated Parmesan and sauce at table. Serves 8.

PASTA WITH BRAISED BEEF SAUCE

(Genovesa con maccheroncelli)

Sauce:
  2½ pounds lean beef
A mixture of:
  1 pound onions, chopped
  5 tablespoons chopped salt
    pork
  2 tablespoons chopped carrot
  1 tablespoon chopped celery
  ½ cup butter
  3 tablespoons lard

Bouquet garni:
  1 sprig basil
  2 sprigs marjoram (or
    parsley)
Salt and pepper
Extra oil
½ cup dry white wine
1 pound maccheroncelli,
    broken (or other short,
    thick macaroni)

Sauce: Truss up the meat well so that it keeps its shape during cooking. Put it in a casserole with the chopped mixture, the butter, and the lard, the bouquet garni, and a few tablespoons of water; season with a tablespoon of salt and a little pepper. Bring to the boil and simmer in the casserole (covered), stirring often. After about 15 minutes, the onion should be reduced to a pulp; remove the lid, raise the heat, and complete the browning of the meat, adding sufficient oil. Pour in the wine and allow it to evaporate over a low heat. Continue simmering, adding, as needed, a little water to prevent the pan juices thickening too much until the meat is properly cooked.

Strain and reserve the pan juices, which serve as the sauce for the pasta. Cook the maccheroncelli (or other pasta) in lightly salted boiling water, strain when al dente, and serve hot with the sauce. The meat is served as a separate course. Serves 6.

PASTA WITH MARINARA SAUCE

(Linguine alla marinara)

1½ pounds linguine (or vermicelli or spaghetti)
Salt
Sauce:
  3 cloves garlic, crushed
  Pinch pepper (but better hot peperoncino pepper)

1 scant cup oil
1 tablespoon orégano (or 2 tablespoons chopped parsley)

Cook the pasta in boiling, lightly salted, water; drain when al dente and season with the following sauce, which is prepared at the last moment.

Put the crushed garlic in a pan with the piece of hot red pepper (peperoncino—or paprika) and lightly sauté in oil. As soon as the garlic is golden, pour the oil on top of the pasta which is already in the serving dish and hot, sprinkling over all the orégano. Mix well and serve. Serves 6.

PASTA WITH TOMATO MARINARA SAUCE

(Vermicelli alla marinara con pomodoro)

The preparation is the same as for pasta with marinara sauce* except that when the garlic is well browned 1 pound sieved, drained tomatoes are added. This should continue cooking slowly for 10 minutes or more. Serves 6.

CANNELLONI AMALFI STYLE

(Cannelloni all'amalfitana)

Dough:
¾ pound sifted flour
4 eggs
Few drops oil
½ tablespoon salt
Salt
Filling:
½ pound ricotta, sieved
½ pound mozzarella, diced
Salt and pepper
Pinch nutmeg
2 ounces prosciutto, cut into
strips
2 eggs

2 tablespoons butter to butter
pan
Sauce:
¾ pound peeled tomatoes,
drained
2 tablespoons chopped basil
3 tablespoons softened butter
½ cup grated Parmesan
2 tablespoons melted butter

Dough: Prepare the pasta dough, wrap it in a damp cloth, and let it rest for 30 minutes. Roll out into thin sheets and cut in 4- by 5-inch rectangles; cook in boiling, lightly salted water, drain, and lay out on a damp cloth and allow to cool.

Filling: Put the ricotta, the mozzarella, a pinch of salt, pepper and nutmeg and the prosciutto in a casserole; add the eggs and combine with a fork until a smooth paste is obtained. Firmly wrap the pasta around the filling in the form of tubes and lay out in a buttered pan.

Sauce: Make a light sauce with the tomatoes, basil, and 3 tablespoons of butter and pour over the cannelloni along with a few tablespoons of grated Parmesan and, over all, melted butter. Put in a warm oven until well browned; serve, sprinkling the remainder of the Parmesan individually at the table. Serves 6.

CLAM SOUP NEAPOLITAN STYLE

(Zuppa di vongole alla napoletana)

4½ pounds clams
½ cup oil
3 cloves garlic, crushed
1 cup dry white wine

Freshly ground pepper
6 slices of bread, browned in
oven
2 tablespoons chopped parsley

Scrub and wash the clams. Heat the oil in a fireproof pan and add the garlic. When the garlic is golden, pour in the white wine and a pinch of pepper and reduce heavily. Then add the clams and sauté them over a brisk flame, shaking the pan until the clams open and their liquid combines with the pan juices.

Brown the bread in the oven and distribute in the soup plates. With a slotted spoon, distribute the clams in each plate and pour the pan juices over them; sprinkle chopped parsley also. Serves 6.

MARINARA MUSSELS NEAPOLITAN STYLE

(Cozze marinare alla napoletana)

½ cup oil
4 cloves garlic, sliced
¼ inch hot peperoncino or
teaspoon red pepper

3½ pounds mussels, scrubbed,
bearded, and washed
½ cup dry white wine
2 tablespoons chopped parsley

Heat the oil in a pan and add the sliced garlic and the piece of hot red pepper (or paprika). As soon as the garlic colors, put in also the mussels and the wine. Allow to cook for a few moments and add the parsley and a few tablespoons of water (or fish stock).

Allow to cook gently until all the mussels are open. Serve in warmed bowls, along with the pan liquids. Serves 4 to 6.

LITTLE MULLETS PARTENOPEA

(Cefaletti alla partenopea)

12 small mullets, prepared for
   cooking
Oil
Salt and pepper
A pounded mixture of:
   3 cloves garlic

Pinch of pepper
1 teaspoon orégano
1 sprig parsley
1 tablespoon oil
1 teaspoon vinegar

Cook the mullets on the lowest of heat in plenty of oil, a little salt, and a pinch of pepper. Prepare a paste of pounded garlic, the pepper, orégano, parsley, with a tablespoon of oil and a little vinegar.

When the mullets are half cooked, distribute over them the pounded mixture and continue simmering at the lowest possible heat for a few minutes. Serves 6.

FISH SOUP NEAPOLITAN STYLE

(Zuppa di pesce alla napoletana)

3 pounds of fish—bass, squid,
   halibut, soles, shrimps,
   clams, mussels, etc.*
1 cup oil
1 small onion, chopped
1 pound peeled tomatoes,
   drained
2 cloves garlic, sliced
3 sprigs parsley, crushed
Salt and plenty of freshly
   ground pepper

4 pints of fish fumet*
   (prepared with chopped
   fish bones, fishheads, a
   carrot, a small onion, a
   stalk celery, salt, and
   sufficient water for 4 pints
   of fish stock after 20
   minutes' cooking)
8 slices bread, crusts removed,
   fried in oil
1 tablespoon chopped parsley

Clean and fillet the soles, bone, and chop the larger fish; shell and devein the shrimps. Beard and scrub the clams and mussels and sauté them in a pan with a little oil; strain the liquid through a warm, damp cheesecloth.

Pour most of the oil into a fireproof pot (leave a little oil to fry the bread in) and brown the onion; add the squids with a little of the strained liquid and cook, covered, for a few minutes. Then add the tomatoes and after a few more minutes the fish, the mussels, clams, shrimps, the garlic, parsley, a little salt, pepper, and the fumet. Bring to the boil and simmer for another 10 minutes.

Fry the bread slices and put them in the soup plates, distribute the fish and seafood on the plates and cover with the soup; sprinkle over all chopped parsley and serve. Serves 6 to 8.

BABY OCTOPUS NEAPOLITAN STYLE

(Polpo alla napoletana)

Baby octopuses	*Lemon*
Oil	*Freshly ground pepper*

This is a simple fisherman's meal; gut the baby octopuses well; wash and boil till tender. They are eaten seasoned with oil, lemon juice, and freshly ground pepper in quantities according to taste. An aged red wine, rather than a white, accompanies this dish admirably.

BIG NEAPOLITAN FRY

(Frienno e magnanno)

This is a Neapolitan specialty for which there are no rules, no set recipes. It is a dish, if it can be called a dish, for great occasions, great festas.

It starts with a mixed fry of fish: first sardines, fresh anchovy, then larger fish, followed by chitterlings, slices of calf liver, sweetbreads, and calf brains: then breaded mozzarella cheese, hardcooked egg yolks covered with béchamel and breaded croquettes of potato, rice, cauliflower, artichokes, zucchini, and zucchini flowers.

All these ingredients are fried, one at a time, in a huge frying pan with oil and lard, and brought to the table hot and crisp as soon as cooked—thus making a continuous-service meal.

FRIED EGGS WITH MOZZARELLA AND SPAGHETTI NEAPOLITAN STYLE

(Uova fritte alla napoletana)

Sauce:
1 peeled tomato, drained
Pinch of basil, crumbled
2 tablespoons oil
1 teaspoon grated Parmesan
2 slices mozzarella

Salt
1 egg, beaten
Flour
1 teaspoon butter
6 ounces spaghetti
2 fried eggs

Prepare a light tomato sauce in a pan by combining the tomato and basil in warm oil, and simmer for a moment. When cooked, mix in some Parmesan.

Take 2 slices of mozzarella, season with a little salt, dip in beaten egg and then in flour and brown lightly in butter.

Cook some spaghetti al dente and put 6 ounces in a small dish, the 2 slices of mozzarella, and finally a fried egg on each slice of mozzarella. Serve hot. Serves 1.

VEAL CUTLETS WITH SPINACH AND CROUTONS

(Braciole di vitello con spinaci e crostoni)

1 pound spinach, cleaned and
washed
Salt
½ cup butter
Salt
6 slices of bread of equal
dimensions to the fillets
and ½ inch thick

½ cup milk, generous
7 eggs
6 slices (¼ pound each) of
fillet or noisette of veal,
lightly pounded

Cook the spinach in very little water and a pinch of salt; drain, eliminate excess water, and sauté the spinach with 3 tablespoons butter and a pinch of salt.

Soak the bread in the milk and then in a beaten egg, then fry with the remaining butter. In the same frying pan and the same butter, add the veal cutlets, lightly salted, and sauté them till golden on both sides over a lively heat.

Put the cutlets in the center of a large fireproof dish and around them lay out the fried bread. On each piece of fried bread place a mound of spinach; in the hollowed-out centers of each mound of spinach place an egg yolk. Sprinkle each egg yolk with a little salt. Put the ovenproof dish in a hot oven for 3 or 4 minutes (till the eggs are cooked) and serve. Serves 6.

STEAKS WITH PIZZAIOLA SAUCE

(Bistecche alla pizzaiola)

2 tablespoons oil	4 cloves garlic, crushed
6 steaks (rump or flank), cut 1 inch thick	¾ pound peeled tomatoes, drained
Salt and freshly ground pepper	Salt
Sauce:	1 teaspoon orégano

Smoke the oil in a pan, and sauté the steaks lightly on both sides; reduce the heat and continue cooking for 4 minutes. Remove the steaks and season them with a little salt and pepper; reserve and keep warm.

Put the garlic cloves in the frying pan and brown them, mixing in the tomatoes and seasoning with a little salt and orégano. After 8 minutes of gentle cooking, replace the steaks in the frying pan and allow to cook together with the tomatoes for a few minutes. Serve the steaks and sauce together. Serves 6.

SMALL RUMPSTEAKS NEAPOLITAN STYLE

(Bistecchine alla napoletana)

½ cup oil
6 ounces ham, chopped
¼ pound mushrooms, cleaned
    and finely sliced*
Salt and pepper
1 cup chopped parsley

12 small rumpsteaks (3 ounces
    each) of beef, veal or
    lamb, lightly flattened
Salt
1 lemon

Oil a fireproof dish and sprinkle in first some ham, followed by a layer of mushrooms; sprinkle with oil and season with ½ tablespoon salt and a pinch of pepper. Distribute chopped parsley over the surface and finish the preparation, laying the little rumpsteaks, lightly salted, on top.

Put the dish into a hot oven for 15 minutes; turn the steaks over and salt them lightly; squeeze a lemon over the steaks and put the dish back into the oven for another 8 minutes. Serve in the fireproof dish. Serves 6.

RABBIT ISCHIA STYLE

(Coniglio alla maniera di Ischia)

½ cup oil
1 rabbit, young and plump,
    skinned, eviscerated and
    chopped into 2-ounce
    chunks
1 pound peeled tomatoes,
    drained

Salt and pepper
1 sprig rosemary
3 basil leaves, crushed
½ cup dry white wine

Heat the oil in a pan; add the rabbit chunks and sauté over a lively flame until golden brown. Add the tomatoes, season with a tablespoon of salt, a pinch of freshly ground pepper and then, after a few minutes, add the rosemary, the basil, and the dry white wine. Simmer this sauce and reduce it by half; then add sufficient water to cover the rabbit chunks. Cover the pan and simmer till all the water has been absorbed and the sauce has reached its proper consistency—not too thick, not too liquid.

Put the rabbit in a warm serving dish, pour the sauce over it, and serve hot. Serves 6.

SWEET PEPPERS PARTENOPEA

(Peperoni alla partenopea)

6 sweet peppers (yellow and red)	2 tablespoons pine nuts
	½ cup oil
2 tablespoons small capers	Salt and pepper
2 tablespoons pitted black olives	1 cup bread crumbs
6 fillets desalted anchovy,* chopped	

Give the sweet peppers a preliminary roasting on the grill, peel them, clean them, remove the seeds, and wash them under running water; chop and dry well with a cloth.

Put the chopped sweet pepper, the capers, the pitted olives, the chopped anchovy fillets, and the pine nuts in a pan with 2 tablespoons of oil and a pinch of salt and pepper and cook over a low heat, mixing the ingredients together.

Oil a fireproof dish with half the remaining oil and put a layer of the above mixture in it; sprinkle with bread crumbs and pour over the rest of the oil. Put the pan in a hot oven and remove when the surface is brought to a golden brown. This side dish can be served either hot or cold. Serves 6 or 8.

BOILED ONIONS NEAPOLITAN STYLE

(Cipolle lessate alla napoletana)

12 medium-sized onions	Salt and pepper
Salt	1 tablespoon chopped parsley
Sauce:	1 tablespoon chopped
½ cup oil	orégano

Peel the onions and simmer them in lightly salted water for 30 minutes; drain and cut them in two. Place on a serving dish and pour over the sauce made of oil, salt and pepper, parsley and orégano beaten together with a fork. An excellent side dish for mixed boiled meats.*

ZEPPOLE COOKIES NEAPOLITAN STYLE

(Zeppole alla napoletana)

2 cups water	2 tablespoons semolina
3 tablespoons oil	4 egg yolks
1 bay leaf	½ cup sweet marsala wine
1 cup superfine sugar	Olive oil and lard for deep-
Salt	frying
½ pound flour	Confectioners' sugar

Put the water, oil, bay leaf, sugar, and a pinch of salt in a saucepan and bring to the boil. Mix the flour and the semolina. Remove the pan from the heat and drop the flour mixture all together into the boiling liquid and stir vigorously with a wooden spoon until a paste is obtained.

Put the saucepan back on the stove and simmer, stirring continuously for 7 or 8 minutes. When the dough becomes dry and smooth, remove from the stove and discard the bay leaf; allow to cool, meanwhile beating the egg yolks into the dough one at a time, along with the marsala. Pour the mixture onto a lightly oiled working surface and allow it to cool completely.

Then, knead the dough again and shape it into a rope the thickness of a finger; chop into 6-inch lengths and form into rings. These are ready to be dropped into the frying pan to be deep-fried; half oil and half lard is an excellent fat for this purpose. During the frying, the zeppole should be pricked with a sharp-pronged fork so that uncooked dough can escape from inside. These little "eruptions" on the surface are a characteristic of the Neapolitan zeppole.

As soon as they are crisp and golden, they should be removed with the slotted spoon, drained, sprinkled with confectioners' sugar and piled high. Serve hot. Serves 6 to 8.

Puglia

Puglia, for centuries, has been a place to loot. Not that it was very rich, but there was always plenty to eat there—wheat, olive oil, wine, fish, and other basic foodstuffs. It was looted by Lombards, Normans, Byzantines, Hohenstaufens, Spaniards, and Bourbons—the list for Puglia (and for most of southern Italy for that matter) is seemingly unending. The temptation, however, was great; Puglia has an enormous amount of flat land which is a great rarity in Italy.

Puglia has the biggest wheat production in all Italy and the olive groves seem to have no end. The production of wine is greater than that of Piedmont and Lombardy combined. In fact, up to fifteen years ago, except for the university city of Bari and the naval base at Taranto, Puglia consisted only of market towns and a completely rural civilization.

The last decade has seen incredible changes; among these is the fact that you can now actually get to Bari in five hours from Rome by six-lane highway, instead of in ten hours by winding roads. Taranto has become a major industrial town with enormous steel foundries, and Bari has turned into a brisk commercial and light industry center which sells not only to Italy but, in traditional spirit, has close contacts with North Africa and the Mid-East. Modern methods and shrewd investment have doubled the agricultural production and, despite heavy emigration, the population is growing fast. Unemployment is no longer that terrible, soul-killing specter that it used to be in so many homes.

Social change as profound as this inevitably has had its effect; initially, on a gastronomic level, the results were ingenuous. So many emigrants had gone to Milan to make their fortune and succeeded that there was an effort to import the Milan cuisine of the successful into Puglia. But this was, fortunately, soon abandoned in favor of a return to the patriarchal food of the past, improved with meats and fishes that grandfather couldn't afford or could afford but rarely.

Adriatic Puglia has a chill winter, but the worst is mitigated by the sea; the southern coast (the instep of Italy with Taranto) is far milder, and both coasts have long, hot summers which bring good crops of soft fruit and table grapes.

The hot summer means that the grapes are sweet for eating and make high-proof wine. The wine, on the whole, tends to be too strong for most people's taste, and, consequently, enormous quantities of it are used for making Turin's famous vermouths, and for cutting into weaker wines of northern Europe and northern Italy. However, with the new wealth of Puglia, some of the wines are being tamed and domesticated. For many years, the Rivera whites and rosés have been widely known and the Aglianico del Vulture, too: the wines of San Severo have an even longer tradition. However, one red wine, Torre di Quarto, has found its way, quietly and with no roll of drums, onto gourmets' dinner tables, thus proving that, with a careful selection of grapes and proper oenological handling, southern wine can more than rival that of the north. We shall hear much more of Puglia wines in the future.

The patriarchal food to which Puglia has returned is based on pasta made at home with their own hard-grain flour; and, in particular, on their timbales. Fresh fish is available in great quantities, while the mussel-breeding beds of Taranto are so big that they supply most of Italy's needs. You will, therefore, find in the recipes a natural co-existence of pasta and mussels. But where grandfather's modest circumstances allowed him only fresh anchovy (which are delicious), with today's wealth, luxury fish such as dentice (bass) are the order of the day, though more than anything, the people of Puglia enjoy fish soups, which are as enormous as they are tasty as they are satisfying.

In the north, in the Gargano Mountains, in winter a great deal of game is found, from hare to pheasant and partridge, which helps out a regional menu that is still light on the meat side in the most elegant of ways.

Antipasti
>PIZZA TARANTO STYLE   281
>(Pizza Tarantina)

Soups
>THICK FENNEL BROTH FOGGIA STYLE   281
>(Simuledda alla foggiana)

>PASTA AND CHICK-PEA SOUP LECCE STYLE   282
>(Minestra di lasagnette con ceci alla leccese)

>GREEN SOUP BARI STYLE   283
>(Minestra verde alla barese)

Pastas and other farinaceous dishes
>PASTA AND MUSSELS   283
>(Pasta con le cozze)

>MACARONI AND SWEET PEPPER SAUCE   284
>(Rigatoni piccoli rigati coi peperoni)

>BAKED MACARONI   285
>(Maccheroni al forno)

>STUFFED MACARONI   286
>(Rigatoni imbottiti)

>MACARONI ANDRIA STYLE   287
>(Maccheroni alla maniera di Andria)

Fish
>MUSSEL SOUP TARANTO STYLE   287
>(Zuppa di cozze alla tarantina)

PIZZA TARANTO STYLE

(Pizza Tarantina)

1 pound mealy potatoes   *¾ pound peeled tomatoes,*
½ pound sifted flour   *drained*
2 teaspoons baking powder, *½ cup grated Parmesan*
   dissolved in a tablespoon *Salt*
   warm water   *½ tablespoon orégano*
½ tablespoon salt   *Pinch of pepper*
½ cup oil
½ pound mozzarella cheese,
   sliced

Boil the potatoes, peel them, dry them, and pass them through a food mill. Make a mound of flour on the working surface of the tabletop and mix in the potatoes. Scoop out a hole in the top of the mound and pour in the dissolved baking powder and the ½ tablespoon salt; knead well, adding a little warm water as required, till a smooth dough is obtained.

Lightly oil a pan, spread out the dough in it, well leveled all over, and sprinkle over half the oil. Then lay the slices of mozzarella cheese, the tomato, and, above these, the grated Parmesan on the dough. Season with salt and orégano and sprinkle pepper lightly all over. Allow to rise in a warm place for about an hour and then put in a medium oven and remove after about 30 minutes. Serve immediately. Serves 6.

THICK FENNEL BROTH FOGGIA STYLE

(Simuledda alla foggiana)

5 pints stock   *¾ pound potatoes, peeled and*
1 pound fennel hearts   *sliced*
   (preferably wild),   *½ cup corn-meal flour*
   coarsely chopped   *1 cup grated Parmesan*

Bring the stock to the boil and toss in the fennel hearts and sliced potatoes; bring back to the boil, and sprinkle in the corn-meal flour a little at a time, stirring continuously. Turn down heat and simmer for 20 to 25 minutes. Serve hot with grated Parmesan. Serves 6 to 8.

PASTA AND CHICK-PEA SOUP LECCE STYLE

(Minestra di lasagnette con ceci alla leccese)

*1½ pounds chick-peas,
    soaked*
3 sprigs rosemary
2 cloves garlic, bruised
1½ tablespoons coarse salt
½ cup oil

*1 teaspoon freshly ground
    pepper*
4 fillets desalted anchovy,
    mashed*
10 ounces dry lasagna

Having soaked the chick-peas for several hours, put them in a fireproof pot covered with plenty of water; add 2 sprigs of rosemary tied with a white thread, a clove of garlic, and 1½ tablespoons of coarse salt. Bring to the boil, turn down heat, and simmer for two hours or more (cooking time depends on the type of chick-pea). Remove the rosemary.

Pour the oil into a little casserole, adding the other sprig of rosemary (tied also with a white thread), a clove of bruised garlic, and a teaspoon of freshly ground pepper. As soon as the garlic browns, remove from the heat and mix in the anchovy, and pour the whole contents of the little casserole into the pot of chick-peas, removing first the rosemary and the garlic.

Bring the chick-pea soup to the boil and scatter in the dried pasta (lasagne) strips; turn down heat a little, add a little hot water if required and remove from stove when the pasta is al dente. Serves 6 to 8.

GREEN SOUP BARI STYLE

(Minestra verde alla barese)

2 pounds lean pork
5 pounds (in equal parts)
   fennel hearts, celery,
   cauliflower flowerets,
   turnip tops, chicory (or
   spinach), all washed, and
   coarsely chopped

1 onion stuck with a clove
1 small carrot
1½ tablespoons coarse salt
Croutons
3 tablespoons grated Parmesan

Put the piece of lean pork in a very large pot with plenty of water. Bring the water to the boil, turn down heat and simmer; remove scum as it comes to the surface. Then add the vegetables, the onion stuck with a clove, the small carrot and season with 1½ tablespoons salt. Bring to the boil, turn down heat and simmer for three hours.

Remove the meat, which is served as a separate dish, along with vegetables sautéed in oil.

The green soup is served with little fried croutons and grated Parmesan. Serves 6.

PASTA AND MUSSELS

(Pasta con le cozze)

2 pounds mussels
Salt
1½ pounds short macaroni
½ cup oil
2 cloves garlic, bruised
1½ pounds peeled tomatoes,
   drained

1 scant tablespoon salt
A pinch of freshly ground
   pepper (or a piece of hot
   red pepper—peperoncino)
2 tablespoons chopped parsley

Scrub and beard the mussels in plenty of running water; shuck them with an appropriate knife and remove from shells, allowing the liquids in the shells to drop into a pan. Filter this liquid through a damp cheesecloth and pour it back into the pan and reduce over a low heat. Put the mussels in the liquid, allow to cool and reserve.

Bring the lightly salted pasta water to the boil and toss in the pasta. In the meantime, pour the oil into a pan and brown the garlic; then discard it. Add the tomatoes, seasoned with a scant tablespoon of salt and a pinch of pepper (or hot red pepper), and cook gently, stirring well. Then add the mussels and their reduced liquids and bring to the boil; turn down heat and simmer for 8 to 10 minutes.

Drain the pasta when al dente and pass to a warmed serving dish; pour over all the mussel and tomato sauce and take to table. Sprinkle chopped parsley, mix well and serve. Serves 6.

MACARONI AND SWEET PEPPER SAUCE

(Rigatoni piccoli rigati coi peperoni)

Sauce:
  2 *pounds sweet peppers,*
    yellow, red, or green
½ *cup oil*
Salt
  2 *cloves garlic, sliced fine*
  2 *pounds peeled tomatoes,*
    drained

Salt and pinch of freshly
    ground pepper
1½ *pounds macaroni*
  2 *tablespoons chopped parsley*
½ *cup grated Pecorino (or*
    Parmesan)

Char the sweet peppers over a grill and plunge them in cold water; peel them carefully, removing the seeds and stem and cut into strips. Put a tablespoon of oil and a pinch of salt in a frying pan and sauté the strips of sweet peppers lightly; reserve and keep warm.

Pour the remaining oil into a pan and lightly brown the garlic slices; add the tomatoes, a pinch of salt and a pinch of freshly ground pepper and simmer for 30 minutes. Then add the sweet pepper strips and their cooking oil and allow to cook together with the tomatoes for a few minutes.

In the meantime, cook the pasta in lightly salted boiling water, drain when al dente and pass into a warmed serving dish; pour the sauce over all, sprinkle with chopped parsley, and carry to the table. Mix well and serve immediately with grated cheese. Serves 6.

BAKED MACARONI

(Maccheroni al forno)

2 tablespoons chopped onion	6 ounces salame (or
¾ cup oil	mortadella), sliced thin
2 pounds peeled tomatoes,	½ pound mozzarella cheese,
drained	sliced thin
1 scant tablespoon salt and	1 cup grated Pecorino cheese
a pinch of pepper	6 tomatoes, cut in half and
1¼ pounds macaroni, short and	parboiled
thick	2 tablespoons bread crumbs

Brown the onion in a pan with ½ cup oil; add the tomatoes, a scant tablespoon salt, and a pinch of pepper. Bring to the boil and simmer for 30 minutes, adding a little water if needed.

Cook the pasta in lightly salted boiling water; drain when nearly al dente. Oil a fireproof dish with a tablespoon of oil and put in a first layer of pasta; follow this with layers of sauce, some slices of salame (or mortadella), mozzarella cheese, and grated Pecorino between each layer of pasta. On reaching the last layer of pasta, cover it with the parboiled tomato halves, sprinkle with bread crumbs and a little oil. Put the pan in a hot oven till browned. Serve hot. Serves 6 to 8.

STUFFED MACARONI

(Rigatoni imbottiti)

Filling:
- ¾ cup oil
- 2 tablespoons chopped onion
- ¾ pound lean beef, minced
- 1 teaspoon salt and a pinch of pepper

A mixture of:
- 3 ounces mortadella, chopped
- 3 ounces mozzarella, chopped (or other soft cheese)
- 2 ounces provolone, chopped (or other sharp cheese)

Sauce:
- 1½ tablespoons chopped onion
- 1 clove garlic, chopped
- ½ tablespoon chopped thyme
- 2½ pounds peeled tomatoes, drained
- Salt
- 1½ pounds large macaroni
- Salt
- ¾ cup grated Pecorino (or Parmesan)

Filling: Pour ¼ cup of oil into a casserole and lightly brown the onion. Add the minced beef, seasoned with a teaspoon of salt and a pinch of freshly ground pepper, and sauté together till the meat is browned and flavored; allow to cool and pass the contents of the casserole into a mixing bowl. Combine with the mixture of mortadella, mozzarella, and provolone. Reserve.

Sauce: Brown, in another pan, the mixture of onion, garlic, and thyme with the remaining oil; add the tomatoes, seasoned with a little salt, bring to the boil, and simmer on a low heat for 30 minutes, stirring often and adding a little water if necessary. Reserve.

Cook the macaroni in lightly salted boiling water; drain when half cooked. Allow to cool. Stuff the macaroni tubes with the minced beef and cheese filling.

To combine: Oil a fireproof dish with a tablespoon of oil and place in it a first layer of stuffed macaroni; continue with layers of sauce, grated cheese, and macaroni until all are used up. Put the pan in a medium oven for about 25 to 30 minutes. Serve hot directly from the fireproof dish. Serves 6 to 8.

MACARONI ANDRIA STYLE

(Maccheroni alla maniera di Andria)

Sauce:
  1½ tablespoons chopped
    onion
  1 clove garlic, chopped
  ½ cup oil
  2 pounds peeled tomatoes,
    drained

Salt and pepper
3 sprigs ruta (or substitute
  sage)
1¼ pounds short pasta (5-
  inch macaroni)
1 cup grated Parmesan or
  Pecorino

Sauté the onion and garlic in a pan with the oil. Add the tomatoes, a little salt and pepper and bring to the boil; turn down heat and simmer for 30 minutes.

Pour plenty of water in a large casserole, season with salt and ruta (or sage) leaves and bring to the boil. Sprinkle in the pasta and cook till al dente; drain and transfer to warmed serving dish. Mix in first the Pecorino (or Parmesan) and then the sauce. Serves 6.

MUSSEL SOUP TARANTO STYLE

(Zuppa di cozze alla tarantina)

2½ pounds large mussels
½ cup oil
1 tablespoon chopped onion
2 cloves garlic, bruised
1 tablespoon chopped parsley

½ cup dry white wine
Freshly ground pepper
6 slices bread, rubbed with
  garlic and toasted
Salt (if necessary)

Scrub, beard, and wash the mussels in plenty of water. Heat the oil in a pan; add the onion and the garlic (discard latter when golden brown). Add the parsley and, immediately, the wine and pepper. Reduce the wine heavily and add the mussels. Turn up the heat and sauté the mussels, shaking the pan till they open.

Distribute 6 slices of garlic toast in soup plates, cover them with mussels and pan juices; when pouring the pan juices adjust for salt and filter them or beware of possible sand residues at the bottom of the pan. Serves 6.

MUSSELS CAPRICE

(Cozze capricciose)

2 pounds smallish mussels	1½ tablespoons Dijon mustard
½ cup dry white wine	2 potatoes, boiled with
¼ pound mayonnaise*	minimum salt

Scrub and beard the mussel shells and wash them well with plenty of water. Put them in a large pan with the wine, cover, and allow to cook gently, shaking the pan every now and then to encourage the shells to open.

Remove from the heat. Remove the mussels from their shells and filter the pan liquid through a damp cheesecloth into a little casserole. Reduce the pan liquids and cool; combine them with the mayonnaise and the mustard and mix this sauce with the mussels in a suitable bowl. Transfer to a serving dish and decorate with slices of boiled potato. Serves 6 to 8.

MUSSELS BARI STYLE

(Cozze alla casalinga barese)

2 pound mussels	3 tablespoons oil
½ cup dry white wine	1 tablespoon vinegar
1 small onion, chopped	Mussels pan juices, reduced
1 tablespoon chopped parsley	1½ tablespoons chopped
Pinch of powdered thyme	capers
Pinch of powdered bay leaf	½ tablespoon chopped parsley
Pinch of freshly ground pepper	1 small onion, chopped
Sauce:	

Scrub and beard the mussels and wash them in plenty of water. Put them in a pan with ½ cup white wine, the onion, the parsley, a pinch of thyme and bay leaf, and a pinch of freshly ground pepper. Heat and, as the mussels open, remove them one by one and allow to cool; remove from their shells and reserve.

Put the pan back on the heat and reduce the pan juices; filter them through a sieve and reduce them again; then let them cool.

Prepare, in a mixing bowl, a little sauce of 3 tablespoons oil, 1 of vinegar, the mussels pan juices, capers, parsley, and onion.

Put the mussels in a serving bowl and pour over all the sauce. Keep in a cool place and serve cold. Serves 6.

PUGLIA BAKED MUSSELS

(Cozze alla pugliese)

3 pounds mussels	Salt and pepper
½ cup oil	1 cup bread crumbs, sautéed
1 cup béchamel* mixed with 2	in plenty of oil for 2
tablespoons grated cheese	seconds and spread out in
2 cloves garlic, crushed	a cold plate
½ cup dry white wine	
3 tablespoons tomato paste,	
dissolved in ½ cup warm	
water	

Scrub and beard the mussels, wash them in plenty of running water, and place them in a pan with a tablespoon of oil. Over a lively heat, stir the mussels, and, as they open, pass them one by one into a colander, allowing the liquids to drip into a pan underneath it. As they cool, remove from their shells. Allow the liquid to rest for a while and then filter through a damp cheesecloth. Reserve both mussels and liquid.

Prepare the béchamel sauce, blend with the Parmesan, and reserve.

Brown the crushed garlic cloves in a pan with the remaining oil and then spoon in the mussels, stirring for a few moments before pouring in the wine and filtered liquid from the mussel shells; on a low heat, reduce the liquids almost completely. Add the tomato paste dissolved in water, add a little salt and pepper, and continue simmering till the sauce thickens. Then remove from the stove and mix the béchamel-and-Parmesan sauce in well.

Pour the whole mixture into a low fireproof dish and smooth down the surface with a spoon; sprinkle the bread crumbs over all and put into a medium oven till lightly browned. Serve hot. Serves 6.

RAGOUT BARI STYLE

(Ragù alla barese)

2 pounds mixed meats (equal parts pork, lamb, beef, veal)	1½ pounds peeled tomatoes, drained
5 tablespoons oil	2 tablespoons salt and a pinch of pepper
3 tablespoons chopped onion	

Chop the meat into ½-ounce cubes. Heat the oil in a pan and brown the onion; add the meat and brown well on all sides. Then add the tomatoes with 2 tablespoons salt and a pinch of pepper and simmer, covered, for about an hour, adding, if necessary, a tablespoon or so of water.

Strain off most of the liquids and pass through a damp cheesecloth; this sauce can be used with spaghetti or egg pasta of any type.

The remaining stewed meat is served hot with boiled potatoes, preferably new potatoes, and vegetables in season. Serves 4 to 6.

LAMB AND SPAGHETTI FOGGIA STYLE

(Agnello con spaghetti alla foggiana)

2 cloves garlic, crushed	2 tablespoons chopped parsley
½ cup oil	1½ pounds spaghetti
2¼ pounds lamb (shoulder or breast) cut in chunks	Salt
1½ tablespoons salt and a pinch of pepper	

Brown the crushed garlic in oil; add the chunks of lamb and sauté them over a lively heat. When golden, pour in sufficient cold water to cover the meat and season with 1½ tablespoons of salt, a pinch of pepper and the parsley. Bring to the boil, turn down heat, and simmer gently for 45 minutes, until the sauce is reduced heavily; pass the sauce through a sieve. Reserve both meat and sauce, and keep warm.

Cook the spaghetti in plenty of lightly salted boiling water; drain when al dente and put in a warmed serving dish and pour over the lamb sauce. Serve the chunks of lamb on the same plate as the spaghetti.

Accompany this dish with green vegetables sautéed in oil, served separately. Serves 6 to 8.

DUCK AND LENTILS BARI STYLE

(Anitra con lenticchie alla barese)

¾ pound dried lentils	1 sprig parsley chopped
Salt	2 tablespoons oil
A mixture of:	1 bay leaf
2 ounces ham fat, chopped	2-pound duck, ready to cook
2 tablespoons chopped onion	1 tablespoon salt and a pinch
1½ tablespoons chopped	of pepper
carrot	½ cup dry white wine
1 tablespoon chopped celery	

First wash the lentils and cook them in lightly salted boiling water for 45 minutes; drain well and reserve.

Put the mixture in a pan with the oil and bay leaf, and brown lightly; add the duck, season with a tablespoon salt and a pinch of pepper, and brown it on all sides, turning often. Then pour in the wine and allow it to reduce over a low heat. Pour in sufficient water to just cover the duck; bring quickly to the boil, turn down heat, cover the pan and simmer for about an hour. After 45 minutes, add the lentils, and finish the cooking process together for the last 15 minutes.

Remove the duck, drain it, and cut it in pieces; lay out on a warmed serving dish and decorate with the lentils. Pour the pan juices over all and serve hot. Serves 6 to 8.

RABBIT STEW SWEET-AND-SOUR

(Coniglio in intingolo agrodolce)

6 ounces lard	*¼ cup sugar*
1 rabbit, young and plump,	*2 tablespoons seeded raisins*
chopped in chunks	*3 tablespoons pine nuts*
Salt	*Pinch of pepper*
1 cup vinegar	*1 tablespoon potato flour*

Heat the lard in a pan and add the pieces of rabbit sprinkled with salt; bring them to a golden brown. At this point, all the lard, or part of it, may be discarded; but if a rich sauce is preferred, it may all be left in the pan. Add the vinegar, the sugar, the raisins, the pine nuts, and a pinch of pepper; if a more highly flavored sauce is desired, add also a pinch or two of crumbled thyme, bay leaf, and rosemary. Bring to the boil, turn down heat, and simmer until the vinegar evaporates, stirring and turning the meat often.

In the meantime, dissolve the potato flour in a little water and mix it into a pint of cold water and pour into the pan, stirring well. Cover the pan and simmer till the pan juices are reduced to about a cup of thick sauce. Serve hot. Serves 6.

PARTRIDGE WITH GREEN OLIVES

(Pernici con olive verdi)

3 partridges (10 ounces each)	*4 tablespoons stock**
Salt and pepper	*½ pound green olives*
¼ cup oil	

Pluck the partridges, eviscerate, and wash thoroughly. Truss up the legs around the body with string and season the birds with salt and pepper.

Heat the oil in a casserole till it smokes and add the partridges. Let them cook on a medium heat for 15 minutes, then pour in the stock and continue cooking for another 10 minutes.

Meantime, parboil the olives for 3 minutes and remove the stones. Put them into the casserole with the birds and continue cooking for a further 4 minutes. Serve hot. Serves 3.

STUFFED SWEET PEPPERS BARI STYLE

(Peperoni imbottiti alla barese)

6 sweet peppers, yellow, red or green

Filling:
¼ pound bread crumbs, sautéed in butter
8 fillets desalted anchovy,* chopped
2 ounces pickled capers, very small
2 ounces pine nuts
2 ounces raisins

1½ tablespoons chopped basil and parsley
¼ pound black olives, pitted
Pinch of pepper
Grating of nutmeg
½ cup oil
1 tablespoon salt
1 cup tomato paste, dissolved in 1 cup warm water

Char the sweet peppers on a grill, skin them, remove the stem and seeds. Cut in half lengthwise, lay them out in a large fireproof dish, and reserve. Sauté the bread crumbs, for a few seconds only, in a little hot butter and allow to cool.

Combine, in a mixing bowl, the bread crumbs, the anchovy fillets, the capers, the pine nuts, the raisins (well soaked in warm water), the chopped mixture of parsley and basil, the olives, a pinch of pepper and a grating of nutmeg, and half the oil. Spoon this mixture out and fill the peppers; season with a little salt and dribble over each sweet pepper a little oil, and pour in the 2 cups of water-and-tomato-paste mixture and put the fireproof dish in a moderate oven. Remove after about an hour. This dish is best served cold. Serves 6.

FRUIT FRITTERS BARI STYLE

(Frittelle di frutta alla barese)

3 eggs	Pinch of salt
½ pound sifted flour	1 cup dry white wine
2 tablespoons oil	2 pounds ripe fruit
Grated peel of ½ lemon	Oil for deep-frying
Drop of vanilla extract	Confectioners' sugar

Prepare a batter as follows: mix the egg yolks, the flour, 2 table-spoons of oil, the grated lemon peel, the vanilla, and the salt in a bowl. Mix this well, stirring with a wooden spoon while pouring in the wine, in a thin dribble, until a soft and smooth batter is obtained. Allow this to rest for two hours in a warm place.

Wash, peel, and dice the fruit; dry out in a cloth. Mix into the batter first the diced fruit and then, with care, the egg whites, whisked till stiff.

Heat plenty of oil till it smokes in a frying pan and toss in tablespoonsful of the mixture; drain with a slotted spoon when crisp and golden. Serve immediately sprinkled with confectioners' sugar. Serves 6.

Calabria

Calabria is the toe of Italy and just about as bony as a toe; 91 per cent is mountainous. Needless to say, Calabria has been and still is one of the great emigrant areas of Italy. The land just cannot maintain the population, not even with the new irrigation systems, the final death of the Anopheles mosquito, and the breaking up and distribution of the big estates.

But Calabria is a most desirable and beautiful land; in fact, the Sybarites lived there (on the instep of Italy's foot) and, except in the Sila highlands, which are heavily wooded and with great lakes, where snows fall in winter, the climate is very mild and conducive to growing oranges, lemons, and melons.

But bad government, raids by Tunisian pirates, brigandage, plagues, earthquakes, and destruction of the forests in times of various wars, and every other sort of natural and man-made ill have never given Calabria a fair break.

Only since 1955 has any real land reclamation and useful investment program been started: and, at last, the Sun Highway from Milan now has reached Calabria. This, in itself, should make an appreciable difference.

The major agricultural products are wheat, maize, beans, potatoes, olives, oranges, table grapes, wine, figs, pears, apples, and bergamots (for the eau de cologne industry). In the Sila highlands, which run to 6,000 feet, there is some cattle, pig, and sheep raising and this area is being looked upon as likely to be fruitful for investment and reclamation, along with the four small coastal plains.

Calabrian food is based heavily on homemade pasta (and bread) with highly peppered sauces. The pasta is often stuffed with ricotta and other soft cheeses. Vegetable soups and broths are also important. Meat balls of well-garlicked beef or pork, excellent dried and spiced sausages and sharp provola cheese are their other daily standbys.

For high days and holidays, a stuffed pig or lamb is the order of the day, washed down with some strong rough wine. As with Puglia, Calabria does not have much in the way of top-line wines and the bulk of local wines are drunk locally: but the ruby red Cirò ages very well and is highly respected and the Pillaro, Maidi, Zibibbo, Palizza, Pollino, and Savuto are fighting their way up the ladder for recognition. Calabria does offer fine sweet wines, a variety of Moscatos and Malvasias (malmseys), and a dryish Greco di Gerace white which is of international class.

Calabria offers the simple life. The farmer is usually a small holder with his own pigs and chickens: he is always a hunter and adds to his dinner table with rabbit, hare, and game birds. To most Italian tastes, his wife has a heavy hand with garlic, lard, and hot red peperoncino; but if these are moderated, the recipes are very lively and tasty. She is, however, a recognized master of handling the eggplant and has an enormous variety of homemade cooky recipes, which vary from village to village.

Sauces

Antipasti

Soups

VEGETABLE BROTH LICURDIA STYLE   300
(Brodetto vegetale licurdia)

FULL-STRENGTH BROTH   300
(Brodo pieno)

Pastas and other farinaceous dishes

PASTA AND CAULIFLOWER   301
(Pasta e cavolfiore alla calabrese)

MACARONI PASTORA STYLE   301
(Maccheroni alla pastora)

PASTA WITH TOMATO AND RICOTTA
SAUCE   302
(Perciatelli con pomodoro e ricotta)

Fish

SARDINES CETRARO STYLE   302
(Sarde alla cetranese)

Meats

ROAST STUFFED KID   303
(Capretto ripieno al forno)

LAMB SHEPHERDS STYLE   303
(Agnello alla pecorara)

PORK CHOP ROLLS   304
(Braciole di maiale alla calabrese)

GRILLED VEAL SARMORIGLIO   304
(Fettine di carne sarmoriglio ai ferri)

Vegetables

MIXED VEGETABLES GIANFOTTERE   305
(Gianfottere calabrese)

CALABRIAN RED WINE SAUCE

(Salsa di vino rosso)

2 tablespoons butter	3 sprigs parsley, chopped
2 tablespoons sliced onion	1½ cups water mixed with
2½ cups dry red wine	1 teaspoon meat extract
Salt	1 teaspoon butter mixed with
Pinch of chopped thyme	flour
Pinch crumbled bay leaf	

Heat the butter in a pan and cook the onion gently until translucent; pour in the red wine, season with salt, thyme, bay leaf, and parsley, and reduce by ⅔ over a lively heat. Add 1½ cups of water in which a teaspoon of meat extract has been dissolved; add a teaspoon of butter mixed with a little flour. Bring to the boil and keep boiling for a few minutes.

SAVORY FISH TOASTS

(Crostini di pesce alla calabrese)

Fresh sardines, fresh anchovy	Oil and lard
Salt anchovy	Slices of bread
Salt herrings	Garlic, crushed
	Black pepper

This recipe depends on what you have on hand, rather than on specific quantities. Fillet the fresh fish; desalt the anchovy and herrings.

Smoke plenty of oil in a pan and fry slices of bread; reserve and keep hot. Heat some garlic (to your taste) crushed with black pepper in a mortar, in the same pan; then add the fish, mashing it with a wooden spoon until it becomes a paste. Remove from heat; spread this fish paste on the fried bread and serve hot.

CALABRIAN PIZZA

(Pizza alla calabrese)

Dough:
  10 ounces sifted flour
  ½ cup grated Pecorino (or Parmesan)
  Pinch of salt
  3 eggs, beaten
  A mixture of dry white wine and water, as needed
  2 tablespoons softened lard

Flavoring:
  10 ounces peeled tomatoes, drained
  ½ inch hot red peperoncino (or ½ tablespoon red pepper)
  3 tablespoons melted lard
  1 teaspoon salt

Put the flour in a bowl with the Pecorino cheese, the salt, the beaten eggs; knead with the fingers, adding a mixture of water and dry white wine as needed to obtain a smooth dough. Allow to rest for 30 minutes in a cool place.

Grease pan with 2 tablespoons of melted lard and put the dough in it, pressing down with the fingers to level it. Lay on top of the dough a layer of tomato and hot pepper, and sprinkle over all the 3 tablespoons melted lard and a teaspoon of salt. Put in a hot oven for 30 to 35 minutes and serve immediately. Serves 4 to 6.

VEGETABLE BROTH LICURDIA STYLE

(Brodetto vegetale licurdia)

½ pound carrots	1 tablespoon salt
1 pound potatoes	1 pound small onions
¼ pound lettuce	¼ pound lard
6 pints water	24 small toasted croutons

Peel and wash the carrots and potatoes; clean and wash the lettuce; having chopped them all together, put them in a casserole with 6 pints of water and 1 tablespoon salt. Parboil the onions and reserve.

Put the casserole on the stove, bring to the boil, and cook on a lively heat for 45 minutes. The water will have been reduced by half. Then pass the liquid through a strainer into another pot. Chop and sauté the onions in the lard, browning them well, and transfer them to the vegetable soup along with the lard they were sautéed in.

Adjust for salt and pour the vegetable broth over croutons already distributed in the soup plates. Serves 6.

FULL-STRENGTH BROTH

(Brodo pieno)

5 pints strong beef-and-chicken stock*	1 cup grated Pecorino (or Parmesan)
4 eggs	1 tablespoon chopped parsley
2 cups bread crumbs	

Bring the stock to the boil in a fireproof pot; at the same time beat the eggs with the bread crumbs in a bowl along with half the cheese and all the parsley.

When the stock is boiling, whip the egg mixture into it a little at a time; it will combine with 3 or 4 minutes' whipping with a wire whisk. Serve and pass grated cheese individually. Serves 6 to 8.

PASTA AND CAULIFLOWER

(Pasta e cavolfiore alla calabrese)

2 pounds cauliflower (or other
    green vegetable)
4 cloves garlic, crushed
1 cup oil
3 pints water
1½ tablespoons salt
1 tablespoon pepper

1 pound short macaroni or
    broken spaghetti
2 tablespoons chopped parsley
1½ cups grated Pecorino (or
    Parmesan)
Salt

Prepare the cauliflower, removing the outer leaves and the core;
break off the flowerets and the tender leaves and wash well.

Sauté the garlic in a large pan in oil; pour in 3 pints of
water and add the salt and pepper. Bring to the boil and toss in
the flowerets, the tender leaves, and the pasta; bring to the boil
again and, stirring often, cook the pasta al dente, adding, if
necessary, ½ cup boiling water. Before serving, add the parsley
and the cheese and allow to combine for about a minute. Adjust
for salt and serve hot. Serves 6 to 8.

MACARONI PASTORA STYLE

(Maccheroni alla pastora)

1 pound macaroni, broken into
    5-inch lengths
Salt
½ pound ricotta, or other soft
    cheese

½ cup butter
Plenty of freshly ground black
    pepper or powdered hot
    red pepper

First cook the macaroni in lightly salted boiling water; 2 minutes
before draining the pasta al dente, put the ricotta (or finely chopped
soft cheese) in a serving bowl and add a few tablespoons of
the boiling water from the pasta, sufficient to liquefy the cheese;
then add to the cheese, the butter and plenty of black or red
pepper.

Drain the pasta well; pour it into the warmed serving bowl where the cheese, butter and pepper mixture is already, and mix well. Serve immediately. Serves 4 to 6.

PASTA WITH TOMATO AND RICOTTA SAUCE

(Perciatelli con pomodoro e ricotta)

Sauce:
3 tablespoons oil
4 tablespoons lard
2 tablespoons chopped onion
2 pounds peeled tomatoes, drained
Salt and pepper

1 tablespoon coarsely chopped basil
½ pound ricotta, or other soft cheese
1¼ pounds perciatelli (or bucatini)
1 cup grated Parmesan

Put the oil and lard in a pan and heat; brown the onion and add the tomatoes, seasoning with salt and pepper. Simmer for 20 minutes and, before removing from the heat, add the basil.

Mix ⅓ of the above tomato sauce in a bowl with the ricotta, and reserve.

Cook the pasta in plenty of lightly salted boiling water; drain when al dente and pour into a warmed serving dish. Pour over all first the remaining ⅔ of the tomato sauce, followed by the tomato-and-ricotta sauce, and then 2 tablespoons of grated Parmesan. Take to the table, mix well and serve, passing the remaining Parmesan on the side. Serves 6.

SARDINES CETRARO STYLE

(Sarde alla cetranese)

2 pounds fresh sardines
2 tablespoons oil
Salt

Orégano
½ cup oil

Remove the heads and tails of the sardines; eviscerate and wash well and dry. If largish, remove also the backbone. Lay out in a well-oiled pan (2 tablespoons oil) and sprinkle the fish with salt

and orégano (to taste). Dribble over the ½ cup of oil slowly
and put in a slow oven until cooked. Serve cold. Serves 4 to 6.

ROAST STUFFED KID

(Capretto ripieno al forno)

½ pound lard	*Pinch of pepper*
Bouquet garni:	*1½ pounds cannolicchietti or*
1 sprig rosemary	*avemaria (small dry pasta)*
1 sprig basil	*1 kid (2-to-3-month-old goat),*
1 bay leaf	*ready to cook*
2 ounces lean salt pork,	*Salt and pepper*
chopped in strips	

Heat half the lard in a pan along with the bouquet garni; add
the strips of salt pork seasoned with a pinch of pepper and a little
water. When the salt pork begins to brown, remove from the heat,
discard the bouquet garni, and reserve.

Meanwhile, cook the small pasta cannolicchietti or avemarias
in plenty of lightly salted boiling water; drain when al dente and
season with the salt pork and pan juices.

Take the kid, smear the interior generously with ½ remaining
softened lard mixed with salt and pepper and stuff the kid with
the sauced pasta. Sew up the opening, smear also the exterior
of the animal with lard, salt, and pepper, and put it in a moderate
oven, in a well-larded pan, for about 40 minutes. Serves 6 to 8.

LAMB SHEPHERDS STYLE

(Agnello alla pecorara)

1 cup oil	*3 cloves garlic, chopped fine*
Salt	*Pepper*
3½ pounds lamb (leg and ribs)	*1 pound peeled tomatoes,*
1 teaspoon dry orégano	*drained*

Oil a pan well. Salt the meat and sprinkle over a little orégano,
garlic, and pepper. Sprinkle with oil and brown well on all sides;

add the tomatoes and simmer for 10 minutes. Then pour over the meat sufficient water to cover it, but not more. Cover the pan and bring to the boil. Turn down heat and simmer for about 45 minutes, or until the water has been heavily reduced and forms a fairly thick sauce.

Transfer the lamb to a warmed serving dish; serve the sauce separately. Serves 8.

PORK CHOP ROLLS

(Braciole di maiale alla calabrese)

12 slices pork weighing about 2 ounces each
Salt and pepper
7 ounces Pecorino cheese, diced (or Parmesan)
3 cloves garlic, sliced finely
5 tablespoons coarsely chopped parsley
¼ pound lard

Flatten the pork slices lightly and lay them on the kitchen table; season each with a little salt and pepper and, in the middle of each slice, place some Pecorino cheese, a pinch of garlic slivers, and a pinch of parsley.

Roll the pork into little tubes, tying them securely with a white thread.

Heat the lard in a pan, and sauté the little rolls of pork over a lively heat till golden on all sides; turn down the heat and simmer for about an hour, adding every now and then a tablespoon of water. When cooked, remove the thread and serve, preferably with potato purée. Serves 6.

GRILLED VEAL SARMORIGLIO

(Fettine di carne sarmoriglio ai ferri)

Salt
1 scant teaspoon dried orégano
2 cloves garlic, chopped
¼ cup oil
2¼ pounds beef or veal, cut into 3-ounce slices
2 sprigs fresh orégano

Sarmoriglio is a sauce made from ¼ cup of water, a little salt, a scant teaspoon of dried orégano and 2 cloves garlic and mixed with ¼ cup of oil. Prepare this and reserve.

The slices of meat are then grilled over a grooved pan to catch the meat juices and, at the same time, are sprinkled continuously with the liquid sarmoriglio sauce; this is traditionally done with the orégano sprigs dipped in the mixture.

When all the meat is cooked, season the meat with a little salt, pour the pan liquid (a mixture of meat juices and sarmoriglio), reduced a little, over the meat. Serves 6 to 8.

MIXED VEGETABLES GIANFOTTERE

(Gianfottere calabrese)

3 large eggplant	*2 cloves garlic, bruised*
3 zucchini, medium	*2 sprigs rosemary*
1 small pumpkin	*Pinch of orégano*
3 sweet peppers	*Pinch of saffron*
3 large potatoes	*Other vegetables in season*
10 ounces peeled tomatoes,	*Salt and pepper*
drained	*3 tablespoon chopped parsley*
1 cup oil	*and basil*
2 large onions, chopped	

Wash the eggplant and cut lengthwise into wedges; clean the zucchini and the pumpkin; slice them. Char the sweet peppers lightly, plunge into cold water, peel them, remove their seeds and core and cut into 2-inch squares. Peel the potatoes, cut them into wedges lengthwise and parboil them. Cut the tomatoes into strips.

Heat half the oil in a pan till smoking, and sauté the sweet pepper squares lightly; drain them and pass to a large fireproof pan. Add the eggplant, zucchini, and pumpkin to this pan and cook over a moderate heat.

Pour the remaining oil into the pan where the sweet peppers were cooked and sauté the onion with the garlic, adding the rosemary, orégano, and saffron. When browned, add the tomato and cook for 8 minutes. Pour in a little water and add the parboiled potatoes and all the other vegetables. Season with salt and pepper and allow all the vegetables to cook together, stirring, to gather flavor. Pour the whole mixture into a serving dish, discard the rosemary and the garlic, sprinkle with basil and parsley chopped together and serve. Serves 6 to 8.

ZUCCHINI SALAD

(Zucchine a scapece)

2 pounds small, tender zucchini	1 tablespoon chopped garlic
Oil for deep-frying	1 tablespoon chopped parsley
Salt	Oil and vinegar dressing
A mixture of:	
¼ inch hot red pepper	
(peperoncino), chopped	

Slice the zucchini and deep-fry them in a pan. When crisp and golden, remove with a slotted spoon, drain, and season with salt.

When cold, transfer these zucchini slices to a salad bowl and add a mixture of chopped red pepper, garlic, and parsley, to taste.

Make a simple dressing of ½ cup olive oil and a little vinegar with a pinch of salt and pour this into the salad bowl; mix well and allow the ingredients to marinate for four hours before serving. Serves 6 to 8.

SWEET COOKIES

(Chinulille)

½ pound ricotta	1¼ pounds sifted flour
Grated peel of ½ lemon (no pith)	3 eggs
	2 ounces sugar
Grated peel of ½ orange (no pith)	1 egg, beaten with little warm water
Pinch of salt	Lard for deep-frying
1 tablespoon brandy	2 ounces confectioners' sugar

Sieve the ricotta and pass to a pan; add the grated lemon and orange peel, a pinch of salt, and the brandy; mix and reserve.

Make a mound of the flour on the tabletop and, having scooped out the center, add the eggs and sugar; knead this mixture with the fingers for up to half an hour. Roll out the dough into two large and very thin sheets; brush both these sheets with an egg beaten with a little warm water. Using a pastry bag filled with the prepared ricotta filling, place little mounds of the filling 1½ inches apart on a dough sheet; place the other sheet on top of the first, press down around the little mounds of filling to amalgamate the two sheets and cut out little squares with a cooky cutter.

Deep-fry these sweet ravioli in lard; when crisp and golden, remove with a slotted spoon and drain on a cloth. When cool, sprinkle with confectioner's sugar. Serves 6 to 8.

Sicily

Sicily is the largest region of Italy and is mostly a thousand feet above sea level; consequently, the vast bulk of its 5 million population lives on the coastal plains. Its agricultural production is high—the second out of all the regions of Italy, but for per capita income, it comes sixteenth. The temperature is mild all year round on the coasts, but the interior finds extremes of heat and cold and often lacks rain.

In ancient times, Sicily was the grain supplier of Rome. Later, the island was conquered by the Arabs, but this experience was not altogether negative; they brought with them palm trees, sugar cane, cotton plants and all sorts of fruits as well as their knowledge of irrigation. Even the times under Norman rule (at the same time as the Norman, William the Conqueror, ruled England) were relatively happy and, in fact, Sicily flourished. As the island passed from hand to hand of the various rulers of Europe over the centuries and, despite sporadic efforts at saving the agricultural situation, it declined to the point that rebellion was a commonplace. When Garibaldi and his thousand men landed at Marsala, they met no resistance and much support from the Sicilians for a united Italy.

Here again, as in other regions, only in the last twenty years has any appreciable effort been made to repair the ravages of a millennium: since this is obviously nearly an impossible task, huge investment is being made in industry in the hope of canceling out the unhappy general situation.

Sicily is still, however, a great wheat producer and has also become an enormous exporter of citrus fruits, wine, almonds, olive oil, cheeses, walnuts, and pistachios. But this is all a drop in the ocean faced with the problems which Sicily is likely to face for a long time ahead.

Gastronomically, Sicily is very interesting; the Sicilians still enjoy bread made as it should be made. For the Sicilian, good bread is still the staff of life and whether eaten with sausage or a bunch of grapes, it makes an excellent meal when washed down with some honest wine, which is equally inexpensive.

A great deal of pasta, seasoned with ricotta, sharp caciocavallo cheeses and, above all, eggplant is *de rigueur*. The meat, all over the south, tends to be tough, chiefly because it is sold too soon after slaughtering as there would seem to be a lack of refrigeration facilities for hanging. The Sicilians, therefore, tend to use beef chiefly for sauce making or grind it with spices and add it in the form of meat balls to their savory timbales.

The coastal waters offer a great deal of fish and, in particular, tuna and swordfish which, grilled as steaks, make good eating, if a trifle heavy going.

Sicilian ice cream, particularly the cassata, is world-famous— they say, however, that you need the water from Messina to make it perfect. With the huge almond crops and plentiful sugar, the Sicilians find no difficulty in inventing a thousand recipes for cookies, which are served at festas and also eaten, mid-morning, along with a glass of sweet wine.

For over a hundred years, Marsala was the only Sicilian wine that anybody had ever heard of; chiefly because it was produced by Englishmen and sold in England. Today, the Corvo wines of Palermo are found throughout Italy and many more such as Faro, Partinico and Etna are now making their names, as are the dessert wines of Pantelleria, Alcamo and Syracuse.

Before leaving this most fascinating of lands, one should try the caponata, a simple dish which has no rival and which, for this writer, personifies the bitter-sweet, luxuriant, yet often penniless but always mysterious world of age-old Sicily.

Desserts

SARMORIGLIO SAUCE FOR ROASTS

(Salsa Sarmoriglio per arrosti)

1 generous cup oil   *Pinch of orégano*
Juice of 2 lemons   *4 tablespoons hot water*
2 tablespoons chopped parsley

Beat the oil, the juice of 2 lemons, the parsley and the orégano together well in a bowl; add 4 tablespoons hot water and continue to beat until a smooth sauce is obtained. Pour this into a saucepan of a double boiler and heat. As the sauce begins to show signs of boiling, immediately pour it over the roast.

LENTEN HORS D'OEUVRES

(Antipasto magro alla siciliana)

1 pound potatoes, boiled and   *1 pound tuna, sliced*
* diced*   *1 cup mayonnaise**
Dressing: *10 ounces beets, roasted,*
* 3 tablespoons oil*   * skinned, and sliced*
* 1 tablespoon vinegar*   *1 tablespoon small salted*
* Pinch of salt*   * capers, washed*
* Pinch of pepper*   *¼ pound pitted black olives*
6 hard-cooked eggs, halved   *1½ tablespoons chopped parsley*
* lengthwise*

Season the diced potatoes in a mixing bowl with the oil and vinegar dressing and spoon them onto a serving dish. Place the

wedges of hard-cooked egg fanwise in the center and all around
the slices of tuna. Cover the whole with mayonnaise and decorate
the circumference of the plate with beet slices, with capers on
each. Distribute the black olives over the mayonnaise and sprinkle
parsley over all. Serve cold. Serves 6.

STUFFED GREEN OLIVES

(Olive verdi alla siciliana)

Green olives	*Oil*
A mixture of:	*Salt and pepper*
Tomato and sweet peppers	

Remove the stones from the olives without deforming the olive
and in such a way that they can be stuffed. Skin and seed the
tomatoes and peppers and pass through a sieve.

Make a little sauce in a pan with this purée of tomato and
sweet peppers, cooked together with a little oil, salt, and pepper
and reduced to a thick consistency such as is suitable for filling
the olives.

Quantities of the ingredients here are conditioned by the size
and number of the olives.

CAPONATA PALERMO STYLE

(Caponata palermitana)

1 pound eggplant, young and plump	*1 pound peeled tomatoes, drained*
Salt and pepper	*1 teaspoon pine nuts*
1 cup oil	*2 tablespoons salted capers, washed and dried*
1/4 pound onion, chopped	
1/2 pound celery hearts, chopped	*1/2 cup vinegar mixed with 1 1/2 tablespoons sugar*
6 ounces green olives, pitted	

Dice 1 pound of tender eggplant without removing the skin; put in a fireproof pot and sprinkle with table salt and a few tablespoons of water; drain after 30 minutes, wash under plenty of running water, squeeze out excess liquids, and dry with a cloth. Put ½ cup oil in a pan and make it smoke, toss in the eggplant cubes, lightly seasoned with salt and pepper, and sauté them till golden brown; remove from pan with a slotted spoon and reserve.

Pour another ½ cup of oil into the same pan and brown the onion; then add the celery hearts and the green olives. Allow to cook together to gather flavor for a few instants before adding the tomatoes; bring to the boil, turn down heat and simmer for about 10 minutes, stirring often. Then add the pine nuts, the capers, and the vinegar mixed with sugar. Continue simmering, with the lid on, but stirring often. When the celery is tender (after about 15 minutes), add the reserved eggplant and the caponata is ready. Adjust for salt. Pour into a serving dish and allow to cool. Serves 6 to 8.

STUFFED TOMATOES

(Pomodori alla siciliana)

12 tomatoes, large, mature, and
    preferably of equal size
Filling:
    ¼ cup oil
    2 tablespoons chopped onion
    6 fillets desalted anchovy,*
      mashed
    1½ tablespoons chopped
      parsley

2 tablespoons chopped capers
3 tablespoons pitted and
    sliced black olives
2 tablespoons bread crumbs
1 tablespoon salt
Pinch of pepper
Grating of nutmeg
¼ cup oil
Salt

Wash the tomatoes and cut them horizontally, close to the stem, so as to form a tomato (to be stuffed) with a little lid. Hollow out the tomatoes, removing the pulp and seeds: upturn them to facilitate the drying out of excess liquid.

Pour ¼ cup of oil into a pan and brown the onions. Remove from the heat and mix in the anchovy and the chopped parsley. Put back on the flame and stir for a few seconds before adding the capers, the olives, and the bread crumbs and seasoning with salt, pepper, and nutmeg. Continue simmering this mixture until it begins to boil: then withdraw pan from the heat. Stuff the tomatoes with this mixture and cover them with the little lids.

Smear a pan with half of the remaining oil, lay the stuffed tomatoes in it, sprinkle the rest of the oil over all along with a little salt. Put the pan into a warm oven and take it out after about 30 minutes. These stuffed tomatoes are good hot, and equally good cold. Serves 6.

PIZZA MARINARA CATANIA STYLE

(Pizza marinara alla catanese)

1 pound sifted flour	8 fillets desalted anchovy,*
1 tablespoon baking powder	chopped
1 cup oil	Salt and pepper
Salt	Pinch of orégano
¾ pound peeled tomatoes, drained	1 tablespoon coarsely chopped basil
4 cloves garlic, sliced	

Make a mound of flour on the tabletop; scoop out the center and pour in the baking powder dissolved in a little warm water. Knead in scant ½ cup oil, a pinch of salt, and as much water as is required to obtain a soft dough. Make a ball of the dough, wrap in a cloth and let it rest for two hours where it is not too cold.

Roll out the dough to ¼-inch thickness and lay it out in a lightly oiled pan; on top, spread the tomatoes and sprinkle over it the slices of garlic, the anchovy, and the remaining oil, seasoning with salt, pepper, orégano, and basil. Allow to rise for 25 to 30 minutes, then put into a hot preheated oven for 20 to 30 minutes. Serves 4 to 6.

PASTA AND ARTICHOKE SOUP

(Minestra di pasta e carciofi)

1 pound artichoke hearts,
   quartered
Lemon juice or vinegar
1½ tablespoons oil
A mixture of:
   ¼ pound salt pork, chopped
   2 tablespoons chopped onion
   1 clove garlic, chopped
   ½ stalk celery, chopped

1 tablespoon chopped parsley
¼ pound peeled tomatoes,
   drained
Salt and pepper
10 ounces of pasta (preferably
   small or broken)
½ cup grated Pecorino (or
   Parmesan)

Strip off hard leaves from the artichokes, remove chokes, quarter them, and reserve them in a bowl of water with a few drops of lemon juice or vinegar.

Heat the oil in a pan and add the salt pork, onion, garlic, etc., mixture; brown with a medium heat and then add the tomatoes, some salt and pepper, and allow to cook gently together, mixing often with a spoon, for about 10 minutes. Toss in the artichoke hearts and allow them to cook for a few minutes, taking flavor from the tomatoes and pan juices; then add 4 pints of cold water, bring to the boil and simmer for 10 minutes. Bring to the boil again and toss in the pasta; when al dente, pour the soup into a tureen, allow to rest for a few minutes and serve with grated Pecorino or Parmesan. Serves 6 to 8.

PASTA AND LENTIL SOUP

(Minestra di pasta e lenticchie)

1 pound lentils
Salt
Oil

1 onion, halved
1 stalk celery, sliced lengthwise

This is made in the same way as pasta and artichoke soup,* except that the artichokes are substituted with 1 pound of lentils, which have been boiled in 6 pints of lightly salted water and sautéed in oil with onion and celery stalk. The onion and celery are discarded and both the lentils and the water in which they were cooked (instead of the cold water) are poured into the pot to make the soup. Serves 6 to 8.

PASTA AND FAVE BEAN SOUP

(Minestra di pasta e fave fresche)

This is made in the same way as pasta and artichoke soup,* except that an equivalent quantity of freshly shelled fave beans are substituted for the artichokes.

PASTA AND BROCCOLI AGRIGENTO STYLE

(Tagliatelle coi broccoli alla maniera di Agrigento)

2½ pounds broccoli
Flour
3 tablespoons oil
1¼ pounds dry tagliatelli pasta
Salt

2 tablespoons onion, chopped
  together with a garlic clove
½ pound salt pork, chopped fine
1 cup grated Pecorino (or
  Parmesan)

Remove the leaves and the core from the broccoli; divide up by breaking off the flowerets; wash them well. Dry them, dust lightly in flour, and sauté in lightly smoking oil; reserve and keep warm.

Start cooking the tagliatelle in plenty of lightly salted boiling water.

In another pan, brown the onion and garlic clove with the salt pork; add a little of the boiling water from the pasta to make a smooth sauce. Reserve and keep warm.

When al dente, drain and pass the pasta into a serving dish; pour over the sauce and the sautéed broccoli flowerets and mix.

At table serve with plenty of grated cheese. Serves 6 to 8.

SPAGHETTI CAPRICE SYRACUSE STYLE

(Spaghetti alla siracusana)

Sauce:
2 eggplant, medium-sized
2 sweet peppers, yellow or red
¾ cup oil
3 cloves garlic, bruised
3 pounds peeled tomatoes, drained
2 ounces pitted black olives
2 tablespoons pickled capers, well washed
8 fillets desalted anchovy,* chopped
1½ tablespoons coarsely chopped basil
Salt and pepper
1½ pounds spaghetti
Salt
1 cup grated Pecorino (or Parmesan)

Wash the eggplant and dice them without removing the skin. Char the sweet peppers on a grill and plunge them in cold water; remove the seeds and chop them into squares.

Heat some oil in a pan and sauté the garlic; when browned, discard them. Add the diced eggplant and allow them to dry out slowly and brown; then add the tomato and bring to a gentle boil for 10 minutes. Stirring continuously, add the sweet pepper squares, the pitted olives, the capers, the anchovy and the basil and season with a little salt and pepper. Cook together on a low heat for a few minutes and the sauce is ready. Reserve and keep warm.

Cook the spaghetti in plenty of lightly salted boiling water;

drain when al dente and pass to a warmed serving dish. First add
the grated cheese and mix and then the hot sauce. Serve immediately. Serves 6 to 8.

PASTA WITH SAUSAGES AND EGGPLANT SAUCE

(Pastasciutta con salsiccie e petroniane)

Sauce:
  10 ounces eggplant
  3 tablespoons oil
  1 pound pork sausages
  ¼ pound salt pork, chopped
    very fine

*1¼ pounds fresh egg pasta or
  dry pasta*
Salt
1 cup grated Parmesan

Wash the eggplant, dice without removing the skin, and put
immediately into a frying pan with smoking oil. Sauté till crisp,
drain, and keep warm.

Scald the pork sausages for 5 minutes in boiling water, and
dice into 1-inch cubes; drain and reserve. Put the salt pork in a
frying pan and when brown, add the sausage cubes and sauté
them together to gain flavor.

Meanwhile, cook the pasta in plenty of lightly salted boiling
water; when al dente drain and pass into a warmed serving dish.
Pour over the sausage cubes and their pan liquid diluted a little
with 2 tablespoons of the boiling water from the pasta; sprinkle
over all half the grated cheese and the eggplant cubes and carry
to the table. Mix well and serve immediately. Pass the remaining
Parmesan at the table. Serves 6.

RISOTTO WITH FRESH VEGETABLES

(Risotto alla siciliana "chi cacuoccioli")

½ cup oil
2 tablespoons chopped onion
¼ pound shelled fave beans
¼ pound shelled peas
3 artichoke hearts, quartered

Salt and pepper
1 pound rice (rubbed with
  clean cloth, not washed)
3 tablespoons butter
1 cup grated Parmesan

Heat the oil in a pan and sauté the onion: when golden brown, add the fave beans, the peas, and the artichoke hearts. Add ½ cup water (more if necessary) and cook gently till all the vegetables are done. Season with salt and pepper.

Bring to the boil a pot of lightly salted water and toss in the rice; after about 20 minutes, when the rice is al dente, drain it and pass to a warmed serving dish. Pour over the vegetables and little lumps of melted butter. Mix well and serve the Parmesan cheese at table. Serves 4 to 6.

SALT COD WITH CAULIFLOWER AND POLENTA MESSINA STYLE

(Baccalà con cavolfiore e polenta alla messinese)

10 ounces corn-meal polenta*	½ cup oil
flour	2 tablespoons lemon juice
1½ salt cod (baccalà)*	1 tablespoon salt
1 cauliflower, medium-sized	Pinch of pepper
1 tablespoon lemon juice or	2 tablespoons chopped
vinegar	parsley
Pinch of salt	1 tablespoon vinegar
Dressing:	

Prepare the polenta according to the Note. Keep the cod in water for forty-eight hours, changing the water often. Remove the hard outer leaves and the core from the cauliflower; wash the remainder in cold water.

Drain the cod, clean it, flake it, and cut it in pieces. Tie the cauliflower in a piece of white cloth so that it is not damaged during cooking. Put the cod in a casserole with just enough water to cover it and bring to the boil; turn down heat and simmer for 6 minutes. Then allow the cod to cool in its own cooking liquid. Meanwhile, cook the cauliflower in a pot with plenty of "acidulated" cold water (i.e., with a spoonful of lemon juice or vinegar) and a pinch of salt and simmer till al dente. Drain cauliflower and cool.

Transfer the cold baccalà (well drained) to a serving dish. Fry the polenta. Mix the oil, lemon, vinegar dressing. Serve the baccalà and cauliflower with hot polenta and the dressing separately in a sauceboat. Serves 6.

LOBSTER WITH BRANDY

(Aragosta al brandy alla siciliana)

3 lobsters, about 1½ pounds each	Melted butter
Salt and pepper	¼ cup brandy

Divide the lobsters lengthwise; remove the sand sac and entrails; season with salt and pepper. Butter a pan and place the ½ lobsters in it, shell side down. Pour melted butter over the lobster meat. Place the pan in a moderate preheated oven or on a broiler rack for 15 minutes, adding more melted butter as required.

Transfer lobsters to a large dish, heat the brandy in a small saucepan, ignite, and pour over the lobsters. Serves 6.

PORK FRICADELLES AND VEGETABLES SAUTÉ

(Polpette di maiale con pitaggio)

1 pound lean pork, minced	2 eggs
½ cup bread crumbs, soaked in stock and well drained	Salt and pepper
A mixture of:	2 tablespoons flour
2 cloves garlic, chopped	¾ pound artichoke hearts, quartered
2 tablespoons chopped parsley	10 ounces shelled peas
1 cup grated Parmesan	10 ounces shelled fave beans
	½ cup oil

Combine, in a bowl, the minced pork, the bread crumbs, and the mixture of garlic, parsley, grated cheese, and 2 eggs, adding a tablespoon of salt and a pinch of pepper. Mix well to obtain a smooth paste. Divide this into little meat ball fricadelles of about 2 ounces each and roll them in flour.

Boil the artichoke hearts, the peas, and the fave beans separately in lightly salted water; drain them when al dente (i.e., not fully cooked). Sauté these vegetables gently in a little oil in a frying pan to color them and give them added flavor; remove, reserve, and keep warm.

Heat the remaining oil in the frying pan and sauté the fricadelles, browning them all over; turn down the heat and simmer for 15 minutes, by which time they should be golden and cooked right through.

Pile the sautéed vegetables in the middle of a large serving dish and decorate the edge with fricadelles. Serves 4 to 6.

GRILLED MARINATED CUTLETS

(Braciole sulla graticola alla siciliana)

Marinade:
  ½ cup oil
  ¼ cup vinegar
  Pepper and salt
  1 tablespoon orégano

12 3-ounce cutlets (beef, veal, or lamb)

Prepare sufficient marinade to cover the cutlets (two parts oil to one part vinegar) with salt, pepper, and a generous sprinkle of orégano. Having flattened the cutlets, lay them in the marinade for one hour, turning them occasionally.

Drain the cutlets, lay them on a very hot grill and brown them on both sides; turn down the heat and continue cooking, brushing them with the marinade. Serve very hot with a fresh salad. Serves 6.

FARSUMAGRU VEAL ROLL

(Farsumagru)

2-pound slice of lean veal
1 tablespoon salt
Pinch of pepper
Filling:
  ¼ pound mozzarella (or
    other soft cheese), sliced
  ¼ pound sausage meat (or
    lean salt pork or ham)
  4 hard-cooked eggs, sliced
  4 cloves garlic, chopped
  2 tablespoons chopped
    parsley

Salt and pepper
Pinch of orégano
Salt and pepper
½ cup oil
2 cloves garlic (not peeled)
1 small onion, sliced
2 tablespoons chopped carrot
1 bay leaf
½ cup dry white wine

Put the slice of veal on the working surface and pound it until it is ½ inch thick. Season it with salt and pepper.

Filling: Combine, in a mixing bowl, the slices of soft cheese, the sausage meat (or salt pork or ham), the hard-cooked-egg slices, the garlic and parsley, salt, pepper, and orégano. Mix well.

To combine: Spread this filling on the pounded veal, and roll it so that it forms a cylinder and the filling is securely inside. Tie with string and season the exterior with salt, pepper, and oil.

Oil a pan well and place the stuffed meat in it with the garlic and slices of onion, carrot, and bay leaf around it: add ½ cup of water and put in the oven. Leave in a moderate oven for about one hour, basting occasionally.

Place the farsumagru (string removed) on a serving dish and keep warm.

Pour the wine into the pan juices and reduce them over a lively heat on the stove. Pass these pan juices through a sieve and pour them over the stuffed meat and serve. Serves 6 to 8.

CAPON WITH ANCHOVIES ON THE SPIT

(Cappone con acciughe allo spiedo)

4½-pound capon*	*Salt and nutmeg*
10 tablespoons butter	*Extra butter*
8 fillets desalted anchovy*	*½ cup sweet marsala wine*
1 lemon	*Salt*

Make an incision around the neck of the capon; lay it on its breast and make another cut from the first incision to the breast. Open up the skin around the neck and cut off the head and neck close to the body. Continue working with the knife to open up the skin on the breast, passing along the breastbone, lifting the skin, cutting it and finally removing it.

With great care not to damage the meat, lift the fillets from the breast. Having removed the breast fillets, from the inside cut away the breastbones and remove. With poultry scissors, working still from the inside, remove any other small bones which may be left.

Having completed this operation, close the front part with the skin raised around the neck; the capon appears intact. Combine the butter and the anchovy into a paste; stuff the capon with this anchovy-butter filling, the juice of a lemon and a pinch of salt and nutmeg. Sew up the capon and truss it with a string. Roast it on the spit, well larded with butter with a dripping pan underneath it. As the capon turns on the spit, baste it often with the pan juices and marsala wine. When cooked—one and a fourth hours—season lightly with salt. Serve immediately. Serves 6.

STUFFED ARTICHOKES AGRIGENTO STYLE

(Carciofi ripieni di Agrigento)

12 artichokes	*1 tablespoon chopped parsley*
Filling:	*3 tablespoons bread crumbs,*
3 ounces fillets desalted	*soaked in oil and lemon*
anchovy,* chopped	*juice*
2 ounces salame, chopped	*Salt and pepper*
1 tablespoon grated	*Oil*
Pecorino	*Juice of 2 lemons*
1 clove garlic, chopped	*Salt and pepper*

Trim, remove hard outer leaves and choke, and wash the artichokes; reserve in acidulated water (i.e., with a squeeze of lemon juice or a few drops of vinegar). Prepare the filling by combining the anchovy, salame, Pecorino, garlic, and parsley well with the bread crumbs, seasoning with salt and pepper.

When required, drain and dry the artichokes, and, with a spoon, open up the centers and stuff them with the prepared filling, adding plenty of oil and lemon juice.

Transfer the artichokes to an oiled pan and pour in sufficient cold water to half cover them; season with salt and pepper. Put the pan into a moderate oven for one hour, basting frequently. Transfer to a serving dish, pouring over the pan juices. Serves 6.

FAVE BEANS TRAPPIST STYLE

(Fave alla trappista)

1½ pounds shelled fave beans	*1 onion, sliced*
Salt	*Oil*

Boil the fave beans in lightly salted water. Meanwhile sauté the sliced onion in oil. Drain the fave beans and transfer them to the frying pan with the sautéed onion and cook together for a few minutes. Serves 4 to 6.

SWEET PINE NUT COOKIES

(Pinoccate alla siciliana)

2 cups blanched almonds	*4 egg whites*
1 pound confectioners' sugar	*½ pound pine nuts*
1 teaspoon vanilla extract	*1½ tablespoons butter*

Pound the almonds, the sugar, and the vanilla in a mortar; reduce to a pulp and combine with the whites of 4 eggs, lightly beaten.

Lay out on the table little heaps of pine nuts; fill a pastry bag with the almond-sugar-vanilla mixture and pipe it over the little mounds, making them egg-shaped, half-moon-shaped, or what you will; allow to rest for four to five hours.

Butter a pan well, line up the pine nut cookies in it and place in a moderate oven for about 10 minutes—or until the cookies are golden brown.

STUFFED CANNOLI

(Cannoli alla siciliana)

Dough:	*½ pound very fresh ricotta*
2 cups flour, sifted	*½ cup confectioners' sugar*
¼ cup marsala or other	*Pinch of salt*
strong red wine	*1 tablespoon pistachio nuts,*
1 tablespoon sugar	*sliced lengthwise*
Pinch salt	*2 tablespoons finely*
Fat for deep-frying	*chopped candied fruit*
Filling:	*Chopped pine nuts*

Dough: Make a mound of the flour on the tabletop; scoop out the center and mix in the wine, the sugar, and the salt. Knead until a firm dough is obtained. Roll it into a ball, wrap it in a slightly damp cloth, and allow to rest for two hours.

Then roll it out into sheets of about ¹⁄₁₆ of an inch thick; cut into 5-inch squares and roll around the special cannoli metal tubes (5 inches long by 1 inch in diameter) diagonally.

When all the cannoli have been prepared, heat plenty of oil till smoking for deep-frying. Put them in a few at a time and remove when golden brown. Drain, cool, and reserve. As they get cold, the metal tubes can, with care, be removed.

To fill: Put the ricotta, the sugar, and the salt in a mixing bowl (or blender): mix well until smooth and pass through a fine sieve. Then combine with the pistachio nuts and the candied fruit. Using a pastry bag with an open nozzle, fill the tubes with the filling; sprinkle chopped pine nuts over the filling at extremities of the cannoli. Yields 12–15 cannoli.

Sardinia

Sardinia is almost as large an island as Sicily, but it is very different in almost every aspect. Lying to the west of Italy, its historic contacts were with Spain rather than with North Africa as were those of Sicily. For centuries, Sardinia was a Spanish possession, which only in the early eighteenth century entered fully into the Italian orbit, when it was taken by Piedmont at the Treaty of London after the War of the Spanish Secession. Strangely, by being a Spanish possession, Sardinia missed taking part in the Italian Renaissance; and by being a part of Piedmont, it did not get involved with the Risorgimento which ended in the unity of Italy, because it was already on the winning side. Even Napoleon, when he conquered Italy, left Sardinia alone.

The pastoral-craftsman-hunter world, therefore, lasted in Sardinia much longer than in any other region of Italy. Even the existence of two universities had little influence in the last hundred years, since most of the graduates emigrated to Italy in search of the opportunity to use their abilities.

The Spanish tradition can be felt most today through the wines which have nothing in common with Italian ones but something in common with the Spanish; but, really, they are quite unique. Only in the last few years has their reputation been leaping: not because they are grand fine wines in the classic French sense, but because they are robust, different, and give immense pleasure. The tarry black Oliena wine from the eastern mountains are exciting, just as are the black and rosé Perda Rubias which (without being fortified) reach 17°. There is also the Cannonau, a good strong red table wine of distinctive taste, but the majority of the wines are dry whites. The best known of these whites is the Oristano Vernaccia, but more subtle is the Dorato di Sorso and the Vermentino of Gallura; the Vernaccia is served normally as an apéritif than a table wine because of its high proof. Then there are the strong, full-bodied whites which come from the Campidano plains behind Cagliari and which sell under such names as Nuragus and I Piani. These in the past were exported to the mainland as cutting wines, but now have been studied by oenological experts and domesticated with great success; this is particularly satisfactory as these wines were usually better than the recognized mainland ones they were being mixed with to give extra body and strength. The strong sweet dessert wines, Nasco, Girò, Monica and a variety of malmseys (malvasias), are among the best to be found in Italy.

After grape production for wine making, the major crop in Sardinia is artichokes, which are exported heavily to north Italy. And then in the Nuoro Mountains there are huge flocks of sheep which produce the milk for Pecorino cheese which replaces Parmesan in so many Italian dishes.

Basically Sardinian cuisine is very simple, but, at the same time, it is very sophisticated. Bread is not just bread; there are half a dozen different kinds, and until recent years it was almost always made at home. With a changing world, this is less common, but the various styles are still to be found. The most memorable is *carta da musica* (music parchment) which is an oriental-type unleavened bread, and there is another without fats, and they are made in all sorts of fantastic shapes and sizes. Many breads are especially made for the shepherds who must stay for long periods in the mountains.

For preference, meat is cooked in the open air on a spit, or sometimes in a two-foot-deep pit on which a bed of myrtle is laid. Wood is piled on top and kept burning gently for a few hours till the lamb or pig is cooked.

Game birds are also very popular. One recipe of particular interest not only to shepherds is that for quails which are boiled with lard. This preparation (called *grive*) conserves the birds over long periods (particularly those long periods when the shepherd or hunter is away from home) and also offers a completely new taste to game gastronomy.

One of the delicacies of Sardinia is wild boar and, when young, this is cooked very slowly in olive oil and myrtle leaves. If a suckling pig is very small, they stuff it inside a sheep and roast them together on a spit over a very slow fire so that it does not dry out.

Perhaps Sardinian cuisine is not for the big city, but it is magnificent for country life. The culinary traditions are not peasant or pastoral; they are those of a country aristocracy and they offer gustatory pleasures which are matched by the uniqueness and wholeheartedness of their wines.

ONION AND OLIVE PIZZA

(Pizza con cipolle e olive)

14 ounces sifted flour	*Salt and pepper*
1 tablespoon baking powder	*1 pound onions, sliced thin*
½ scant cup warm milk	*12 fillets desalted anchovy,**
¾ cup oil	*chopped*
Pinch of salt	*6 ounces peeled, sliced tomato*
2 cloves garlic, bruised	*30 green olives, pitted*

Make a mound of flour on tabletop working surface; scoop out the center and pour in the baking powder dissolved in the warm milk, a scant tablespoon of oil, a pinch of salt, and knead until a smooth dough is obtained; allow the dough to rest, wrapped in a damp cloth, for two hours.

Heat 2 tablespoons of oil in a pan, add the garlic (discard this as soon as browned), a pinch of salt and a pinch of pepper; then add the onions and a little water and cook this very slowly till it disintegrates but does not brown.

Roll out the dough and, having oiled a pan lightly, lay the dough in it, leveling it down all over. Then distribute the chopped anchovy all over, followed by the onion sauce, the slices of tomato and the remaining oil. Finally scatter the olives regularly over the surface. Allow to rise for 20 minutes or so and then put the pan in a hot oven for about 25 minutes till cooked. Serves 6.

SARDINIAN BROTH

(Zuppa sarda)

4 pints beef stock*
5 eggs, beaten
Pinch freshly ground pepper
½ pound mozzarella cheese,
    sliced thin

1 scant cup grated Pecorino
    cheese
1½ tablespoons chopped parsley
2 cups diced day-old bread,
    browned in the oven

Bring the stock to the boil in a large fireproof pot. Combine the eggs in a mixing bowl with a pinch of freshly ground pepper, the slices of mozzarella, the grated cheese, and the parsley. Remove the stock from the heat and add egg and cheese mixture, stirring continuously. Replace on the heat and as soon as the soup begins to bubble a little, remove from stove; put the diced bread in deep soup plates and pour the soup on top. Serves 8.

FREGULA BROTH

(Fregula)

10 ounces large-grain semolina
Pinch of saffron
Salt

5 pints stock*
1 cup grated Pecorino (or
    grated dried ricotta)

Put the semolina and the saffron in a wooden bowl and pour over 1 cup of lightly salted water. Knead until a smooth dough is obtained; then, with the palm of the right hand, roll the dough until it begins to break up into small balls the size of peppercorns. Toss these on a wire sieve to remove any semolina flour which has not combined fully, and then put these little balls on a cloth to dry in the sun.

To prepare the soup, bring the stock to the boil, toss in the little balls and cook for a few minutes; when done, remove from the stove, add the grated cheese immediately, and mix in well. Serves 6 to 8.

PORK AND FAVE BEAN SOUP

(Favata sarda)

½ cup oil
A mixture of:
  ¼ pound salt pork, chopped
  2 tablespoons chopped onion
  1 clove garlic, chopped
  1 bay leaf, crushed
  1 sprig mint, chopped
  1 sprig parsley, chopped
  1 teaspoon dried sage
2 pig's feet, cleaned and
  chopped
1 pound pork ribs
1 pound sausages, pricked with
  the prongs of a fork

10 ounces dried fave beans,
  soaked overnight
6 ounces lean salt pork
1 pound fennel hearts, chopped
1 pound onions, chopped
1 pound Savoy cabbage,
  chopped
1 pound peeled tomatoes,
  drained
1 tablespoon salt and a pinch
  of pepper
24 slices bread, browned in
  the oven
1 cup grated Parmesan

Heat the oil in a big earthenware pot and brown the mixture of salt pork, onions, garlic, and herbs. Add the pig's feet, the pork ribs, and the sausages, and allow to cook together for a few minutes. Add the fave beans and sufficient water to cover all the ingredients: bring to the boil and simmer for one hour.

Add the salt pork whole and all the vegetables (fennel hearts, onions, cabbage, and tomatoes) and more water so as to make the soup not too thick; season with 1 tablespoon of salt and a pinch of pepper. Simmer until the vegetables are done.

Toward the end of the cooking, remove the salt pork and dice it; remove the pig's feet and scrape·off remaining meat and chop it; discard the bones and replace the diced salt pork and pig's feet meat in the pot. Remove pork ribs and serve as separate dish. Distribute the toast in soup bowls. Pour over the broth and serve with Parmesan if desired. Serves 6 to 8.

PASTA AND CABBAGE SOUP

(Cavolata alla sarda)

1½ Savoy cabbage
½ pound potatoes
1 pig's foot
6 ounces pork rind
1 onion, sliced
1 bay leaf
½ tablespoon salt
A mixture of:

¼ pound salt pork, chopped
2 tablespoons chopped onion
2 tablespoons oil
*10 ounces cannolicchi (or
    other small pasta)*
*2 tablespoons salt and a pinch
    of pepper*
1 cup grated Pecorino cheese

Remove the hard leaves and the core from the cabbage; chop the remaining leaves into broad strips and wash well. Peel, wash, and slice the potatoes and reserve in cold water. Pass the pig's foot and the pork rind over a flame to remove any residual bristles and parboil both for 10 minutes; cut the rind into strips and split the pig's foot in two lengthwise.

Put the foot and rind in a casserole with plenty of water along with the sliced onion, the bay leaf, and ½ tablespoon of salt; bring to the boil and simmer until cooked (that is, until the pork rind is tender). Drain both pig's foot and rind; strip the meat off the pig's foot, chop it, and reserve. Discard the bone.

Put the salt pork and onion mixture in a deep fireproof pot and sauté in oil; when lightly browned, pour in 4 pints of water, add the cabbage strips, the raw potatoes and bring to the boil. At the same time, combine, in a mixing bowl, the small pasta with the pork rind, pig's-foot meat, season with 2 tablespoons salt and a pinch of pepper, and add to the boiling mixture of cabbages and potatoes. Simmer till the pasta is al dente; serve in soup bowls, sprinkled with grated cheese. Serves 4 to 6.

PASTA AND MEATLESS SAUCE SASSARI STYLE

(Linguine di magro alla sassarese)

2 tablespoons onion and 1
    clove garlic, chopped
    together
½ cup oil
2 pounds peeled tomatoes,
    drained

Salt and freshly ground pepper
1¼ pounds linguine (or
    spaghetti)
3 tablespoons chopped parsley
2 tablespoons grated
    Pecorino cheese

Sauté the onion and garlic mixture in oil and add the tomatoes, seasoned with salt and pepper. Bring to the boil, turn down the heat, and simmer for 30 minutes, adding if necessary a tablespoon of water.

Cook the pasta in plenty of lightly salted boiling water; drain when al dente and transfer to a warmed serving dish. Sprinkle over all the parsley, the cheese, and the sauce; mix well and serve. Serves 6.

PASTA AND SARDINIAN MEAT SAUCE

(Pastasciutta alla sarda)

¼ pound salt pork (or ham
    fat), cut in strips
2 cloves garlic, crushed
1 pound lean beef, chopped
    coarsely
2 pounds peeled tomatoes,
1½ pints stock
1 teaspoon salt and a pinch of
    pepper

1 tablespoon coarsely chopped
    basil
1¼ pounds macaroni (or other
    short pasta)
1 scant cup grated Pecorino
    cheese

Heat the salt pork in a pan and brown the crushed garlic; add the beef and sauté for a minute or two. Pour in the tomatoes and combine for a few moments, and add the stock; season with 1 teaspoon salt, a pinch of pepper, and the basil. Bring to the boil, simmer for 30 minutes, and the sauce should be correctly thickened; reserve and keep warm.

Cook the pasta in plenty of lightly salted boiling water; drain when al dente and transfer to a warmed serving dish. Sprinkle over half of the grated cheese and mix; pour over the sauce and mix again. Serve immediately with the remaining cheese separately. Serves 6.

RAVIOLI NUORO STYLE

(Culorjones alla maniera di Nuoro)

3 pounds potatoes, boiled	1 tablespoon chopped mint
6 eggs	1 cup grated Pecorino
6 ounces butter	Watered milk
Flour	Salt
2 eggs, beaten with a few	2½ cups Sardinian meat sauce*
drops of water	or Roman sugo finto*
Filling:	3 tablespoons grated Parmesan
1 pound onions, sliced	

Having boiled the potatoes and passed them through a strainer, put the purée on the tabletop and knead in the eggs and butter until a smooth dough is obtained. Flour the tabletop and roll out the dough into very thin sheets. Beat the remaining 2 eggs with a little warm water and brush the surface of one of the sheets.

Cook the onion slices in a little water; allow to cool, then mix in the mint and the Pecorino cheese. Combine these ingredients well and put them in a pastry bag; squeeze out little ravioli-sized fillings onto the dough sheet, on which the beaten egg has been brushed,

at 2-inch distances. Lay a second sheet over the first, having damp-
ened it on the inside with a little watered milk; press down with
the fingers around the little fillings so that the 2 sheets combine
and the filling is securely contained. With a cooky cutter cut out
1-inch-square raviolis. Flour a working surface, and as the raviolis
are cut lay them out on it and allow them to dry a little.

Cook them in plenty of lightly salted boiling water; after about
5 minutes, as they come to the surface, skim them off and place
in a serving dish. Pour over the sauce (Sardinian meat sauce or
sugo finto suggested) and sprinkle with a little grated cheese.
Serves 4 to 6.

PASTA WITH RABBIT SAUCE

(Pastasciutta con sugo di coniglio)

Sauce:
½ cup oil
3 ounces lean salt pork,
  chopped
1 small rabbit
1 tablespoon onion,
  chopped with 1 clove
  garlic
Flour
1 bottle dry red wine

1 teaspoon salt and a pinch
  of pepper
Pinch of powdered cinnamon
Bouquet garni:
  2 sprigs parsley
  2 sprigs thyme
3 cloves
1¼ pounds spaghetti (or other
  pasta)
1 cup grated Pecorino cheese

Heat the oil in a pan and sauté the salt pork; having chopped
the rabbit into 1-ounce chunks and dried them, put them in the
pan, and brown on all sides. Add the chopped onion and garlic
and bring to a golden brown and remove from heat. Mix in a
little flour to thicken the pan liquids and replace on the heat;
as the flour begins to color, pour in the wine slowly, stirring,
and season with a teaspoon of salt, a pinch of pepper, a pinch
of cinnamon, the bouquet garni and the cloves. Reduce heat and
simmer for one and a half hours till the sauce is reduced to the
right consistency. Pass the whole through a sieve, reserving the meat

as a second course, to be served with sautéed green vegetables; keep the sauce warm.

Cook the pasta in plenty of lightly salted boiling water; drain when al dente and pass to a warmed serving dish. Sprinkle over half of the grated Pecorino and the rabbit sauce; mix and serve the remaining cheese at table. Serves 6.

FETTUCCINE COOKED IN WILD BOAR BROTH

(Patedda alla sarda)

1½ pounds rump wild boar
1½ pounds veal rump
¾ pound shoulder of mutton
¾ pound shoulder of kid
1 onion stuck with 2 cloves
1 small carrot
1 stalk of celery

1 clove of garlic
2 tablespoons coarse salt
10 ounces of egg-pasta
    fettuccine, broken into
    5-inch lengths
1 cup grated Pecorino cheese

Prepare, clean, and wash the meats and put them in a big fireproof pot and cover with plenty of cold water. Bring slowly to the boil, skim off the scum from the surface and add the onion, carrot, celery, and garlic and the coarse salt. Bring to the boil again, turn down heat and simmer for three hours.

Drain and remove the meat (this serves as a main course, accompanied by fresh vegetables sautéed in oil).

Pass the broth through a sieve and bring back to the boil; toss in the fettuccine, cook until al dente and serve in deep soup bowls with a sprinkle of grated Pecorino over each bowl. Serves 4 to 6.

SARDINIAN RISOTTO

(Risotto alla sardegnola)

¼ pound butter
1 pound rice, rubbed with
    clean cloth but not washed
Salt
2 vegetable-soup cubes and 2
    pints water
2 tablespoons Pecorino grated
    cheese
Sauce:
    6 ounces lean salt pork,
    diced

¼ cup oil
A mixture of:
    1½ tablespoons chopped
    onion
    1 clove garlic, chopped
    ½ tablespoon chopped parsley
    1½ pounds peeled tomatoes,
    drained
Salt and pepper
3 tablespoons grated cheese,
    preferably Pecorino

Heat 5 tablespoons of butter in a casserole, sprinkle in the rice, and allow to cook for 30 seconds, stirring with a wooden spoon. Pour in 2 pints of lightly salted water and add the vegetable-soup cubes; bring to the boil again and, as the rice water thickens, add more water, stirring often. After about 20 minutes, the rice should be cooked; mix in then the remaining butter and 2 tablespoons of grated cheese. Pour into a serving dish, and keep warm.

The sauce is made as follows. Sauté the diced salt pork in a pan with the oil, and when browned, remove, reserve, and keep warm. Put the mixture of onion, garlic, and parsley in the pan and bring to a golden brown; add the tomatoes, season with salt and pepper, and simmer for 20 minutes, then replace the sautéed salt-pork cubes. Pour this sauce over the risotto and sprinkle on grated Pecorino. Serves 6.

BURRIDA FRIED FISH

(Burrida)

2 pounds fish, suitable for frying	2 tablespoons pine nuts
Flour	2 tablespoons chopped walnuts
Oil	Salt and pepper
2 cloves garlic, crushed	Grating of nutmeg
½ cup vinegar	1 tablespoon bread crumbs

Trim, eviscerate, and wash the fish; dust them in flour and fry them in a small quantity of smoking oil. Remove, reserve.

Add ¼ cup oil to the pan juices and sauté 2 cloves of garlic until golden; pour in ½ cup vinegar, adding also 2 tablespoons of pine nuts and 2 tablespoons of walnuts, a pinch of salt, a little pepper, a grating of nutmeg and a generous tablespoon of bread crumbs; combine this mixture with a wooden spoon and cook until the vinegar is reduced by half. Pour the mixture over the fish; allow to cool and reserve in a cool place for at least 48 hours. Serves 6.

LAMB WITH FENNEL HEARTS

(Agnello con finocchietti alla sarda)

2 pounds fennel hearts	½ cup oil
2 pounds of lamb (leg and shoulder)	2 tablespoons chopped onion
Salt and pepper	1 pound peeled tomatoes, drained
1½ tablespoons flour	½ tablespoon salt

Strip off outer skin and boil fennel hearts till al dente. Dice the fennel and reserve the cooking water.

Having chopped the lamb into 1-ounce chunks, season with a little salt and pepper and roll in flour. Pour the oil into a pan and heat till it smokes; add the lamb chunks and sauté over a lively flame till golden brown. Add the chopped onion and mix with a wooden spoon for 2 minutes, then pour in the tomatoes and a few tablespoons of the fennel's cooking water; season with another ½ tablespoon of salt and simmer for about 30 minutes. Then toss in the fennel cubes, allow 2 minutes for them to gather flavor from the pan juices, and serve. Serves 4 to 6.

ROAST SUCKLING PIG

(Porchetta allo spiedo alla sarda)

1 suckling pig (20 pounds)
10 ounces salt pork
Salt and freshly ground pepper

Remove all the piglet's entrails, scrape its skin well, and pass over a flame to remove any residual bristles. Wash well inside and out and dry with a cloth. Season with salt and pepper.

Run a spit through the pig lengthwise and place over heat, preferably a fire of aromatic wood, at about 17 inches' distance. Put the spit mechanism into action and as the heat begins to reach the pork rind, put the salt pork on a long skewer and pass it up and down above the suckling pig so that, as the fat melts, it penetrates the rind and prevents scorching. Continue this process for about three hours. If to be eaten cold, the suckling pig should be laid on a bed of myrtle leaves and covered with plenty more. Serves 20 persons.

BEEF STEW WITH POTATOES

(Stufato di carne magra ghisau con patate)

3 ounces salt pork
1 pint dry red wine
Pinch of pepper
2 pounds potatoes, parboiled
    and cut in wedges
1½ tablespoons chopped parsley
2 pounds lean beef, well hung

½ cup oil
1½ tablespoons flour
¼ pound peeled tomatoes,
    drained
1 pint stock* (or water)
Salt

Slice the salt pork into strips and marinate in the dry red wine and pinch of pepper for 30 minutes. Peel the potatoes, parboil, cut into wedges, dry, and reserve; reserve also the cooking water.

Drain the marinated strips of salt pork and roll them in the chopped parsley; lard the beef with the salt-pork strips, using a larding needle, and dry it with a clean cloth. Heat 2 tablespoons of oil in a pan and, when smoking, add the meat and turn it continuously till browned on all sides; remove and reserve.

Add the remaining oil to the pan juices, turn up heat, and sprinkle in the flour; as soon as it colors, pour in the wine from the marinade and reduce it by ¾.

Replace the meat, add the tomatoes and the stock, season with teaspoon of salt, and bring to the boil; turn down heat and simmer for two and a half hours or more if necessary.

Drain the meat and pass the pan juices through a fine sieve; replace both meat and pan juices in the pan and simmer for another 25 to 30 minutes. Add the potato wedges and a few tablespoons of the potato cooking water (if necessary) and continue cooking for another 10 minutes. Serve very hot. Serves 6.

FILLET OF BEEF WITH ANCHOVIES

(Filetto di bue con acciughe)

2½ pounds beef fillet, trimmed	½ tablespoon salt
Marinade:	½ cup butter
1 pint dry white wine	1 tablespoon salt
¼ pound mushrooms, chopped	1 pint stock*
	6 fillets desalted anchovy,*
1½ tablespoons chopped parsley	mashed
	1 lemon
Pinch of pepper	12 slices of day-old bread

Marinate the beef fillet for an hour, turning occasionally, in the wine, mushroom, parsley, etc. mixture. Tie the fillet securely with string so that it keeps its shape during cooking and put it in a pan with 3 tablespoons of butter; turn up the heat and brown well on all sides. Then pour over the marinade with a tablespoon of salt and simmer till the pan liquid is reduced heavily. Pour in the stock until the fillet is just covered and continue simmering till the pan liquids thicken a little, then add the anchovy fillets, 1½ tablespoons of butter, and a squeeze of lemon. Combine these well with a wooden spoon.

Fry the slices of bread with the remaining butter. Remove the fillet of beef, remove the string, and slice into twelve slices; pass the pan juices through a fine sieve. Lay out the fried bread on a serving dish, lay on each a slice of fillet and a tablespoon or more of hot sauce. Serve immediately. Serves 12.

COLD CHICKEN WITH MYRTLE

(Gallina fredda al profumo di mirto)

3-pound boiling fowl	*½ stalk celery*
1 small onion stuck with a	*1½ tablespoons coarse salt*
clove	*Plenty of myrtle leaves*
1 small carrot	

Pluck and eviscerate the bird, pass it over a flame to remove remaining feathers, etc.; remove the head and feet. Wash and dry it well and truss up so that it maintains its shape during cooking.

Put the bird in a fireproof pot and cover with plenty of cold water; bring to the boil slowly and skim off the scum which rises to the surface. Then add the onion, the carrot, and the celery along with 1½ tablespoons of salt. Bring again to the boil and simmer for 45 minutes. Lay out a bed of myrtle leaves on the serving dish, place the hot boiled chicken on it and sprinkle other myrtle leaves over all. Cover with a large dish or bowl so that the perfume of the myrtle impregnates the bird. Allow to cool and serve cold. Serves 4 to 6.

PARTRIDGE IN OIL

(Pernice sott'olio)

3 partridges (10 ounces each)	1 tablespoon salt
1 small onion, sliced	Vinegar
1 small carrot, sliced	

Having cleaned and trussed the partridges, discard the feet and put the birds, with the onion and carrot and 1 tablespoon of salt, in a casserole with plenty of cold water, bring slowly to the boil and simmer for 35 to 40 minutes. Remove the birds, let them dry in the fresh air, and then cut them in pieces, putting the pieces in a bowl of vinegar.

After three or four hours, when they are impregnated with vinegar, remove them and transfer them to a jar and cover with good-quality oil. They are ready to eat in forty-eight hours, but will be good for some considerable time as long as they remain covered with oil. Serves 3.

BOILED PARTRIDGES WITH GREEN SAUCE

(Pernici lessate con salsa verde)

3 partridges, 10 ounces each, plucked, cleaned and trussed	4 gherkins
	1 small potato, boiled
	1 clove garlic
1 small onion, sliced	1 small onion
1 small carrot, sliced	½ tablespoon salt
Green sauce:	1 cup oil
3 fillets desalted anchovy*	¼ cup vinegar

Prepare and boil the partridges as for partridges in oil,* but do not soak them in vinegar. When boiled they are eaten with a green sauce made as follows: the anchovy, gherkins, potato, garlic, onion, and salt are pounded in a mortar and combined with oil and vinegar to make a smooth green sauce. Serves 3.

STUFFED TOMATOES

(Pomodoro di magro alla sarda)

6 *salad tomatoes, slightly green*	*Eggplant, cooked and diced*
A mixture of:	*Tuna puréed with butter*
Sardines in oil, filleted	*Bread crumbs*
	Oil

Take 6 large salad tomatoes, cut them in half horizontally, remove the seeds and liquid, and put them on a baking tray in a slow oven.

Meanwhile, prepare a mixture sufficient to fill the tomato halves (the quantities depend on the size of the tomatoes) of equal parts of sardines in oil, eggplant, and tuna butter.

When the tomatoes are ¾ cooked, fill them with the prepared mixture; sprinkle over each some bread crumbs and oil and replace in the oven. Turn up heat and remove when well browned. Serves 6.

FAVE BEANS WITH LEAN SALT PORK

(Fave con pancetta magra di maiale)

1½ *pounds shelled fresh fave*	7 *tablespoons lard*
beans	*Salt and pepper*
6 *ounces lean salt pork*	
1 *tablespoon finely chopped*	
onion	

Wash the fave beans; dice the salt pork and chop the onion. Sauté the pork and onion in a pan with the lard; add the fave beans, sprinkle with salt and pepper, and cook over a lively heat till tender. Serve hot. Serves 6.

SARDINIAN BISCUITS

(Biscotti sardi)

6 eggs	½ pound sifted semolina
½ pound superfine sugar	Butter
Grated peel of ½ lemon (no pith)	Flour

Beat the 6 eggs with the sugar in a bowl until frothy; add the lemon peel and, a little at a time, the semolina. Work this into a dough, and, having buttered and floured a large baking pan, shape up long, thin biscuits (about 6 inches long, 1 inch wide and ½ inch thick) and lay them in it. Put in a warm (open) oven for an hour (the Sardinians put them by a wood-burning stove) and then increase the oven heat to moderate until the biscuits are well browned. Serves 4.

SEBADAS SWEET FRITTERS

(Sebadas)

1¼ pounds semolina	Pinch of salt
½ pound fresh ricotta, sieved	Water
½ pound sugar	Oil and lard for deep-frying

Knead the semolina, the ricotta chesse, the sugar, and a pinch of salt into a smooth, slightly stiff dough; adding a little warm water if needed. Allow this to rest for 15 minutes. Break up the dough into walnut-sized quantities and roll into balls. Heat plenty of oil and lard, in equal quantities, in a pan and deep-fry these sebadas balls till golden and crisp. Drain on a cloth and serve immediately. Honey may be used instead of sugar to advantage. Serves 4.

INDEX

PIEDMONT

AOSTA VALLEY

LOMBARDY

ALTO ADIGE

VENETO

LIGURIA

EMILIA ROMAGNA

TUSCANY

OIL

SARDINIA